CANINE
COMMANDOS

CANINE
COMMANDOS

The Heroism, Devotion and Sacrifice of Dogs in War

NIGEL CAWTHORNE

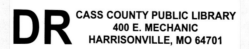

Ulysses Press

Published in the United States by
ULYSSES PRESS
P.O. Box 3440
Berkeley, CA 94703
www.ulyssespress.com

ISBN13: 978-1-61243-055-3
Library of Congress Catalog Number: 2012931424

Printed in Canada by Webcom

10 9 8 7 6 5 4 3 2 1

Acquisitions: Kelly Reed
Managing Editor: Claire Chun
Editor: Barbara Schultz
Proofreader: Lauren Harrison
Production: Judith Metzener
Front cover design: Double R Design
Back cover design: what!design @ whatweb.com
Front cover photo: courtesy of U.S. Army/photo by Staff Sgt. Stacy L. Pearsall *(U.S. Army Staff Sgt. Kevin Reese and his military working dog Grek in Iraq)*
Back cover photos: top courtesy of U.S. Marines/photo by Cpl. Bryan Nygaard *(Cpl. Matthew Flaherty, 1st Battalion, 25th Marine Regiment, posts security with Chica, an explosives detection dog, in Afghanistan)*; bottom courtesy of U.S. Army/photo by Pfc. Adam Halleck, 1BCT PAO, 1st Cav. Div., MND-B *(Palli and handler, Air Force Staff Sgt. Terry Mace Jr., search for weapons caches in Bagdad)*

Distributed by Publishers Group West

CONTENTS

INTRODUCTION

NEWS THAT A DOG NAMED CAIRO had been on the mission with SEAL Team Six to kill Osama bin Laden in May 2011 sparked interest in the contributions and the fate of war dogs. Some three hundred are put up for adoption each year at the end of their active service, and in the weeks following the death of bin Laden, more than four hundred applications were filed. But civilian adoption of war dogs was not always possible. The law allowing these adoptions was only passed in 2000. Before that, dogs were usually put down once their tours of duty were over.

After the Vietnam War, only 204 of an estimated 4,900 war dogs that served in Southeast Asia returned to the United States, according to military dog organizations. The others were euthanized, released by their handlers in an attempt to save their lives, or given to the South Vietnamese army, rendering their fate uncertain. But these days, few are put down. Most are placed in good homes. In 2010, for example, 304 were adopted, while another 34 continued service in police departments or other government agencies. Then, following the bin Laden raid, applications soared and the adoption wait time swelled to six months.

Adopting a military dog is not cheap. Their new owners often have to pay $1,000 to $2,000 to bring a dog back to the US on a commercial flight. Putting a retired dog in a crate on a military cargo flight at public expense is against military regulations because, once the dog is adopted, it no longer belongs to the military. Besides, the government has already picked up the check for the animal's initial purchase, board, upkeep, and training; these costs run to between $40,000 and $50,000 per dog. Sadly, not all ex-military dogs are suitable for adoption by civilians. Some dogs that have performed prolonged service on the battlefield are not safe to be around children. Before they are released to the public, dogs are tested extensively for the symptoms of trauma. For the most part, however, those that have been encouraged to be aggressive during their period of service can be detrained, and most are remarkably docile even after being under gunfire for prolonged periods.

Generally, these dogs are more than ten years old when they retire from the military. Some may simply have been guard dogs at military establishments. Others have been on the front lines and have been credited with saving hundreds of lives. One dog in Iraq, for example, detected a fertilizer bomb on the other side of a door and alerted soldiers who were about to enter the building, preventing them all from being blown sky high. Other dogs have warned troops of the presence of the enemy, spotted booby traps or mines, tracked down a foe, discovered the bodies of the fallen so they can be returned to their loved ones, or simply been a companion in adversity.

We all know dogs that are afraid of thunder, so it comes as no surprise that many are nervous around gunfire. Other dogs feel so deeply connected to their owners and handlers that they are traumatized by human distress. But the dogs in this book are not the nervous type. They are the bravest of the brave, courageous and loyal beyond the call of duty.

War dogs do not start wars. They are not concerned with ideologies or the clash of civilizations; those are human failings. Dogs serve because they live to please human beings. We owe them a great debt.

Nigel Cawthorne
Bloomsbury
March 2012

CHAPTER ONE
WAR DOGS IN EARLY TIMES

DESCENDED FROM THE GRAY WOLF, dogs became domesticated about twelve thousand years ago. First, they were used as hunters, then as herders when sheep, goats, and cattle were domesticated alongside them. Then, as the growth of civilization led to rivalry and war, they accompanied soldiers as war dogs.

The earliest known war dogs were a type of mastiff domesticated in Tibet during the Stone Age. Their use soon spread. In the tomb of Egyptian king Tutankhamun (1333–23 BC), there are depictions of mastiffs with armored collars escorting the pharaoh's chariot, and a decorated wooden casket shows the young king on his chariot pursuing Nubian soldiers who are being harassed by his dogs.

When the Persian king Cambyses II invaded Egypt in 525 BC, he used packs of war dogs to disrupt the Egyptian cavalry. The Greeks used fighting dogs against the Persians at the Battle of Marathon in 490 BC and during the Peloponnesian War of 431–04 BC. During the Corinthian War (395–87 BC), soldiers in the garrison at Corinth were asleep when the Athenians landed on the coast. Fifty war dogs were kenneled along the beach; they attacked the invaders. All but one were killed. But the survivor, Sorter, raced to the citadel and roused the garrison, and the soldiers repelled the Athenians. A grateful city presented the dog with a silver collar, inscribed, "To Sorter, defender and savior of Corinth."

The Romans came up against dogs when fighting the Teutons at the Battle of Versella in 101 BC. They were unleashed by the "blonde-haired women of Wagenburg," according to the Roman consul Marius. The Romans learned their lesson and developed formations of attack dogs wearing spiked collars and body armor. Writing during the first century AD, Pliny the Elder said that these Roman war dogs would not even cower in front of men wielding swords. Dogs were also used on guard duty and as messengers. Attack dogs marched with the legions but, according to Julius Caesar, they met their match when they came up against the mastiffs bred in Britain when he invaded in 55 BC. When Caesar withdrew, the Romans took with them British mastiffs to breed for use in the arena.

Attila the Hun traveled with canine sentinels when he invaded Europe in the fifth century AD. Again, they were swathed in armor and chain mail. The use of dogs as weapons of war continued throughout the Dark Ages that followed the fall of Rome. A manuscript from the eleventh century says, "Dogs were trained to savagely bite the enemy. They were coated with mail and carry a brazen vase on their backs, partially filled with a resinous substance, together with a sponge soaked in spirit. The horses of the enemy, thoroughly upset by the bites of these creatures and the burning fire from the vases, flee in disorder."

By the thirteenth century, Kublai Khan, it was said, had a contingent of thirty thousand Tibetan mastiffs in his army.

The English knight Sir Piers Leigh of Lyme Hall, Cheshire, took his mastiff with him to war in France. When he fell wounded at the Battle of Agincourt in 1415, he was guarded throughout the night by the faithful bitch until his country-men took him to Paris, where he died. The mastiff was taken back to England and is commemorated in a stained-glass window in Lyme Hall.

When the walled city of St. Malo in northern France declared itself an independent republic in the fifteenth cen-tury, it kept three hundred dogs at the expense of the city guard. During the sixteenth century, the Piedmontese kept packs of war dogs numbering three hundred each. Quot-ing the fifteenth-century Italian historian Flavio Biondo, the sixteenth-century Italian naturalist Ulisse Aldrovandi said these war dogs had a "terrifying aspect and look as though they were just going to fight and be an enemy to everybody but their master; so much so that he will not allow himself to be stroked even by those he knows best, but threatens every-one alike with the fulminations of his teeth, and always looks at everybody as though he was burning with anger, and glares around in very direction with a hostile glance."

These dogs were trained from their earliest years to at-tack. A man dressed in a thick coat that the dog would not be able to bite through would first goad the dog, then run away. When the dog chased after him, the man would let himself be caught, then fall on the ground, allowing himself to be bitten.

When the Holy Roman Emperor Charles V—who was also Charles I of Spain—went to war with Francis I, king of France, Henry VIII of England sent Charles four hundred soldiers, along with four hundred dogs with iron collars, though it was not known whether these were meant as guard dogs or attack dogs. The dogs were used to defend Valencia,

Spain, where they fought off enemy dogs. Henry's daughter Elizabeth I of England sent eight hundred dogs with her favorite, the Earl of Essex, to put down a rebellion in Ireland.

Bloodhounds were originally thought to have been bred from dogs that William the Conqueror brought to England in the eleventh century. They were reared in the Abbey of St. Hubert in the Ardennes. More were sent to stock the kennels of Elizabeth I's successor, James I of England, who was also James VI of Scotland. Bloodhounds were trained in England as tracker dogs. Known in Scotland as "slough dogs," they were used against Scottish clansmen who opposed English rule. These dogs had earlier been used to track down Robert the Bruce of Scotland, but he escaped by wading downstream until they lost the scent. The Duke of Monmouth, illegitimate son of Charles II of England, was not so lucky when bloodhounds caught up with him after the Battle of Sedgemoor in 1685. He was beheaded.

Wars Dogs in the New World

Christopher Columbus took twenty bloodhounds with him to the Indies, where he used the dogs to track down the Amerindians. Two of the animals, Bercillo and Leoncillo, were praised for their bravery. Columbus was followed by the Spanish conquistadors, who took dogs with them to the New World and used them to attack the native people. Dogs proved so useful when the conquistadors invaded Mexico and Peru that the king of Spain decreed that the animals should have pensions. Again bloodhounds were favored, while in England bloodhounds were also being trained as tracker dogs.

Toward the end of the seventeenth century, the Maroon Wars broke out in Jamaica. The Maroons were a mixture of runaway slaves from the sugar plantations there and the indigenous Amerindian people. In 1695, the British brought a hundred savage dogs from Cuba to put down the Maroons, but they failed, and the war was ended with a series of treaties.

In North America, the Native American tribes had long used dogs as sentries and pack animals that would drag their loads behind them on a wooden frame or travois. Two dogs could be harnessed together to transport the injured from the battlefield. However, dogs were not used in an offensive role in the Americas until European settlers turned up. In the preamble to an act of the Province of the Massachusetts Bay, passed by His Excellency the Governor, Council, and Representatives in General Court assembled on November 21, 1706, it says, "Whereas upon tryal lately made of rangeing and scouring the woods on the frontiers with hounds and other dogs used to hunting, it has proved of great service to discourage and keep off the Indians..."

The statute was enacted to encourage the breeding and training of a large number of dogs. Settlers who did so would be "paid out of the publick treasury the sum of five shillings per annum, in consideration of their care and charge, for the raising and keeping of every such dog..."

The statute also required that a certificate be sent each year "to the commissary-general, under the hands of the commission military officers, and the town clerk..." The act would continue in force for the next three years "if the war with the Indians lasts so long, and not afterwards."

But the need for dogs continued. In 1755, Benjamin Franklin wrote:

> Dogs should be used against the Indians. They should
> be large, strong, and fierce; and every dog led in a slip
> string, to prevent their tiring themselves out by running

out and in, and discovering the part by barking at squirrels, etc. Only when the party comes near thick woods and suspicious places they should turn out a dog or two to search them. In case of meeting a party of the enemy, the dogs are all then to be turned loose and set on. They will be fresher and finer for having been previously confined and will confound the enemy a good deal and be very serviceable. This was the Spanish method of guarding their marches.

On June 28, 1764, John Penn, lieutenant governor of the colony of Pennsylvania and grandson of its founder, wrote to the paymaster James Young, saying, "You will acquaint the captains that every soldier will be allowed three shillings per month who brings with him a strong dog that shall be judged proper to be employed in discovering and pursuing the savages. It is recommended to them to procure as many as they can, not exceeding ten per company; each dog is to be kept tied and by his owner."

Then, during the American Revolution, William McClay, a member of the Pennsylvania Supreme Executive Council, proposed using dogs to find the Indians who had sided with the British. In 1779, he wrote, "I have sustained some ridicule for a scheme which I have long recommended, viz. that of hunting the scalping parties with horsemen and dogs. The imminent services which dogs have rendered to our people in some late instances seems to open people's eyes to a method of this kind. We know that dogs will follow them, that they will discover them, when hunted on by their masters."

Dogs were still in use in Europe at that time. Frederick the Great, king of Prussia, ordered Field Marshal Keith, a Scotsman, to supply him with collies for sentry work, and the

Turks caused Austrian patrols to flee using dogs during the siege of Dubnitza in 1779.

Napoleon Bonaparte, a keen student of military history, took a tip from antiquity and chained dogs around the walls of Alexandria in Egypt, after he took the city in 1798, to warn him of any counterattack. Before the Battle of Aboukir the following year, he wrote of General Marmont, saying, "You should have a large quantity of dogs which can be made use of by posting them in front of your fortifications."

French Poodles

In Europe, the poodle had become the unlikely choice as a dog of war. A *Pudel*—German for poodle—named Boy had been lost by the Royalist Commander, Prince Rupert of the Rhine, at the Battle of Marston Moor in 1644, during the English Civil War. During the Napoleonic wars, many officers took their poodles into battle with them. After the Battle of Marengo in 1800, Napoleon wrote in his memoirs, "I walked over the battlefield and saw among the slain a poodle killed bestowing a last lick up his dead friend's face. Never had anything on any of my battlefields caused me a like emotion."

He saw another dog sitting by the body of his dead master licking the hand of corpse, perhaps hoping to revive him: "This soldier, I realized, must have had friends at home and in his regiment; yet he lay there deserted by all except his dog... Tearless, I had given orders which brought death to thousands. Yet, here I was stirred, profoundly stirred, stirred to tears. And by what? By the grief of one dog."

A black poodle named Moustache came to fame with a regiment of French grenadiers. One night when they were asleep in the Valley of Babo in Italy, his barks awoke them, just in time to fend off a surprise attack by the Austrians. Later, when a messenger entered the camp, Moustache growled and had to be restrained from attacking the man. After the messenger left, it was discovered that he was, in fact, a spy. Moustache then tracked him down and he was captured.

But it was at the Battle of Austerlitz in 1805 that Moustache showed his true colors. When a young French standard-bearer was cut down in the middle of the battle, Moustache dashed into the fray. He could not save the standard-bearer, but he could save the flag. He tore it from the hands of an Austrian and, though injured, returned to the French lines with the regimental colors in his teeth.

For his daring, Moustache was awarded a tricolor collar with a silver medal by Marshal Jean Lannes. On one side, the inscription read, "Moustache, a French dog, a brave fighter entitled to respect." On the other side, it said, "At the Battle of Austerlitz, he had his leg broken while saving the flag of his regiment."

Later, Moustache was introduced to Napoleon and amused the emperor with his latest trick: Every time the name of one of Napoleon's enemies was mentioned, he raised his leg. Moustache was killed by a cannonball during the storming of Badajoz in Spain. He was buried where he fell, along with his collar and medal, and with full military honors. His gravestone said simply, *"Ce git le brave Moustache"* ("Here lies the brave Moustache"). But after Napoleon's armies were pushed out of Spain, the gravestone was smashed and the body dug up and burned by order of the Inquisition.

After the Battle of Talavera in 1809, a large poodle was found lying on the grave of a Spanish officer. The dog was refusing food, and part of his ear had been shot off during the battle. General Thomas Graham, a Scot in the Duke of

Wellington's army, gave orders for the dog to be brought to his quarters, but the servant returned empty-handed, saying the dog would not allow him to come near. General Graham then ordered the servant to take as many soldiers as were necessary to fetch the dog. Eventually, General Graham sent the dog back to Scotland to his friend Robert Graham of Fintry, a patron of the poet Robert Burns. The poodle found a home in Edinburgh, where the local garrison honored him as a war hero.

A poodle named Sancho was found nearly starved to death on the grave of a French officer after the Battle of Salamanca in 1812. He was adopted by the Marquis of Worcester and taken back to London. Another poodle picked up in Spain died during Napoleon's retreat from Moscow that year.

The British had also taken to poodles by this time. In 1819, a Lieutenant Action had his poodle with him during an attack on Porto Bello in Panama. The dog, Leo, was clipped to resemble a lion. One night, during a surprise attack, his master was bayoneted and killed. But, according to *The Court Journal*: "His faithful Leo made a vigorous attack on the barbarous miscreants, and likewise fell, covered with wounds, in the vain endeavor to defend his master."

Another poodle, named Thoutou, the mascot of the Zouaves, a French North African regiment, was credited with the arrest of several Austrian spies during Napoleon's Italian campaign. He had begun his career with the Zouaves in an expedition against the Beni-Raten tribes in the Kabylie region of what is now Algeria. His job was to flush out enemy snipers from the thickets around the Zouave camp and make nightly patrols with the French sentries.

As a puppy, Thoutou had been tortured by Arabs and, it was said, could smell them from any distance. They infuriated him, and this made him very useful on sentry duty. He was with the 3rd Zouave Regiment when a man in Zouave uniform rode up, saying he was from the 1st Zouave. Naturally the regiment invited him to stay for lunch, but when Thoutou returned from searching the thickets, he was suspicious. He sniffed the air, then launched himself at the visitor's throat. The embarrassed hosts managed to pull him off, but the attack made them suspicious. While Thoutou continued to growl, they questioned the stranger. It soon became plain that he was not who he said he was. Rather, he was an Arab spy and he was led away to face the commandant.

Later, Thoutou was with the Zouaves when they were attacking an Arab position at Palestro. The enemy had hastily drawn up their artillery behind a water-filled ditch—so hastily that the horses were still attached to the gun carriages. As the Zouaves approached, the Arabs opened fire. Thoutou, who was at the rear, gave his handler the slip, bounded up, and jumped into the water. Inspired by his example, and without waiting for orders, the Zouaves followed, holding their rifles above their heads.

When Thoutou reached the far bank, he scrambled up it and began snapping at the horses' legs. They pulled at the gun carriages, preventing the Arabs aiming their guns at the men in the ditch. The Zouaves then scrambled up the bank to attack the artillery men, and the battle was won with consummate ease—thanks to Thoutou.

Thoutou went on to serve in further campaigns in Morocco and Mexico, where half his tail was shot off by a dumdum bullet. Eventually he was demobilized and settled in France near Versailles. By then he had served in fourteen campaigns and, apart from his severed tail, had suffered no serious injury, though the French Army record says that he suffered "two wounds and three contusions."

A handsome setter named Dash, who belonged to Lieutenant William Hay, served with the 12th Light Dragoons for four years in the Peninsula War against Napoleon. He was eventually killed at the Battle of Waterloo in 1815 when his regiment charged to rescue the survivors of the Heavy Cavalry Brigade.

When the Light Brigade charged at Balaclava, a fox terrier owned by an officer in the 17th Lancers escaped from his batman and joined the charge toward the Russian guns, then returned with his master. Both had miraculously escaped death.

Sallie

Dogs took to the field again during the American Civil War. A pug-nosed brindle bull terrier puppy named Sallie joined the 11th Pennsylvania Volunteer Infantry Regiment when they began training in 1861. She was just four or five weeks old. Raised by Yankee men, it was said that there were only three things she disliked: rebels, Democrats, and women.

She would sleep in the captain's tent and, at the drum roll for reveille, Sallie was always the first out of quarters to attend roll call. She joined in the drills and would station herself alongside the regimental colors at dress parade.

At the Battle of Cedar Mountain in 1862, she did not scurry to the rear, but remained with the colors throughout the engagement or ran around the front lines, barking at the enemy. She did the same at Antietam, Fredericksburg, and Chancellorsville. No one ever thought of sending Sallie to the rear in times of combat.

Sallie marched alongside the 11th Pennsylvania at review of the Union Army in the spring of 1863 and was acknowledged by President Lincoln. During the first day's fighting at Gettysburg, the 11th Pennsylvania was driven back from Oak Ridge. Sallie got separated from her unit, but refused to go through Confederate lines and returned to Oak Ridge, standing guard over the Union dead. She was found there by the 12th Massachusetts Volunteer Infantry three days later.

The following May, at Spotsylvania, Sallie was wounded in the neck. Then, on February 6, 1865, when the 11th Pennsylvania made a concerted attack upon the rebel lines at Hatcher's Run, Sallie was at the end of the first line of attack. As the men in the second wave advanced under heavy fire, they came upon Sallie's body. She had been killed instantly by a shot through the head. Still under withering fire, they buried her where she lay on the battlefield. Many of the battle-hardened veterans wept.

In 1890, the surviving members of the 11th Pennsylvania Volunteer Infantry dedicated a monument on Oak Ridge. On the front of it is a bronze likeness of the little dog Sallie, keeping watch out over those who had fallen. There was also thought to have been a Confederate dog at Gettysburg who was killed and buried with full military honors. But history is written by the victors, and there are no confirmed records of this.

Another Union dog entered the history books though. It belonged to Lieutenant Louis Pfieff of the 3rd Illinois Infantry. He was one of the twenty thousand casualties at the Battle of Shiloh in April 1862. When Pfieff's widow came to claim his body, she searched all day among the thousands of hastily dug graves. At dusk, she had almost given up when she saw her husband's dog coming toward her. He then led her to the grave he had been watching over for twelve days.

Jack

Jack was the mascot of the 102nd Regiment of the Pennsylvania Veteran Volunteers, Washington Infantry. The black and white terrier was seen racing across battlefields in Virginia and Maryland. His comrades, the volunteer firemen of Niagara, Pennsylvania, claimed that Jack understood bugle calls, and after a battle he would help locate the dead and wounded of his regiment.

According to a regimental historian, Jack was wounded at the battle of Malvern Hill, but recovered. Then he was captured by Confederates at the Battle of Savage's Station on June 29, 1862, but somehow escaped. Jack survived the Battle of Antietam on September 17, 1862, where some 23,000 men were killed, missing, or wounded.

Jack's luck appeared to be running out when he was severely wounded at Fredericksburg three months later, but he was nursed back to health. Then, at Salem Church, Virginia, he was taken prisoner by the Confederate Army for the second time. According to wartime protocol, a Yankee prisoner could be traded for a Confederate prisoner. Six months after his capture, Jack was exchanged for a rebel at Belle Isle.

In his book *Camp, March and Battle-Field; or, Three-and-a-Half Years with the Army of the Potomac,* the Reverend A. M. Stewart writes:

> Several times, during our retreat, Jack, our regimental
> dog, came alongside of my horse, turned up his
> envious doggish eyes, the shining of which could
> be seen, notwithstanding the darkness; whine in a
> distressed and peculiarly uneasy manner—then ran
> backwards and forwards, to right and left, came back
> near me, and repeated his uneasy gestures and noise,
> as much as to say—"Chaplain, my doggish head

can't exactly comprehend the present state of affairs; something out of joint about the business. Can't you enlighten this old soldier?"

Poor Jack, however, with all his uneasiness, soon got sadly at fault—wandered in the dark with a squad of the men, and was taken prisoner. With his fellow prisoners to Richmond, Jack was, however, ere long paroled or exchanged; got safely to Annapolis; thence to his old home and haunts in Pittsburg, and finally back in front to the regiment; where he assumed his former position with as much familiarity and dignity as though he had never been a captive.

After he rejoined his regiment, he stayed with them through the Wilderness and Spotsylvania campaigns, and the siege of Petersburg. Jack's regiment considered he had done such sterling service that they collected $75 to buy him a beautiful silver collar, which was presented to him with due ceremony.

On the evening of December 23, 1864, Jack disappeared from his regiment, which was on furlough at Frederick, Maryland. The men searched all over for their mascot, but Jack had simply vanished and was never seen or heard from again. A photograph of Jack hangs in the Allegheny County Soldiers and Sailors Memorial Hall in Pittsburg, Pennsylvania.

Hospital Dogs

During the Civil War, a German observer had seen both sides use what he called a "Large American Dog"—a crossbred Irish wolfhound. The German Army employed them during the Franco–Prussian War of 1870. One such creature, which stood thirty-six inches high at the shoulder, was presented to Queen Victoria.

The Germans also used collies and retrievers as hospital dogs to carry first aid equipment. The dogs would go out onto the battlefield to search for the missing and wounded. They were trained to return to their handler with a wounded man's cap, then run back and forth to show where he lay. Or they would stay by the injured man and bark. At night, they would be put on long leashes and direct their handlers to the casualties.

Inspector General Czernicky of the French Army Medical Service said that he wished he had dogs to perform this task. French casualties were left to die on the battlefield untended and undiscovered. However, the French used dogs for other purposes, and the animals were often injured in the fray. A visiting British major saw wounded dogs being tended alongside human casualties with every bit as much care and attention.

Every French Army Corps, said Major A. D. Dawson, "had its completely organized, fully staffed, and equipped camps of dogs, administered like any other recognized arm of the service... They are real soldiers, these dogs of France, cheery and enduring in their work, jolly and sportive in their leisure, and devoted body, soul, and spirit to the officers and men who train and lead and direct them."

Large dogs were used on both sides in the Russo–Turkish War of 1877–78.

Dick

At the Battle of Rorke's Drift in January 1879, commemorated in the movie *Zulu*, where 139 British troops took on

4,500 South African tribesmen, there was a fox terrier named Dick. According to James Reynolds of the Army Medical Department, who won a Victoria Cross (VC) that day, Dick never wavered as shots and spears continued falling around them, or even when the Zulus set fire to the hospital. He only left Reynolds's side once—to bite a Zulu who came too close. Dick received a special mention in the citation for Reynolds's VC for "his constant attention to the wounded under the fire where they fell."

Bobbie

A white short-haired terrier named Bobbie was presented with a campaign medal by Queen Victoria in 1881. He was the only survivor of the last stand of the 66th Regiment of Foot at the Battle of Maiwand in Afghanistan, a country that produces heroic dogs to this day. It was at this battle that Sherlock Holmes's amanuensis, Dr. Watson, was said to have been injured, forcing him to leave the army and return to England, where he chronicled the triumphs of the great detective.

The Battle of Maiwand, during the Second Afghan War, was one of the British Army's greatest defeats. They wanted control of Afghanistan to protect the long northwest frontier of British India from the encroachment of the Russians and Persians, the modern-day Iranians. The immediate cause of the war was the assassination of Lord Cavagnari, the British resident in Kabul in 1879, by Ayub Khan, the local Wali or governor.

Bobbie was the mascot of 66th Regiment of Foot that had been posted to Karachi that year. He was a stray and had been adopted by Sergeant Peter Kelly nine years earlier in the port of Valletta in Malta on his way out to India on the troopship *Seraphis*. They had since seen service together all over the subcontinent.

By January 1880, Bobbie was a fully trained war dog. He went out on patrol to warn the soldiers of an approaching enemy or of the perils of venomous snakes, quicksand, or bogs. He was also used to being around pack animals—donkeys, mules, horses, and camels. That month, Lieutenant Colonel James Galbraith and the 66th Foot were ordered to move up to Sibi on the northwest frontier where they were to meet E Battery of B Brigade of the Royal Household Artillery. They traveled on the Indian Peninsula Railway. D detachment of the 66th was already at Sibi with six howitzers from Hyderabad that the British East India Company was to give to the Wali of Kandahar, their new favorite in Afghanistan.

From Sibi they had to take the Khoja Pass across the mountains into Afghanistan. It was a dangerous trip; they could only travel in the dark of night because it was too hot to march and haul the guns during the day. They were also under sporadic attack by the Indian hill tribes, who had recently massacred the garrisons at Dubbrai and Gatai. At Dubbrai, the 66th's scout found Major Wauby dead with his pet dog, badly wounded, lying across this body. The dog survived and was eventually returned to Major Wauby's widow.

It took the 66th three days to negotiate the Piskin Valley, which was full of quicksand. Bobbie went ahead to test the ground. From the Khoja Pass at the top of the valley, they could see Kandahar. It had taken ten days to get to the Pass from Sibi, and already their losses were mounting.

The Wali of Kandahar, Sher Ali, was delighted with his new guns and immediately sent a force of three thousand irregulars to Helmand to preempt any attack by Ayub Khan, the Wali of Kabul. Colonel St. John, the political officer at

Kandahar, had little faith in Sher Ali and advised General Primrose, commander of the garrison there, to send a brigade to support the irregulars. General Primrose telegraphed General Sir Frederick Roberts in Kabul, asking what he should do. Roberts got in touch with the viceroy and the East India Company, who referred the whole matter back to London. It was not until July 1 that General Primrose finally got authorization to send out a brigade. But they were not to cross the Helmand River, only to prevent Ayub Khan from doing so. This would leave the garrison at Kandahar undermanned, as two companies of the 66th also had to man the garrison at Khalat-i-Gilzai.

On July 4, the brigade moved out. In command was Brigadier General Burrows, leading the 3rd Bombay Light Cavalry and the 3rd Sind Horse. Major Blackwood led E Battery of B Brigade of the Royal Household Artillery with their new guns. Lieutenant Colonel Galbraith led the 66th Regiment of Foot, followed by Major Preston and a field hospital. There were also half a company of the Bombay Sappers and Miners under the command of Lieutenant Henn of the Royal Engineers, and units of the 1st Bombay Grenadiers of 30th Bombay Infantry, also know as Jacob's Rifles.

There were 3,453 men in all. The 66th fielded 497 men and 19 officers. Also in the column was Bobbie, now ten years old, with a ribbon around his neck and a medallion on his chest. He was followed by two other dogs named Billy and Nellie. The infantry were carrying the latest breech-loading Martini-Henry rifles, while the cavalry carried curved sabers. They wore colorful uniforms and were accompanied by a band. Their ammunition, tents, and stores were carried by 350 donkeys, 100 mules, 500 ponies, 2,000 camels, and more than 100 bullocks. The whole column stretched for over three miles.

Again they traveled at night, depending on dogs to lead the way. They has to cross a desert that was 1,500 feet below Kandahar and ford a river until, after nine days, they caught up with Sher Ali's men in Helmand. That night, fighting broke out among Sher Ali's men. General Burrows decided to disarm them, but before he could do so, two thousand of them deserted, taking the new howitzers to join Ayub Khan.

The cavalry and five of the six companies of the 66th Foot, led by Bobbie, headed out after the deserters; they fled for the hills, leaving the howitzers behind. There was no way they were going to return them to Sher Ali, so gunners from E Battery began training men from the 66th Foot on how to lay down fire.

General Burrows now felt that he could no longer depend on Sher Ali's remaining men and on July 26 moved his troops to an old fort at Mahmudabad, where they set up a defensive position. That night, they were surrounded by camp fires, indicating the presence of the enemy. The following morning, they heard the drumming of hooves as four thousand cavalry approached. Then came eight thousand infantry, plus thirty guns, six of which were the latest breech-loading twelve-pounders made by Armstrong in England. There were another twenty thousand irregulars, as well, including the turncoats from Sher Ali's army and bands of religious fanatics known as Ghazis.

While the British were outnumbered more than ten to one, General Burrows was confident he would prevail. His men were well-trained and disciplined. Ayub Khan's were not. However, the Ghazis staged a feint, pretending to charge to distract the British from a force sent up a dry watercourse to outflank them. But the 66th were alerted by the barking of a dog, probably Bobbie. This was repulsed in furious fighting.

The Afghans' artillery fire proved withering, while the British howitzers soon ran out of ammunition. The British infantry fired their breech-loaders until they were too hot to hold. Meanwhile, the Afghan sun beat down. There was no time to take a drink, and the defenders' tongues swelled, while gun carriages—and anything else that moved—were used to carry the wounded to the rear.

Another enemy attack was repulsed. Then Ayub Khan changed tactics. He sent the Ghazis against the Indian infantry on the end of the line. They broke, crashing into the 66th as they fled. The 66th broke momentarily too, but reformed. Two of the Household Artillery's guns were overrun and hauled away. Major Blackwood was hit twice before he was dragged from his horse and disappeared among the enemy.

Sergeant Kelly was hit in the head. Bobbie defended him until Kelly could be carried to the rear. Then Bobbie returned to his unit. The British now tried to cross the watercourse to set up defensive positions on the other side, but the British were scattered. The survivors took refuge in the ruins of the village of Khig. By then, the 66th had been reduced to just eleven men and two dogs—Nellie and Bobbie. They pulled back into the walled garden of Maiwand for their last stand.

Realizing they were doomed, the British opted for an honorable death. In a lull in the fighting, they emerged from behind the ruins of a wall and set up, as best they could, a defensive square. They loaded and fired, only to be cut down by a fusillade from the Afghans. Nellie was killed, along with her master. In the end, there was just one survivor: Bobbie, who continued snarling at the enemy and snapping at their horses' fetlocks. Almost the last thing the injured saw as they headed back to Kandahar was this brave little dog still fighting for Queen and country.

It took two days before the wounded got back to Kandahar, where they dug in for a siege. Of the British and Indian force, 21 officers and 948 soldiers were killed. Eight officers and 169 men were wounded. The Grenadiers lost 64 percent of their strength, and the 66th lost 62 percent, including 12 officers. The cavalry's losses were much smaller, but the horses suffered badly. Five officers' horses were killed and two wounded. Sixty-two battery horses were killed; five more died of their wounds. Eleven horses were shot due to wounds or exhaustion. Another eighty-three horses were shot at Kandahar because of their wounds. Among the pack animals that were lost were 1,676 camels, 355 ponies, 291 donkeys, 79 bullocks, and 24 mules.

General Roberts was sent from Kabul to raise the siege of Kandahar. He covered the three hundred miles in just six weeks. Ayub Khan, not believing that the British could make such quick time in those conditions, was quickly overrun.

The very evening the siege was lifted, a white-haired terrier limped into camp. Bobbie's coat was still matted with blood. The first thing he did was seek out Sergeant Kelly. The dog had been injured. A bullet had gouged a rut down his spine. But somehow he survived.

In October, the remnants of the 66th returned to Bombay. They set sail for England on January 20, 1881, arriving in Portsmouth on February 18 after losing four more of their complement on the way. The survivors of the Battle of Maiwand were presented to Queen Victoria on August 17. Bobbie got a new coat for the occasion, complete with regimental blazon.

They met the Queen at Osborne, her summer home on the Isle of Wight. She inspected Bobbie's wound. Then he was lifted onto a table so that she could hang the campaign medal on its ribbon around his neck. That evening, referring to Bobbie as a Pomeranian, she made an entry in her diary. It read:

> At eleven, I gave six good conduct medals to sergeants and corporals who had, all but one, been in the 66th Regiment in the retreat after Maiwand, and had showed great gallantry. I stood in front of the house with my back to the portico, a sergeant with the colors next to me, and two hundred of the 66th Regiment (now called the Berkshire, with white facings instead of green) under the command of Colonel Hogge, were formed up in a square, facing me. They had their little dog, a sort of Pomeranian, with them, which had been with them through the campaign and it is quite devoted to the men. It disappeared after Maiwand but came back with Sir F. Roberts when he entered Kandahar, and instantly recognized the remaining men of the regiment. Bobbie, as he is called, is a great pet and had a velvet coat on embroidered with pearls and two good conduct stripes and other devices and orders tied round his neck. It was wounded in the back but had quite recovered. The men marched past; Lieutenant Lynch was presented who was badly wounded at Maiwand and is almost the only officer to the regiment who came back alive.

Bobbie's remains had been preserved and are now in the Duke of Edinburgh's Royal Regiment Museum in Salisbury, along with items rescued from the battlefield and two paintings of the Last Stand, one prominently showing Bobbie. He remains the only war dog to have been decorated by a reigning monarch.

Don

A dog named Don patrolled Cuba with the US Cavalry during the Spanish-American war of 1898. Captain Steel, his commanding officer, said, "Dogs are the only scouts that can secure a small detachment against [being] ambuscaded in these tropical jungles." It was a role they would excel in, in the following century.

Mafeking

The British used dogs as sentries and scouts in their invasion of Sudan in 1899 and in the Boer War of 1899–1902. An Irish terrier who came to be known as Mafeking distinguished himself at the siege of Mafeking (now Mafikeng), 150 miles west of Johannesburg. The small British garrison there under Colonel Robert Baden-Powell—later founder of the Boy Scouts—was besieged by the Boers from October 12, 1899, to May 27, 1900. The troops had kept the dog as a rat-catcher and watchdog that fed himself by scavenging because rations were short. But Mafeking was destined for greater things.

One day when the town came under bombardment by the gunners of the Staats Artillery, the dog shunned the safety of the bombproof shelters and marched out toward the outer defense line. Soldiers tried to grab him, but he evaded them and continued on toward the enemy's guns. But once he was over the last defensive parapet, the Boers' guns felt silent. Even the Boers' famed snipers held their fire. No one, it seemed, wanted to risk harming the dog. When he eventually returned to the British lines, and to the safety of a shelter, the bombardment opened up again.

A few days later, when Mafeking was far back in town, a shell landed near him and he was hit by shrapnel. The unconscious terrier was carried to a field hospital, where he made a full recovery. On his first day out of the hospital, he headed for no-man's-land again, as if he intended to silence the guns once more. But this time he was caught and tied up in a shelter.

Then one night, he entered a dormitory building and began biting the sleeping soldiers and pulling the blankets off them. He barked until they were all awake and snarled at them, driving them out of the building. Moments later, the building was hit by a shell. Mafeking had saved their lives.

The British soldiers began to believe that this dog had psychic powers; if he had, however, they certainly did not work on his own behalf. He was hit a second time by shell fragments. This time it took him longer to recover because there was little nourishing food left in the town. Soldiers in the garrison were reduced to eating oats and grains husks, flavored with glycerin and thin gravy made from boiling up the bones and hides of the horses they had already eaten. Nevertheless, Mafeking did recover and, after the war, was taken back to England.

In the Russo–Japanese War of 1904–05, the Russians sent out dogs carrying medical supplies to find wounded men lost in the wilds of Manchuria. Some of the dogs were supplied by Major E. H. Richardson, the noted dog trainer of the British Army. The Germans used dogs again in their genocidal campaign against the Herreros in German South-West Africa (now Namibia) between 1904 and 1907. And during the various Spanish–Moroccan wars, the native Rifs put their own clothes on dogs and sent them running along the front lines. Through the heat haze and sand kicked up by the wind, the Spanish mistook them for the enemy and opened fire, revealing their positions.

CHAPTER TWO
WORLD WAR I

WHILE BRITAIN, GERMANY, AND FRANCE had used thousands of dogs on active service in World War I, America's only official canine contribution was to deliver four hundred sled dogs to the French Army.

Again, as during the Franco–German war, Germany used dogs to carry medicine, and this time France did as well. The Germans called them *Sanitätshunde*, or "sanitary dogs." They carried a small canteen of water or spirits and first-aid equipment in a bag on their chest or a small saddlebag on their back. The dogs were trained to ignore dead bodies. If a man was unconscious or could not move, they were to fetch a handler. But they were not to bark, as that might attract enemy fire.

Initially, the French dogs were taught to retrieve the wounded man's cap or helmet. A dog named Captain with the French Red Cross rescued thirty wounded men in single day this way. A dog named Prusco went further. He dragged wounded men into the shelter of trenches or shell holes before heading off to find his master. After one battle, he rescued a hundred men. If the dog could not find a cap or a helmet, they were trained to take some other item of clothing or a bandage, though some dogs tried yanking out the injured man's hair.

The Germans had another system. Each dog would carry a short leash known as a *Brindel*, sometimes rendered as *Brinsel*. If he returned with it in his mouth, the wounded man was alive and needed tending. If the leash hung free, only dead men had been found.

One of the German war dogs found lasting fame. A German shepherd puppy was found abandoned in the trenches after an American attack. He was taken back to the US where he eventually became a movie star under the name Rin Tin Tin.

Dogs were also used to carry messages—though sometimes pigeons would carry the reply back to base, saving the dog the danger of making a return trip. One dog, an Irish terrier named Paddy, completed a nine-mile journey to deliver a dispatch even though he had been partially blinded by gas. The most famous messenger dog of the war was a French mongrel named Satan, who was credited with saving a lost battalion.

Satan

The French, who were holding a small village outside Verdun, had found themselves surrounded by the Germans. The phone lines were cut and their last messenger pigeon was dead. A German artillery piece on a nearby hill soon found its mark. Dozens of men lay dead. Then, through the smoke of the battle came Satan. He was wearing a bulbous gas mask and had two pigeons flapping in their carriers on his flanks, giving him the appearance of some hideous winged messenger.

As he approached the French lines, German riflemen opened fire. In the hail of bullets, one hit home. Satan staggered, but recovered. Then he resumed his mission, this time taking a zigzag path. A second bullet smashed his shoulder. But now he was only yards from the French lines. Again, he picked himself up and stumbled on. When he reached the stranded French unit, he was tended by army doctors while messages were tied to the pigeons' feet. One bird soared into the air but was immediately shot down by German rifle fire. The second pigeon miraculously dodged the bullets and carried its message back to headquarters. The French artillery were called in to barrage the German positions. Then the infantry attacked, relieving the village. Fearing an all-out counteroffensive, the Germans pulled back. Satan had saved the day.

Rags

When the US joined the war in 1917, efforts were made to employ dogs. The American Red Cross offered to supply trained dogs to rescue the wounded, but the plan was blocked by the US Senate. A program for the French Army to supply the American Expeditionary Forces with dogs was also dropped. Individuals donated dogs, but as none of them had been trained work under gun- and shell-fire, they were next to useless at the front.

However, there was one great American canine hero of World War I, though he was not American by birth. Sergeant James Donovan with the American Expeditionary Force signal corps serving with the 1st Infantry Division was out in Paris on Bastille Day, July 14, 1918. During the blackout in Montmartre, he tripped over a Highland terrier that he mistook for a pile of rags. Minutes later, three Military Policemen turned up and asked to see his pass. Donovan, who was AWOL at the time, had to think fast. Picking up the dog, he explained that he was out searching for the 1st Division's mascot. Asked what the dog's name was, he said, "Rags."

Back in camp, Donovan was sent to the front to string telephone wires between the 26th Infantry Regiment, who were advancing, and the 7th Field Artillery Brigade, who were to give them artillery support during the Battle of the Marne. Though Donovan tried to leave Rags behind in the safety of headquarters, the dog insisted on following his new master along the trenches. So Donovan decided to put him to good use. As the telephone wires he laid were often broken by shell-fire and runners could not get through, he trained Rags to carry messages back to the 7th Field Artillery. And Rags was clever enough to return with a reply.

Rags quickly learned to imitate the men around him. When he came under shell-fire, he would throw himself on the ground with his paws splayed. Soon the doughboys would see him do this before any of them had heard the sound of an incoming round. They realized that Rags's acute sense of hearing meant that he could hear incoming shells long before humans could, and the dog became an early-warning system.

He was also a clever dog who refused to play "fetch" just to amuse the soldiers; he looked on bemused when a collie, the mascot of a machine-gun company, chased after a grenade and was only saved when his quick-thinking handler executed a masterly flying tackle. The collie and his master were both covered in dirt and shrapnel.

In July 1918, during a counterattack near the Paris–Soissons road, Sergeant Donovan, Rags, and the remnants of an artillery unit found themselves surrounded by Germans.

The only surviving officer, a young artillery lieutenant, wrote a note, saying, "I have forty-two men, mixed, healthy and wounded. We have advanced to the road but can go no farther. Most of the men are from the 26th Infantry. I am the only officer. Machine guns at the rear, front, left, and right. Send infantry officer to take command. I need machine-gun ammunition."

The note was attached to Rags's collar, and he took off toward the 7th Field Artillery. They conveyed the message to headquarters. An artillery barrage began, and reinforcements were sent to rescue the beleaguered unit. Rags instantly became a hero.

Later, when Donovan was involved in hand-to-hand fighting, Rags came to the rescue, biting the German on his leg and on the hand that was holding a Mauser. With Rags's aid, the trench was taken and an enemy howitzer captured.

Sergeant Donovan made Rags a gas mask that fitted around his nose, but the dog did not like wearing it. He went up in a balloon on a reconnaissance mission, and when it was shot down by a German plane, Rags made a parachute jump into Donovan's arms, making him the world's first para-pup. Rags also learned to salute, raising his right paw. This impressed Major General Charles P. Summerall, the new commanding officer of the 1st Division. However, Rags did not endear himself to Colonel Theodore Roosevelt, Jr., the eldest son of the former president, after a spat with his cat.

When a captured German major kicked Rags, Sergeant Donovan challenged him to a fistfight. When Donovan seemed to be getting the worst of it, Rags intervened to save his master.

In September of 1918, Rags and Sergeant Donovan were involved in the final American campaign of the war. Rags carried a number of messages and, on October 2, 1918, he took one from the 1st Battalion of the 26th Infantry Regiment to the 7th Field Artillery. The resulting artillery barrage led to an important objective, the Very–Epinonville Road, being secured. This saved the lives of numerous doughboys.

A week later, Sergeant Donovan and Rags again came under intensive shell-fire. When a messenger carrying a note asking the artillery for support was cut down, Rags led Donovan to the fatally wounded man and took over his task. A shell splinter cut Rags's left forepaw. Another piece of shrapnel careened off his gas mask and cut his ear, while a needle-like splinter imbedded itself in his eye. He was gassed. Then another shell blew Rags into a shell hole—and into the arms of another signalman. The little terrier still had the vital message clasped between his teeth. And, thanks to Rags, the message finally got through.

Sergeant Donovan had also been injured in the attack and the two of them found themselves reunited at a dressing station. But when the ambulance men refused to take Rags to a hospital, his comrades made a fuss. Eventually, orders were received from headquarters that, due to his bravery, the dog should be accorded all the privileges of a soldier. He was to be evacuated along with Sergeant Donovan. However, their ambulance was attacked by an enemy plane. Bullets narrowly missed Rags and Donovan but killed a man on the bunk below them.

At each stage of their evacuation, Rags and Donovan were accorded the same level of treatment. Anyone who balked was informed of the "orders from headquarters" concerning Rags's treatment. As the injured dog moved through the system, it was assumed that the "order from headquar-

ters" came from General John J. Pershing, officer commanding the AEF, himself.

At the American field hospital in an old monastery behind the lines, Rags was given a special cot made out of a
packing case that slid under Sergeant Donovan's hospital
bed. A doctor welding a magnifying glass and tweezers removed the splinter from Rags's eye. Then the head of the hospital rustled up a veterinarian to look after the dog's general
health. Eventually, his paw healed, though he remained blind
in his right eye and deaf in the right ear.

Soon Rags was well enough to run out in the grounds of
the monastery, chasing hares and pigeons. He also occupied
himself by barking at the minnows in a nearby stream. On
one occasion he dived in, only to be attacked by an eel that
wound itself around him, and an officer had to wade in to
save Rags from drowning. The French chef at the hospital
duly cooked the eel and served it up to the commandant.
Later, Rags tangled with the goats used to provide milk for
the patients and the ward's cat.

Though Rags recovered quickly, Sergeant Donovan did
not. The gas had partially paralyzed his lungs, and it was decided that he should be sent back to the States as soon as
possible. By then the war was over. A dog-loving colonel from
the 1st Division smuggled Rags aboard the ship carrying Sergeant Donovan from Brest to New York, despite orders ban-
ning animals from hospital ships. Rags then accompanied
Donovan to Fort Sheridan in Chicago, where gas victims
were being treated.

At the base there, word spread of Rags's heroism, and
he was treated accordingly. Rags made his home at the firehouse, and the commanding officer bought him a collar with
"First Division Rags" written on it.

Early in 1919, Sergeant Donovan died, but Rags continued showing up at the door of the hospital every day, looking for his master. Eventually, some one got the idea of showing him Donovan's empty bed. After that, he no longer turned up at the hospital.

Rags stayed on as the post's dog, living in the firehouse and eating in the mess hall. The following year, Major Raymond W. Hardenbergh arrived at Fort Sheridan with his wife and two daughters. The family adopted Rags, who went with them on several postings. In 1924 they arrived at Governor's Island in New York Harbor, where the 16th Infantry Regiment of the 1st Division, with whom Rags had served in World War I, were stationed. From there, Rags began being taken on the ferries to Fort Hamilton in Brooklyn, Fort Wadsworth on Staten Island, and to Battery Park.

In Manhattan, Rags became something of a celebrity, and the *New York Times* carried a number of articles about him. In October 1926, he was given an award at the Long Island Kennel club honoring his wartime achievements. Two years later, he marched down Broadway with a reunited 1st Division on the tenth anniversary of World War I. He moved with the Hardenberghs to Fort Hamilton. Numerous politicians and generals, including his old comrade General Summersall, visited to have their pictures taken with Rags. As ever, Rags made a quick round of the mess halls to find out which one had the best food and the most generous staff, and he could be seen saluting as the flag was lowered each evening. In 1930, the book *Rags: The Dog Who Went to War* was published. As his fame grew, Rags was presented with more medals and awards, and in 1931, he was inducted into the Legion of Dog Heroes by the New York Anti-Vivisection Society.

In 1934, Hardenbergh, by then promoted to Lieutenant Colonel, was transferred to Washington, D.C., to serve in the War Department. Rags died there in March 1936. He was nearly twenty years old. Rags was buried with full military honors and a monument to him was erected at the Aspen Hill memorial park and animal sanctuary in Silver Spring, Maryland, near the Hardenberghs' home. His gravestone says simply, "Rags—War Hero, 1st Division Mascot, WWI, 1916–1936."

Stubby

Rags may have been the most courageous dog to serve with the US forces during World War I, but he was not the most decorated. That distinction belongs to a dog named Stubby, whose military career began in a most unpromising fashion. A pit bull with some other breed of bulldog thrown in, Stubby was a stray on the streets of Hartford, Connecticut. Meanwhile, the 1st Connecticut Regiment from Hartford and the 2nd Connecticut Regiment from New Haven had recently combined to form the 102nd Infantry of the 26th Yankee Division, and they were training on the campus of Yale University.

With them was Private J. Robert Conroy. The dog took a shine to him began to follow him around town. Even though soldiers were not allowed to have pets, Conroy decided to adopt him and named him "Stubby" for his short, docked tail. He smuggled the dog into the barracks and made up a bed for him under his own bunk.

Stubby was soon discovered, but the platoon sergeant was a dog lover and it was not difficult to see that the dog was a boon to morale. The men made no attempt to hide him and added his name to the regimental strength. He trained with the men—participating in drills, answering bugle calls, and learning to salute with his right paw resting on his eyebrow. Stubby also underwent full combat training; he was at Conroy's side in the midst of simulated combat and soon got used to the din.

There was no way the men of the 102nd were going to leave him behind when they were shipped out to France. They smuggled him onboard the troopship SS *Minnesota,* and he was hidden in the coal bin until they were well out to sea. While the men were scared that their commanding officer would order them to throw him overboard, no action when taken when Stubby was seen walking on the deck, and one of the ship's machinists made him a pair of dog tags. The CO eventually spotted him when they arrived in France. He asked Conroy how the dog had gotten so far. Conroy came clean. Despite the clear breech of discipline, the CO regularized the situation by making Stubby the official mascot of the 102nd Infantry.

By the time the American Expeditionary Force reached northern France, the war in Europe had dragged on for three years. The front was a sea of mud. The winter of 1917–18 was particularly harsh. It was all Conroy could do to keep Stubby warm and alive. But his training had prepared him well. Stubby was not afraid of the crack of bullets or the whine of shells. Like Rags, he could offer early warning of incoming shells, thanks to his acute hearing. The men took cover when Stubby lay down and put his paws over his ears.

On the first day of their offensive that spring, the Germans used gas. They released it at dawn so it rolled across the trenches like morning mist. But Stubby had an acute sense of smell. He ran up and down barking until he woke Conroy and some of the men. They soon realized what the fuss was all about and donned their gas masks. He saved many lives that morning, though for some it was too late. No one ignored his warning again.

Stubby himself succumbed to the gas and was taken to the hospital. There was little they could do for him, except to bathe his eyes. Eventually, though, with loving care, he recovered. Conroy then tried to fashion a makeshift gas mask for Stubby, but he could not manage to fit one around the dog's blunt nose. Gas masks were not issued to American war dogs until World War II.

During the battle to take Seicheprey, Stubby was barking at the Germans from the top of the trench, when one threw a grenade his way. He dived for cover, but the shrapnel grazed his forelegs. After the battle was won, Conroy took Stubby to the field hospital. Again he pulled through, and six weeks later he was back at the front.

There are more stories of Stubby's heroics—how he sought out the injured on the battlefield and comforted the dying. On one occasion, he clamped his teeth into the backside of a German infiltrator. Conroy then took the German prisoner, though he had a hard time persuading Stubby to let go of his catch. The German had been mapping the Allied trenches. For his part in the capture, Stubby was promoted to sergeant; he now outranked his master.

He later the received further commendations, both from the Americans and the French. The women of the town of Château-Thierry, which was liberated from the Germans by the AEF in July 1918, showed their gratitude by making Stubby a chamois coat on which his medals were pinned. These included the Château-Thierry Campaign Medal, the French Medal of Verdun, the St. Mihiel Campaign Medal, and the Republic of France Grande War Medal. It also carried the Yankee Division YD Patch, his sergeant's stripes, and a Wound Stripe, the forerunner of the Purple Heart, which was reintroduced in 1932. On the rear, Stubby's coat briefly carried an Iron Cross, though this was never explained. He served in the front line for a year and a half and participated in seventeen battles in four campaigns. He also received an award for saving a civilian. While on leave one day in Paris, Stubby bounded up and knocked a young girl out of the way of a runaway taxi.

In the last days of the war, Conroy was hit in the head by a stray bullet. Stubby went with him to the hospital and stayed by him throughout his recuperation in Paris. Then he had to be smuggled home on a troopship. More accolades awaited him. In 1921, General John Pershing presented him with a special gold medal awarded by the Human Education Society, and he was presented to three presidents—Woodrow Wilson, Warren Harding, and Calvin Coolidge.

The YMCA offered Stubby lifetime membership, plus three bones a day for the rest of his life. He was also given lifetime membership of the American Legion and attended every American Legion convention and marched in every American Legion parade up until his death. And he helped the American Red Cross recruit members and sell Victory Bonds.

However, not everyone recognized Stubby's fame. One day, he was refused entry to the Hotel Majestic in New York. Conroy was told that they did not allow dogs. Conroy replied, "A dog? This is no dog. This is a war hero." The ban was lifted.

Conroy went on to study law at Georgetown University, where Stubby became the mascot of the football team and provided halftime entertainment. He died in Conroy's arms in 1926 and was given a nine-hundred-word obituary in the

New York Times. It took up three columns under the headline "Stubby of the A.E.F. Enters Valhalla: Tramp Dog of No Pedigree Took Part in the Big Parade in France."

Before Stubby was cremated, his skin was removed by a taxidermist and stretched over a plaster mold. Stubby was then put on display in the Red Cross Museum. After a subsequent ignominious period in a storage room in the Smithsonian, he is now a centerpiece at the exhibition *The Prices of Freedom: Americans at War* at the National Museum of American History in Washington, D.C.

CHAPTER THREE
WORLD WAR II

THE PRINCIPAL PLAYERS IN WORLD WAR II were all dog lovers. President Franklin Delano Roosevelt famously had a Scottish terrier named Fala. The dog accompanied him everywhere, eating his meals in Roosevelt's study and sleeping in a chair at the foot of his bed. Fala was even on hand to witness his president signing the "Declaration of United Nations," calling for the unconditional surrender of Germany and Japan, though he slept throughout the ceremony.

Fala had also been onboard the USS *Augusta* off Newfoundland in August 1941 when Roosevelt signed the Atlantic Charter with British Prime Minister Winston Churchill, outlining the future conduct of the war should the United States join in. At the time Fala was below decks with Churchill's poodle, Rufus, who was nicknamed "Paprika" for the brownish red color of his coat. Churchill himself was compared to a bulldog.

In the trenches, during World War I, Hitler had adopted a stray bull terrier he called Fuchsl, which means "little fox." He was upset when the dog went missing, believing his pet to have been stolen. As head of the Nazi Party, he kept a number of German shepherd dogs. He relished their resemblance to a wolf, claiming kinship, as the name Adolf means "noble wolf." His favorite was a bitch named Blondi, who accompanied him everywhere. However, his mistress Eva Braun, like Roosevelt, preferred Scottish terriers.

During Stalin's exile in Siberia as a youth, he was given a little dog called Stepan Timofeevich, or Tishka for short. He joked that he liked to discuss international politics with the dog when there were few other sympathetic people around to talk to. Later he used this as a pet name for his second wife, Nadya. Stalin even had a dog named after him—the Black Russian terrier, bred to work as a guard dog and police dog, was also known as "Stalin's dog."

The quotation "The better I get to know men, the more I find myself loving dogs" is attributed to the French leader General Charles de Gaulle. And in Japan, under Hirohito, school children were taught about the faithful dog Hachiko to encourage fealty to the emperor.

However, an appreciation of dogs did not necessarily equate with a strong canine military presence. The US armed forces' dogs were notoriously ill-prepared for war. On December 7, 1941—the day the Japanese attacked Pearl Harbor—the US military had just fifty sled dogs in Alaska, and another forty in Greenland that had accompanied Admiral Richard E. Byrd on his expedition to Antarctica in 1939.

It was not that the American military did not acknowledge the role of dogs in war. During the interwar period they had studied countries that had used war dogs effectively—particularly Germany. Soon after Pearl Harbor, a group called Dogs for Defense was set up that encouraged people to donate suitable pets to help the war effort, and in March 1942, the US Quartermaster's Corps began training dogs for the newly established War Dog Program, known unofficially as the K-9 Corps—though it was later officially designated the K-9 (Canine) Section, with the word "Canine" in parentheses for people who did not get the joke. Technically, in military terms, a corps must comprise two or more divisions.

Chips

One of the first American dogs to be sent overseas was Chips, who was donated by Edward J. Wren of Pleasantville, New York. Chips's mother was a husky; his father was part German shepherd, part collie. His "brand number" was 11A, though the dogs' service number was tattooed on, rather than branded.

Chips arrived at the canine reception center in Front Royal, Virginia, early in 1942. After being trained as a sentry, he was sent to the 30th Infantry, 3rd Infantry Division, at Camp Pickett, Virginia, where he was assigned to handler Private John P. Rowell. Chips was part of a canine detachment, along with Pal, Watch, and Mena, a bitch dubbed by the press K-9 WAC (Women's Army Corps). She later gave birth to a litter of nine of Chips's puppies, though some attributed them to Watch. After this, it was decided not to send unspayed bitches on active duty.

In October 1942, the dogs were shipped out on Operation Torch, the invasion of French North Africa. They landed on the beaches of Morocco at Fedallah. The intense fire from the Vichy shore batteries caused Mena to cower. She proved useless as a war dog and was shipped home. But Chips remained unfazed and soon took up sentry duty.

The dogs proved invaluable as sentries. Infiltrators were sometimes killed by Senegalese or French Colonial troops on sentry duty. But with dogs guarding the perimeter, no one dared.

Chips and the 30th Infantry were appointed to guard the Casablanca Conference, January 12–23, 1942, where President Franklin D. Roosevelt met British Prime Minister Winston Churchill to discuss in the prosecution of the war. Then Chips joined Brigade General George S. Patton's Seventh Army for Operation Husky, the invasion of Sicily.

Landing at Beach Blue near Licata on the southern coast, Chips and Private Rowell were approaching what appeared to be a grass-covered hut at around 4:20 a.m. It was, in fact, a camouflaged pillbox. Then a machine gun opened up. Chips slipped his leash and attacked the emplacement single-handedly. After a few moments, the machine gun fell silent. An Italian soldier appeared with Chips snarling at his heels. He had bite marks on his arm and throat. Three other Italians appeared with their hands up.

Plainly a fierce fight had taken place. Chips suffered powder burns and a minor scalp wound where one of the Italian soldiers had tried to shoot him. But Chips had gotten the better of them—they had surrendered, not the dog. He was given medical treatment and returned to duty that evening. Later that day, with Chips's help, Rowell rounded up ten more prisoners of war. Chips was credited with being directly responsible for the capture of many other enemy prisoners by alerting the men of I Company of the 30th Infantry Regiment to their presence. As news of his exploits spread throughout the landing force, the press began promoting Chips as a "hero dog."

Chips was the subject of two speeches in Congress that urged the donation of more dogs for the war effort. He was recommended for the Distinguished Service Cross, and was awarded the Silver Star and the Purple Heart. But objections were raised, notably by the national commander for the Military Order of the Purple Heart, who complained that giving a medal to a dog demeaned its human recipients. So, although Chips's citations were not revoked, no more dogs received US awards for heroism during the war.

In Italy, Chips saw action in both the Naples–Foggia and Rome–Arno campaigns. It was there that he met General Dwight D. Eisenhower, then commander in the field. But when Eisenhower tried to pet him, Chips nipped the general's hand. This was attributed to combat stress, and Chips was sent to the rear where he resumed sentry duties.

Nevertheless, Chips was back in action again in southern France after the D-Day landings and moved on through the Rhineland and into Germany during the campaigns there. He returned to the United States in October 1945 and was demobilized at Front Royal on December 10 and returned to the Wren family, at their request.

Despite the ban on giving medals to dogs, Chips was awarded, unofficially, a Battle Star for each of his eight engagements, and an American Theater Ribbon with an arrowhead, showing that he had taken part in an amphibious landing. But war had taken its toll. Chips died on April 12, 1946, due to kidney problems and heart failure.

Gander

Pal was a large Newfoundland dog who lived in Gander, Newfoundland. He belonged to the Hayden family and was a favorite with the local children, towing their sleds during the long Canadian winters. In everyone's eyes, he seemed a very unlikely war hero. But in 1941, war was to come to Gander.

Until then, Gander comprised just ten houses and a one-room school. In 1936, an airstrip had been built there. It was the most easterly airstrip in North America and, after the outbreak of World War II, it came to be of immense strategic importance. As a Dominion in the British Empire, Canada had gone to war with Germany in 1939. Gander became a refueling depot for transatlantic flights. Then, as German U-boats menaced shipping on the North Atlantic, Gander became a base for the surveillance planes that went out hunting submarines, and in 1941 the Royal Canadian Air Force took over. The Royal Canadian Navy also sited their wireless post in Gander, listening out for radio transmissions to and from German submarines. The Canadian Army sent troops to guard the facilities. And, although the United States had yet to join the war, the US sent troops there, too. Barracks were built. The runway was extended. A hospital, a bakery, and a laundry were added.

Pal's master, Ron Hayden, was manager of Shell Oil at Gander Airport and supervised the refueling of planes. Pal would often go to work with him and help the war effort by pulling a sled carrying a forty-five-gallon drum of fuel. He became a firm favorite of the troops based there. Then one day, during some particularly exuberant playtime, Pal jumped up and accidentally scratched a girl's face. The wound, though not deep, required the attention of a doctor and Ron Hayden decided that Pal had to go.

The Royal Rifles of Canada, then in charge of security at Gander Airport, agreed to take him as their regimental mascot, and he was put in the charge of nineteen-year-old rifleman Fred Kelly. Pal settled in well in the barracks, sharing the men's food and even their beer. He particularly enjoyed using their showers. And they taught him a number of tricks including how to stand on his back legs and put his paws on their shoulders. This would become a useful skill later.

Then came news that the Royal Rifles were being posted overseas. At first it was rumored that they were going to North Africa, the only theater where the British and Germans were fighting on land. It turned out that they were being sent to Hong Kong. In the run up to the attack on Pearl Harbor, it was clear that the Japanese, who were already at war with China, intended to expand their offensive and take over the British and Dutch possessions in the Far East. As the wealthiest British colony in the Far East, Hong Kong was clearly under threat and troops were being sent to defend it.

The men of the Royal Rifles decided to take Pal with them, even though it was against regulations. Wherever they were going, the journey would involve a long train ride then a voyage on a troopship. They knew that if Pal was discovered, he risked being abandoned at a railroad station in the middle of nowhere or, worse, being flung overboard in the middle of the ocean. Nevertheless, they were adamant that they were not going to leave him behind. And to remind them of home when they were fighting on the other side of the world, they changed Pal's name to Gander.

Newfoundlands are large dogs. Gander weighed 120 pounds—almost as much as his diminutive handler Fred Kelly—and he had a thick, shaggy black coat. He could not be hidden away like Rags or Stubby. So the Royal Rifles managed to get him on the army list as Sergeant Gander. That meant he would get his own seat on the train and his own berth on the ship. He would be issued his own rations and be listed in the travel orders. And he would get his own kit bag in which he could keep his dog bowl, dog brush, drinking water, a towel, soap, and anything else a dog may need on his travels.

The Royal Rifles were based in Quebec. Before they were sent overseas, they were first paraded through the streets behind Fred Kelly and the regimental mascot Gander. At the station, Kelly's detachment crowded around, screening Gander from the eyes of the officer. During roll call, Kelly shouted out "Sir!" when Gander's name was called. Then two soldiers started a scuffle to distract the officers when he was smuggled onto the train. The 962 men of the Royal Rifles of Canada were then joined by the 911 men of the Winnipeg Grenadiers to make up "C" Force under the command of Brigadier John K. Lawson.

It took three days for the train to reach Vancouver, British Columbia, and there was not a lot for a big dog to do on a train. The corner of one of the rest rooms was turned into a dog's bathroom. Now three years old, Gander had to go through toilet training all over again.

At the harbor in Vancouver, a longshoreman spotted two men guiding what he thought was a bear up the gangplank of the troopship HMCS *Prince Robert* and refused to allow it onboard. The men howled in protest, as they had seen a staff officer take a small lapdog onboard. Gander was just a larger version, they argued. As the large hairy animal they were smuggling up the gangplank was not, in fact, a bear, he was allowed aboard.

Soon everyone on the *Prince Robert* knew that Gander was onboard, so Kelly let him roam the decks. Although having a dog on a troopship was against regulations, the men of the Royal Rifles were young; some were only sixteen. They were going away from home for the first time to face unknown dangers and they were afraid. The authorities soon conceded that Gander was an invaluable morale booster.

When the *Prince Robert* reached Hong Kong, Gander had to be restrained from jumping in the harbor to cool down. Then the Royal Rifles marched up to Sham Shui Po Barracks, where Gander took first pick of the bunks, before going to lie on the floor of the shower block to get cool. Rifleman Kelly and Gander were sent to guard the border between Hong Kong and Japanese-occupied Canton. Gander was used to pull ammunition carts and was rewarded with bottles of beer. But he was in constant danger from the Chinese who tried to abduct him. It seems they wanted him for the dinner table. As a result, Gander greeted all Chinese people with bared teeth.

Then the Japanese attacked Pearl Harbor. Belatedly a British intelligence officer in Hong Kong picked up a radio message that said, "The Army and Navy division of the Imperial Headquarters jointly announced at six o'clock this morning [Tokyo time], December 8, that Imperial Army and Navy forces have begun hostilities against American and British forces in the Pacific at dawn today."

Hong Kong came under air attack that day. News then arrived that the Japanese were massing in Canton. The British then pulled back from Kowloon, the part of Hong Kong that is on mainland China, to Hong Kong Island. "C" Force were sent to defend the Lye Mun Gap, where the strait between the island and the mainland is less than five hundred yards wide.

Japanese bombers appeared overhead as Rifleman Kelly and Gander withdrew from the mainland on the Kowloon ferry. The British had just one destroyer in Hong Kong harbor and three torpedo bombers. The airport was destroyed by the first bomber attack. Next the Japanese dropped leaflets advising the British to surrender. The British took no notice.

There were more air attacks, and the artillery began its bombardment. The Royal Rifles were occupied with bringing up ammunition, while Gander spent his time comforting anyone who showed signs of stress.

By December 10, the Japanese had taken over Kowloon without opposition. Seeing their withdrawal from the mainland as a retreat, the Japanese again asked the British to surrender. They refused. Then the Japanese artillery began their barrage in earnest, taking out the British ammunition dumps and strong points. The Japanese then informed the British that they intended to invade Hong Kong Island across the Lye Mun Gap on December 18.

True to their word, the Japanese began landing on Hong Kong Island on the evening of December 18. Fred Kelly and the rest of the Royal Rifles were occupied in covering the beaches with heavy gunfire. No one had time to look after Gander. But, by then, he had seen his friends cut down by bombs and shells; now they were falling to Japanese bullets and bayonets. He grew angry. Standing six feet tall on his back legs, Gander attacked the enemy. The Japanese would later call him the "Black Devil."

Gander's growling attack took the Japanese by surprise. They were too shocked to raise their rifles. Despite Gander's aggression, the Canadians were forced back. They were in danger of being surrounded, but their main concern was the evacuation of wounded. Kelly and Gander were taking cover in a ditch when they saw a group of wounded Canadians in the middle of the road about two hundred yards away. They were pinned down by crossfire. Gander jumped to his feet. Kelly yelled at him to get down, but the dog took no notice. He bounded toward the wounded men. They were men he knew.

Then the Japanese appeared. They raised their rifles in the direction of the wounded. Gander bared his teeth and charged at them, sending them fleeing. His fearless action allowed other Canadians to move forward and rescue the wounded.

Kelly could not understand why the Japanese did not shoot Gander and was sure that he could not be that lucky again. He took him and tied him up in a pillbox, where he would be relatively safe. From there he kept watch over the wounded.

The following day, the Canadians withdrew to the hills on the south side of the island. Unable to get a clear shot in the dense undergrowth there, the Japanese began throwing hand grenades. Gander was with a group of wounded men under Captain Garvey, when a grenade fell just short of them. A man grabbed it and threw it back. Two more landed close by. They, too, were returned. Then a fourth landed in the middle of them, but it rolled away just out of reach.

Everyone was convinced that they were all they were going to die when Gander rushed forward. He picked up the grenade in his mouth and scampered away. The grenade exploded in his mouth, killing him instantly. But he was out of range of the wounded Canadians, who emerged unscathed. Gander had given his life for them.

The fighting continued. The Canadians were forced back, and no one could retrieve Gander's body. Kelly knew nothing of his canine companion's heroism. As far as he was concerned, Gander was safe in the pillbox. Only later did he learn what had happened.

"When they started shelling, he must have gotten scared and ran out of the pillbox," he said. "It was pitch dark. I didn't see him run and if I had I would have tried to stop him. But I didn't see him go or save Garvey and his men. That damned dog was a friend to all of us."

Kelly's friends were afraid to tell him that Gander was dead, but the following morning he could see his body lying out in the open.

"I could see that he was dead and I hated that I couldn't go near," said Kelly. "To think he was gone hurt me so much, and I'm not ashamed to say that I cried. I missed my old pal very much."

On December 25, 1941, Hong Kong fell to the Japanese. Fred Kelly and the other survivors were taken to prisoner-of-war camps. They spent nearly four years in captivity. Those who survived the experience returned to Canada in 1945.

Sergeant Gander's death was recorded in the list of "C" Force soldiers who were killed or missing in action, or died of wounds, on December 19, 1941. He is listed simply as "Sgt. Gander, age nk [not known], Location of battle death, nk, 1941/12/19, No military grave or memorial." Indeed, he was forgotten—by history at least, though not by his comrades—for fifty-four years.

In the year 2000, an exhibition was mounted in the Canadian War Museum commemorating the eight hundred Canadians who had been killed and wounded in the Battle of Hong Kong. Veterans were discussing the heroism of Sergeant-Major Osborn, of the Winnipeg Grenadiers, who had earned the Victoria Cross, Britain's highest award for bravery, during the battle. He had thrown himself on a grenade, killing himself but saving others. Then one of the men said, "Just like that goddamn dog." They then decided that Gander deserved a medal too.

On October 27, 2000, Gander was posthumously award the Dickin Medal. The award had been instituted in 1943 in the United Kingdom by British animal-welfare pioneer Maria Dickin to honor the contribution of animals in war. She had started the People's Dispensary for Sick Animals (PDSA) in London in 1917. The medal was called the animals' Victoria Cross. Made of bronze, it carries the words "For Gallantry" and "We Also Serve" within a laurel wreath, suspended on a ribbon of striped green, dark brown, and pale blue. It is awarded to animals that have displayed "conspicuous gallantry or devotion to duty while serving or associated with any branch of the Armed Forces or Civil Defence Units." It was accepted on Gander's behalf by Fred Kelly. The citation read:

> For saving the lives of Canadian Infantrymen during the Battle of Lye Mun on Hong Kong Island in December 1941. On three documented occasions, Gander, the Newfoundland Mascot of the Royal Rifles of Canada, engaged the enemy as his regiment joined the Winnipeg Grenadiers, members of Battalion Headquarters "C" Force and other Commonwealth troops in their courageous defense of the Island. Twice Gander's attacks halted the enemy's advance and protected groups of wounded soldiers. In a final act of bravery, the war dog was killed in action gathering a grenade. Without Gander's intervention many more lives would have been lost in the assault.

Rifleman Khan

A German shepherd dog, unofficially designated Rifleman Khan, was awarded the Dickin Medal for his actions in the Battle of Walcheren Causeway in November 1944, when Canadian and Scottish regiments cut off the Germans, allowing the Allies access to the port of Antwerp.

After the landings in Normandy on D-Day, June 6, 1944, one of the most vital tasks was to take the Channel ports so the Allied troops landing on mainland Europe could be supplied. Antwerp was a key gateway for vital supplies, as the Allies' armies pushed on through Belgium, Holland, and into Germany itself. Before Antwerp could be taken, the German 15th Division would have to be driven from Walcheren Island and the causeway linking it to the mainland. However, the British had been beaten there twice before—once by the Spanish in 1585 and again, in 1799, during the Napoleonic wars.

In 1944, the 1st Canadian Army was given the job of opening the route to Antwerp. Clearing the Germans from Walcheren Island was to be the responsibility of the 31,000 men of the 2nd Canadian Corps. With them were two Scottish battalions, the 6th and 7th Cameronian (Scottish Rifles). Rifleman Khan was with the 6th.

As a puppy, Khan had been the pet of the Railton family in Tolword, Surrey, in England. In 1942, after appeals for dogs had been made in the press, he was handed over to the War Dog Training School, where he was considered a star pupil. Officially designated War Dog 147, he was then assigned to dog handler Lance Corporal James Muldoon of the 6th Cameronians. They had landed in Normandy and seen a great deal of action as the Allied armies pushed out across Western Europe. Khan had already shown that he was cool under gunfire, but at Walcheren he proved his worth.

On October 31, the 2nd Canadian Corps took the eastern end of the causeway that carried the railroad and highway out to Walcheren which was held, it turned out, by 150 Germans who were all on special rations due to a stomach complaint. The causeway was about 40 yards wide and 120 yards long. It was flat and straight, offering no cover. Deep ditches filled with water ran along either side. Beyond that were sodden mud flats where it would have been impossible to walk, let alone mount a charge.

Though there was little defending the eastern end of the causeway, the western end was fortified. There were more

German positions along the main dyke, covering any movement along the causeway.

Three attempts were made to rush along the causeway to Walcheren. They were met with artillery, mortar, and machine-gun fire. Losses mounted. The 2nd Canadian Division alone had suffered 3,600 casualties in the previous five weeks and had to be withdrawn. Plainly, a new plan was required.

The fortification at the end of the causeway would have to be outflanked. Troops would have to cross the Sloe Channel by boat, then wade ashore across a mile-long mud bank along a path marked out by sappers. The Germans had been expecting this and had laid mines there. Most of the mines had been dislodged by flooding caused by Allied air raids, but still the sappers would have to feel their way forward through the mud to locate those remaining, before rigging up a safety line for the rest of the troops to follow.

The assault was to be made on the dark, cold night of November 2. The 6th Cameronians pushed off in their landing craft at 3:30 a.m. Almost immediately, the small armada came under intense fire. Lance Corporal Muldoon and Khan crouched low in their landing craft. They were sitting ducks.

In the middle of the channel, an artillery shell hit the vessel and sliced it in half. Men were thrown high in the air, before landing in the waters of the Sloe, where they foundered under the weight of their heavy equipment while searchlights raked the water, directing machine-gun fire.

The shell had hurled Khan into the water, but unencumbered by heavy equipment, he swam ashore, where his paws sank deep into the mud. Men who had struggled ashore also found themselves stuck there, raked by machine-gun fire. But Khan, who was lighter, managed to extricate himself. He ran up to higher ground and began looking for his handler. Then, above the din of battle, he recognized a voice.

Lance Corporal Muldoon could not swim. He was desperately struggling in the water, crying out for help. Khan's acute ears picked up his cries, and his sharp eyes spotted his handler sinking beneath the dark water.

Khan ran down across the mud and flung himself back into the water. He paddled out to the struggling figure and seized the neck of his tunic in his teeth. Then he paddled back to shore, dragging his master with him. Not content with getting his handler to dry land, Khan urged him on to higher ground. Many men lost their lives that night, including Colonel Sixsmith, the company commander. But Lance Corporal Muldoon survived, thanks to Rifleman Khan, who was nominated for the Dickin Medal. It was awarded four months later on March 27, 1945. The citation read, "For rescuing L/Cpl Muldoon from drowning under heavy shell-fire at that assault of Walcheren, November 1944, while serving with the 6th Cameronians."

Two years later, Rifleman Khan wore his medal as he and Corporal Muldoon led the regiment in a victory parade though its hometown of Lanark in Scotland.

Ricky

The Germans had developed nonmetallic mines that could not be detected by conventional magnetic mine detectors. So the British trained dogs to search for soil that had recently been disturbed. They were then taught to halt and refuse to advance until the way ahead had been cleared.

One of these "M-dogs" was a short-legged Welsh collie named Ricky, who, like Rifleman Khan, had been loaned to the military by his owner for the duration of the war. The training was intensive. Not only did the dog have to sniff out explosives and point its nose at it until its handler came along, the animal had to remain calm and disciplined under fire. A dog running wild in a minefield would put everyone at risk. Many dogs were rejected.

After Ricky and his handler had finished their training, they were sent to Normandy after D-Day. They worked their way through France and Holland. The Germans had filled the Netherlands with mines—it was their last line of defense before the Allies entered Germany itself. Not only were the roads mined; but also the banks of the rivers and canals, and nonmetallic mines were particularly hard to detect among the shingle and mud that led down to the water.

On December 3, 1944, Ricky was working along the banks of the Nederweert River. He discovered a number of mines that were clumped together in clusters. But while Ricky was pointing them out, someone who was probing for mines set one off. The officer leading the party was killed by the explosion. Ricky was blown sideways off the bank and lay on the mud for some time, motionless. When help arrived, it was discovered that he had been hit on the head by a piece of shrapnel. He was bleeding profusely and there were fears that he'd lose his eyesight. But once Ricky was bandaged, he went back to work again unfazed. If he had panicked, he could have set off more mines, imperiling the lives of the rest of the patrol. He, too, was awarded the Dickin Medal. His citation read, "This dog was engaged in cleaning the verges of the canal bank at Nederweert, Holland. He found all the mines, but during the operation one of them exploded. Ricky was wounded in the head but remained calm and kept at work.

Had he become excited he would have been a danger to the rest of the section working nearby."

Fleabite

The US Army boasted a Pomeranian name Fleabite among its canine contingent. How such a small dog was accepted into the Army in the first place is not known. Nor is it recorded how Fleabite evaded the stringent British quarantine laws to arrive in England before the Normandy landings. But somehow he turned up with the troops on the beaches on D-Day. He had been trained to handle live firing and showed no fear when out on maneuvers. He showed such courage that, even before D-Day, he was promoted to sergeant.

On June 6, 1944, Fleabite arrived on the beaches at the front of the landing craft. He proved his worth by indicating which shells were going to land close by and which would fall farther away, so that the troops knew when they needed to take cover. He was sheltering in a foxhole with some troops, when suddenly he leaped out and ran for it. The rest of the men did likewise. Seconds later, the foxhole was hit by an 88mm shell. Unfortunately, Fleabite's master did not clear out in time and was badly wounded. He was sent back to a hospital in England and was told that Fleabite was not allowed to go with him.

But Field Marshal Bernard Montgomery, who was in overall command of the Anglo-American ground forces in the invasion of Normandy, was an animal lover. He had heard of this extraordinary little dog that had saved so many lives. He was in the area at the time and wanted to see the creature for himself. When he heard what had happened, he issued orders for Fleabite to return to England with his master.

Bobo

With the brand number Z303, Bobo and his handler Sergeant John Coleman led a reconnaissance patrol safely into German-held territory. Their mission accomplished, the patrol started back to their own lines. Scarcely a hundred yards from the outpost, Bobo alerted sharply and definitely straight ahead, then to the left, then to the right. A German patrol was surrounding the outpost, and a scout was sent in to warn the men who were holding it. The enemy was dispersed, and the patrol proceeded back to headquarters.

Peefke

A German shepherd named Peefke, brand number A595, was on patrol with the US Army in the Italian Alps when he suddenly stopped. There was no sign of the enemy, and the trail seemed empty. But when his handler looked more closely, he saw a nearly invisible trip wire stretched across the path. The wire was attached to three German "S" mines, which could have killed the entire patrol. Peefke is credited with saving hundreds of other lives during his service. Sadly, he was killed in action by a direct hit from an enemy hand grenade on March 20, 1945.

Silver and Pal

Other dogs also gave their lives. Silver, brand number A595, was given credit for preventing serious casualties by alerting his unit prior to a bayonet attack. She was killed in action on February 17, 1945, in a foxhole by an enemy grenade. And Pal, brand number 8M2, was killed by enemy action on April 25, 1945, at San Benedetto Po, Italy. Blocking shrapnel with his own body, he prevented the serious wounding of several men. Without Pal, the entire advance patrol would have been wiped out.

Rob

On February 8, 1945, the war dog Rob was awarded the Dickin Medal by Major Philip Sydney, himself a holder of the Victoria Cross. The citation read:

> War Dog 471/322. Special Air Service. Took part in landings during North African Campaign with an Infantry Unit and later served with a Special Air Unit in Italy as patrol and guard on small detachments lying-up in enemy territory. His presence with these parties saved many of them from discovery and subsequent capture or destruction. Rob made over twenty parachute descents.

Rob is probably the most decorated dog in British history. He is the only dog to have been recommended for any award by the War Office. Indeed, he was decorated eight times. In addition to the Dickin Medal, which is awarded by the PDSA, he also received a red collar and silver medallion inscribed "For Valour" from the Royal Society for the Prevention of Cruelty to Animals.

However, like the US Navy SEALs, the British Special Air Service is a ferociously secretive organization. Details of their operations are withheld from the public. So no one is entirely sure what Rob did to earn his medals—and some have maintained that he did not deserve them at all.

Born in July 1939, Rob was later described in *Shropshire Magazine* by his owner, Mrs. Heather Bayne, as "an ordinary cattle collie, born and bred in Shropshire. He was mostly black with a white face, one ear white with black spots, white waistcoat and 'stockings,' and a long black bushy tail with a white tip."

His mother, Jess, was a farm dog described by Mrs. Bayne as a "maid of all work." Rob was the larger of a litter of two pups and was sold to Mrs. Bayne for five shillings, then the equivalent of one dollar. At today's prices that would be about twenty dollars. Mrs. Bayne spoiled Rob. She let him sleep on a soft armchair and eat off her best china. She would talk to him and cuddle him, but her husband, Basil, a farmer, put him to work driving cows, rounding up pigs, and keeping chickens out of the vegetable garden.

Rob was happy to go to work with his master on the back of the tractor. But he had a gentle side, too. Once when a brood of chicks got lost in a patch of nettles, Rob picked them up carefully with his teeth and returned them to their coop without hurting them.

When Mrs. Bayne gave birth to a son, Rob displayed no jealousy about the affection that was lavished on the newcomer. Instead, he abandoned the comfy chair that had been his bed and slept across the threshold of the nursery, guarding the child.

In 1942, the British government asked for dogs to help with the war effort. As several members of her family were already serving overseas, Mrs. Bayne decided that Rob should also do his part. The War Office said they would take him for the duration of the war and, after three months, he was summoned to the War Dog Training School at Northaw, Middlesex, a hundred miles from his home in Shropshire in the west of England.

Rob showed a particular aptitude for military training; he passed classes in patrolling, sentry work, and delivering messages to handlers on the move. After graduation, he and his handler were sent to an infantry regiment in North Africa. When the Axis forces surrendered in Tunis in May 1943, all the military dogs were taken to a holding center at Constantine in Algeria, two hundred miles to the west.

The Special Air Service had been formed in July 1941 and had proved its worth fighting behind enemy lines in North Africa with the Long Range Desert Group. After the end of the North African Campaign, the SAS was stationed at Sousse, some sixty miles south of Tunis. The regiment's quartermaster, Captain Tom Burt, noticed that supplies were disappearing and decided that he needed a guard dog. Two were sent from Constantine. One was rejected because it had a skin disease. The other had the war dog number 471/322 tattooed inside his ear. This was Rob. He went on guard duty, proving his worth immediately. He could tell the difference between friend and foe, and it was said that "Italian prisoners of war walked sideways passed him, and pilfering Arabs became honest men overnight."

Rob would also ride around the camp in Captain Burt's jeep, bracing himself for every bump and turn as if he was still on farmer Bayne's tractor. Though he was clearly enjoying himself, he did not bark uncontrollably and Captain Burt thought he had the potential to be of greater use to the regiment.

It is not recorded who first thought of turning Rob into a "para-pup." All of Rob's handlers with the SAS were killed. But someone smuggled him onto a plane the next time the SAS were having a practice parachute drop to see how he could cope with the noise, movement, and vibration.

The US had toyed with the idea of sending dogs into battle with airborne troops, but found initially that the dogs enjoyed the parachute ride so much they would bark, costing the descending troops the element of surprise. However, American troops in North Africa did have canine parachute harnesses, which had been developed by the Quartermasters Corps for the San Carlos War Dog Training and Reception Center. The SAS borrowed one. It weighed ninety-three pounds, but Rob did not seem to find it uncomfortable. There was plenty of room for him to move his legs and paws.

Now used to air travel, Rob lay quietly at his handler's feet as the plane gained height. When the door was opened and the jump began, Rob calmly waited while his static line was attached. Then suddenly he was out of the plane, descending the eight hundred feet to the ground with his handler behind him. He did not even seem disconcerted when his parachute opened, jerking him upward. He made a perfect landing and was quickly released from his harness by another member of the team.

After that, the commanding officer gave his permission for Rob to join the team officially, and the dog began parachute training in earnest, making seventeen practice jumps in North Africa. However, the American dog handlers asked for their harness back, also enquiring how Rob was faring with it. When they were told how well he had done, they asked whether he could be sent to their kennels. But the SAS were not about to give him up. The harness remained on permanent loan. The US then reconsidered its position on airborne dogs, and a number saw action in Europe after D-Day.

During his training, Rob had learned, on landing, to lie still and wait for his handler to come and release him. Then he was to round up the rest of the patrol—a vital task if they were landing in darkness. Rob loved his role, and those who flew with him said that he would be first through the door of the aircraft on a parachute jump if he got to choose. Rob was now officially a "sky dog," whose existence was restricted to the "Very Secret List." However, the War Office wrote to Mrs. Bayne telling her that Rob was "fit and well, and doing a splendid job of work."

With the war in North Africa at an end, the Allies turned their attention first to Sicily and then to mainland Italy. Again, the activities of the SAS remain secret, but it is said that Rob made three parachute jumps into occupied Italy, though other accounts of his exploits say it was two parachute jumps and one landing by sea.

The SAS certainly made one landing in Italy. They went ashore from an American cruiser that was on its way to Taranto, the home port of the Italian Navy. Another team, under Lieutenant Alastair McGregor, dropped down near Chieti, on the east coast. Rob was with them.

By then, Italian dictator Benito Mussolini had been deposed and Germany was increasing its grip on its former ally. As the SAS team floated toward the ground, they saw German vehicles coming toward them, but the local Italians hid the SAS, relieving them of their parachutes to make silk underwear. At the time, hundreds prisoners of war who had been freed from the camps were traveling southward to meet the advancing Allies. Rob, it seems, was sent with them.

The Allied advance was held up that winter by a series of defensive lines the Germans had established across the Italian peninsula. Lieutenant McGregor and his party distracted the attention of a special SS squad that had been sent to round up the escaping prisoners of war. They ambushed the Germans, who were aided by the local *carabinieri* (the Italian military police). Only McGregor and Private McQueen made it back to Allied lines. They had been in enemy territory for four months and had been posted as "missing in action."

After the war, Lieutenant McGregor did not return to live in Britain. But when an article about Rob was published in the newspapers, his mother wrote to Mrs. Bayne, saying that her son was always talking about Rob's exploits and his bravery, so there seems little doubt that he was on that mission.

In an attempt to outflank the German defensive lines, the Allies planned an amphibious landing on the beaches at Anzio. But first it would be necessary to knock out the German reconnaissance airplanes based at San Egidio, more than a hundred miles to the north. On the night of January 12, 1944, a six-man SAS team led by Major Tony Widdrington and Lieutenant Hughes landed on the shores of Lake Trasimeno, twenty miles to the west. They ran into trouble when they met a German sentry crossing the River Tiber and were separated.

Major Widdrington and Lieutenant Hughes reached the airfield alone. On the night of January 19, they got through the wire and planted Lewes bombs on the seven German planes there. But before they could make their escape, one of the bombs went off, killing Major Widdrington. Lieutenant Hughes suffered temporary blindness and a concussion. He was captured and taken to a hospital in Perugia. Hitler had issued an order that all saboteurs landing by parachute be handed over to the Gestapo for summary execution, even if they were captured in uniform. This was a flagrant breach of the Geneva Conventions. However, a sympathetic German doctor had Lieutenant Hughes classified as an escaped prisoner of war and kept him out of the hands of the Gestapo. Hughes then escaped and reached the Allied lines, earning himself the Military Cross and bar. But the incident left him blind in one eye and deaf in one ear for the rest of his life.

After the newspaper article about Rob appeared, Major Widdrington's mother also wrote to Mrs. Bayne, saying that her son had often written to her about Rob's courage, but concluded that she would say "no more than that because he [her son] had died."

The SAS were withdrawn from Italy and returned to North Africa. But while the rest of the regiment was then sent back to Britain, Rob was left behind. Eventually, the captain of a Norwegian freighter agreed to take Rob to Scotland, where he was put in quarantine. Meanwhile the SAS headed for Belgium, then Holland. Many of the men Rob had known were killed at Arnhem. The battle was over before Rob was released from quarantine into the care of Captain Burt's batman, Sam Redhead.

After he had been presented with his medals, Rob was taken on tour to raise money for the returning prisoners of war he had already aided in Italy. He was stationed at Rednal and made one last parachute jump over the hills of Llangollen in Wales.

After the war ended, Rob should have been returned home. Travel arrangements were made and Mr. Bayne received notice that Rob would soon be returning. But, by then, Rob had become the SAS's mascot. Another letter followed asking permission to retain Rob for another tour of duty. However, in October 1945, the SAS was officially disbanded, though it was resurrected the following year.

In the meantime, on November 27, 1945, Rob was returned home. By then his Dickin Medal had gone missing, though the War Office eventually provided a replacement. Back on the farm, Rob had lost his old herding skills, now preferring to lead from the front. But he was good with Mrs. Bayne's children and still had an uncanny instinct for warning humans of danger. One night, he woke the household with his barking, then ran out into the night to round up some valuable yearlings that had escaped from their shed. On another occasion he fetched Mr. Bayne when a cow had slipped and fallen in its stall, tightening its chain around its neck.

Rob died in January 1952. The PDSA offered the family a plot in their pet cemetery, but the Baynes preferred to have him buried at home. He now lies under a marble gravestone whose inscription reads:

To the dear memory of Rob, war dog no. 471/322, twice VC, Britain's first parachute dog who served three and a half years in North Africa and Italy with the Second Special Air Service Regiment. Died 18th January 1952 aged twelve and a half years. Erected by Basil and Heather Bayne in memory of a faithful friend and playmate 1939–52.

But then doubt was cast over Rob's war record by Quentin Hughes, the lieutenant who had served with him in the SAS in Italy. After returning to Britain, he became commander of the regiment's headquarters squadron before a jeep accident forced him to retire from the army. He went on to become an architect and writer. In 1998, he published his autobiography *Who Cares Who Wins*—a play on the SAS's motto "Who Dares Wins."

In it, he said that far from doing twenty parachute jumps, Rob did little more than act as a companion for Captain Burt. His reputation was concocted when Rob's owners, who had lent him to the Army Veterinary and Remount Services to help the war effort, wrote asking if they could have their dog back. Burt, who had grown attached to the dog, was upset at the prospect of losing him, so he and Hughes contrived to keep him in the regiment by sending him on a parachute jump. Hughes would then write to the family to say that Rob's services were indispensable.

"We had a suitable parachute harness and I phoned through to the RAF and made arrangements for Rob to have a short flight," Hughes wrote in his memoir. "Unfortunately, quite a strong wind blew up during the flight and the RAF decided it would be dangerous to drop Rob on that day."

Hughes resolved to write the letter regardless, thinking it would be the end of the matter, but Rob's owners were so proud that they passed the letter on to the PDSA, who then awarded Rob the Dickin Medal.

Little notice was taken of the book until 2006 when a portrait of Rob and his Dickin Medal appeared in an exhibition called "The Animals' War" at the Imperial War Museum in London. Hughes had died in 2004, but his friend and colleague Mickey King told the newspapers that he remembers the former officer laughing about the hoax: "Quentin said that nobody survived twenty parachute drops, let alone a dog. You were lucky to survive three."

Professor Simon Pepper of the University of Liverpool, a friend and colleague of Quentin Hughes for more than thirty years, said, "If he was still alive he would be laughing like hell to see this. He would say: 'Why didn't they talk to me? I could've saved them the embarrassment.'"

However, the Imperial War Museum said the information was taken in good faith from the PDSA citation and the information that the story of Rob's heroism was a hoax came from only one source. Rob and his medal remained on show at the exhibition and, in 2008, the children's book *Rob the Para-dog* was published by Blue Hills Press.

Other Para-Pups

There were other para-dogs during World War II. They trained to parachute alongside the troops, then undertake guard, mine-detecting, and patrol duties. Their acute senses gave the paratroopers early warning of the presence of the enemy, and they undoubtedly saved many lives.

Most of these dogs belonged to the Scout Platoon of the 13th South Lancashire Regiment Parachute Battalion. Their dogs included Bing—whose real name was Brian—Flash, Monty, Ranee, and Bob, a captured German dog. All were German shepherds. Ranee was the only bitch. The platoon was initially commanded by Jack Sharples and later by Peter Downward, and its members were all dog lovers, especially the handlers, Ken Bailey, Lloyd Neale, Bill Rutter, and Wally Walton. Several of the dogs were dropped into Normandy in June 1944, and later over the Rhine in March 1945.

The 9th (Essex) Parachute Battalion had two para-dogs named Bereda and Glen. Their handlers were Jimmy Gardner and Emile Corteil, while the 1st (Canadian) Parachute Battalion had a dog named Johnny with handler Peter Kawalski. These dogs were all Alsatians. Both Glen and Johnny are known to have dropped into Normandy.

It is not known how much the dogs enjoyed the parachuting, but it has been said that Bing sometimes had to be encouraged out of the aircraft with a helpful nudge to his rear. Both Bing and Rob were awarded the Dickin Medal for their service.

Salvo

The US Airborne also had a para-pup, a fox terrier named Salvo. His first drop was in Cleveland, Ohio, where he jumped from 1,500 feet and landed safely without a scratch. His owner was Second Lieutenant Hugh Fletcher, a bombardier navigator from Cleveland, whose wife worked at the Dayton Signal Corps Inspection Office. Lieutenant Fletcher rigged up a special mini-chute for Salvo. It had a sixty-inch canopy, deployed by a static line, and was tested to twenty-five pounds. According to Lieutenant Fletcher, Salvo loved his parachute jumps.

Salvo went into action in the European theater, when he was just one year old and was given the honorary rank of second lieutenant. By May 1945, Salvo had clocked up more than five hundred hours in the air and had served on two battle operations in a Marauder medium bomber over western Europe. While stationed in England, Salvo also became a father. His mate was Duchess, an Air Corps mascot.

Antis

As relationships between dogs and their owners during wartime go, few could rival the bond between Czechoslovak airman Václav Robert Bozděch and his dog Antis. The German shepherd spent eleven years on air bases in France and Britain, and Bozděch said that during their time with 311 (Czechoslovak) Squadron, Antis saved his life over a thousand times.

Bozděch was born in Bohemia in 1912. After World War I ended in 1918, Bohemia became part of the new country of Czechoslovakia. Bozděch graduated from technical college in 1929, and then he was drafted for two years compulsory military service. Following basic training, he became a mechanic in the Czechoslovak Air Force. Demobilized, he went to work for the car manufacturer Skoda.

When Hitler came to power in Germany, Czechoslovakia came increasingly under threat. In October 1937, Bozděch returned to Czechoslovak Air Force and trained as an air gunner. Britain and France had promised to defend Czechoslovakia against German aggression. Nevertheless, the country was dismembered by the Munich Agreement of September 1938. In March the following year, Germany swallowed up the rest of Czechoslovakia. Determined to fight on, Bozděch and many other Czechoslovaks left. He made the long walk to Poland, but with only a small air force, the Polish had no need for new recruits. However, Bozděch heard that France was welcoming expatriate airmen. He obtained a visa from the French consulate in Krakov and then took a boat to Calais, arriving there in July 1939.

Once in France, Bozděch found that there was another problem. France feared that employing Czechoslovak airmen might be seen as a provocation by the Germans. So they had to sign a five-year contract with the French Foreign Legion, including a clause that allowed them to join Czechoslovak unit in the event of war. Consequently, Bozděch was shipped out to the Legion's base at Sidi-bel-Abbès in Algeria.

On September 1, 1939, Germany invaded Poland. Two days later, Britain and France declared war on Germany. Bozděch, who had retrained as a radio operator, then found himself in a Czechoslovak unit in the French Air Force. His plane was returning from a bombing raid over Germany when it crashed in no-man's-land on the German and French borders. As the crew headed back toward France on foot, they came across a ruined farmhouse that had been destroyed by German shelling. Inside, they found a small black and tan puppy. Bozděch picked him up and put him in his flying jacket. The puppy found the warmth comforting and by the time they got back to the airfield, he was asleep.

The puppy quickly became a favorite among the airmen. They then had to decide what to call him. It was clear that he was a German shepherd, but he had disproportionately large ears, so it was suggested that he be named after a plane. The Czechoslovak Air Force had flown Russian PE-2 bombers, which were called Ants after their Russian designation ANT. So the puppy was called Ant, but Bozděch strengthened this to Antis, a name the little dog responded to.

Antis began to accompany Bozděch on sorties, sleeping at his feet throughout the action. As the Germans stormed into France, the Czechoslovak airmen commandeered a horse and trap and headed south, taking Antis with them. Eventually they found their way to Gibraltar. From there they caught a boat to England. There were strict quarantine rules in force in the UK, but thanks to a sympathetic crew, Bozděch managed to smuggle Antis ashore in a kit bag. When the whimpering of a puppy could be heard from the pile of luggage, a fellow airman—a well-known joker—began making whimpering sounds as if he were a homesick dog.

By that time the Czechoslovak government-in-exile was established in Britain, and the Czechoslovak airmen were allowed to form their own squadrons in the RAF. Bozděch and Antis were sent for training at RAF Cosford in the West Midlands. But Antis had to wait patiently outside while his master attended English language classes. Meanwhile, Bozděch spent his spare time giving Antis obedience training.

Bozděch was then to become a fighter pilot with 312 (Czechoslovak) Squadron, stationed at RAF Duxford in Cambridgeshire where Antis became the squadron mascot.

As the Battle of Britain came to an end and the Germans began bombing British cities, 312 Squadron were moved to Speke Airfield outside Liverpool. After visiting a girlfriend in the city, Bozděch and Antis were caught in an air raid. Unable to find an air-raid shelter, they flung themselves to the ground, taking cover as best they could; Bozděch shielded Antis's body with his own. When the air raid was over, they were uninjured, but then began the awful business of searching for casualties. Antis began whining. He was unhurt and Bozděch realized that he had picked up on the distress of someone in the vicinity.

There was a huge pile of rubble nearby. Antis began digging, then stopped and started barking. Taking this as a hint, everyone started digging. They found four people—alive. But the area was unsafe. Seconds later, a wall collapsed in a great cloud of dust and masonry. Antis disappeared from sight. When the dust settled, he reappeared barking. He had found a mother and child, but sadly, both were dead.

One night, there was an air raid on the airfield and Antis disappeared. Bozděch had injured his hand at the time and was relieved of duty. He spent his time searching for Antis. Since he had first plucked the dog from the ruined farm house, Antis had rarely been far from the airman's side, and he soon became convinced that Antis must have been killed in the air raid. But he continued searching for his body. The search was impeded by a torrent of rain. Although the aircraft would hardly take to the skies in those conditions, they still had to be maintained, and a mechanic was out in the dark when he tripped over what it thought was a pile rags. On closer inspection, it was Antis.

The mechanic carried the dog inside and called for Bozděch. As his master approached, Antis recognized his footsteps and raised his head. Bozděch comforted him. Then the medics stepped in. The dog was weak but uninjured, and with proper care, he recovered. As far as they could make out, during the air raid, Antis had been blown into a bomb crater. Weakened by the blast, he was unable to get out and lay there, gradually growing weaker and dehydrated. When it began to rain, the water revived him and he managed to clamber out of the crater. Then he collapsed exhausted where the mechanic found him.

Determined not to be separated from his dog again, Bozděch transferred to 311 (Czechoslovak) Squadron, which was with Bomber Command. He became an air gunner again and could have Antis at his feet during sorties. They flew a Wellington bomber from East Wretham Airfield, a satellite of RAF Honington in Suffolk. The Czechoslovaks were billeted in local farmhouses where Antis had fun chasing the farmyard animals. He was indulged by all and, that Christmas, lapped the dregs from everyone's glasses, getting so drunk Bozděch had to put him to bed.

Bozděch and Antis flew on Wellington 1698-C—known as "C for Cecilia." In February 1941, they were sent out to bomb the Channel ports. Antis had strict orders to lie still at Bozděch's feet no matter what flak was thrown at them. It was a dangerous business, and the air gunner and his dog were particularly vulnerable. On the first raid, only five of the six planes returned.

The raids continued into April. For his part in the missions, Bozděch was awarded the Czechoslovak Medal for Valor, then the Czechoslovak War Medal. There would be no medals for Antis though. Under RAF regulations, he was not officially allowed to fly with his master, though everyone knew about it.

This was okay when they flew in raids near the coast of France, as these were conducted at a relatively low height. But as they flew raids deeper into Germany, they flew higher and needed to breathe through oxygen masks. Antis had to be left at home. But he soon learned to recognize the sound of the 1598-C when she was still miles from the airfield, and would be there to welcome his master home. However, in June 1941, they were sent on a raid on Hamm in Germany where the plane was hit by antiaircraft fire. Instead of making its way back to East Wretham, the damaged plane had to put down at RAF Coltishall in Norfolk. During the raid, Bozděch had been hit in the head by shrapnel and was taken to a hospital in Norwich.

For two days, Antis waited outdoors at East Wretham, expecting 1598-C to return. He would not eat or drink. He snarled at anyone who tried to get him to move and stayed out on the airfield day and night, rain or shine. When news came that Bozděch was in the hospital, the squadron's chaplain contacted him. Bozděch was well enough to come and collect his dog, and the two of them stayed together until he was fully recovered.

After two weeks, Bozděch was well enough to take to the air again. The squadron was making a raid on the harbor at Bremen. Antis recognized that they were making preparations to go. This time he would not be left behind and crept onto the plane when no one was looking. He made himself comfortable in a hammock used for injured crewmen. Soon he was fast asleep.

Everything was fine until they reached the Dutch coast and were climbing to 15,000 feet. Antis was feeling unwell; he needed oxygen. Bozděch felt a cold nose on his arm. He was surprised to see Antis and could see that he was in distress. Quickly, he pulled off his oxygen mask and held it over Antis's snout. But Bozděch needed both hands to fire the gun. He got Antis to sit between his legs so that the oxygen mask could rest over his nose and mouth. Then, when Bozděch felt light-headed, he could grab the mask and take a breath. This was not the ideal solution. But fate intervened. The plane was hit by a violent electrical storm. A lightning bolt knocked out some of its electrical systems. They had no choice but to turn back, dump the bombs in the sea, and head for home.

Somehow the plane limped back to East Wretham. When the crew discovered that Antis had been onboard, they gave him the credit for bringing them luck. After all, last time they had been out without him, they had been hit. From then on Antis was a vital member of the crew, and an extra oxygen mask was rigged up for him.

Together, dog and master made bombing raids over Hamburg, Hanover, Essen, Münster, Cologne, and Brest, with Antis lying silently at Bozděch's feet in his gun turret. Bozděch got a bar for his War Cross. On one occasion a piece of shrapnel hit Antis's oxygen mask and clipped his nose and left ear. Though he was obviously in pain, Antis made no noise or fuss. No one noticed his injuries until he had made his victory dance around the field at East Wretham when they got back.

They made a bombing raid on Mannheim. After dropping its bomb load, the plane came under sustained antiaircraft attack. The fuselage was peppered with flak. As the pilots struggled to regain control, they were caught in a searchlight and German fighters moved in for the kill. Though the plane was badly damaged, they managed to escape. The engines had just enough power to carry them back to England. When the crew checked each other over, they found that, miraculously, they were uninjured—all except for Antis.

Throughout the long flight home, Bozděch had often reached down to give Antis a stroke. He was as warm and docile as ever, and there was no reason to think anything was wrong with him. As they came in to land, Bozděch undid Antis's oxygen mask, expecting a lick on the hand. Instead he found that Antis was unconscious. Looking down, he could see a pool of blood. A shell splinter had left a deep gash in Antis's chest. It must have happened hours before but, again, Antis had made no fuss.

"Never once had he tried to hinder or distract the men from their duty," said Bozděch. "Silently he had lain there, staring mutely at his master and bearing his pain with a fortitude not often found even amongst the bravest of men."

There was no veterinarian on the base, so Bozděch took the stricken dog to sick bay. There, in the care of a doctor and nurse, he made a full recovery. They story of the brave dog who had been injured in the skies appeared in the newspapers. It was great for morale. But Bozděch made himself scarce. He knew that it was against regulations to take a dog onboard and he did not want to lose his companion.

Bozděch had now completed thirty-two sorties. He and Antis were sent to Number 8 Air Gunnery School at RAF Evanton in Scotland, where Bozděch was to train new air gunners. Antis quickly became a celebrity, winning a local dog show in October 1942. Again Antis and Bozděch, the heroes of Bomber Command, were celebrated in the newspapers. Then Antis misbehaved himself. He was caught worrying sheep. It was a capital crime. If convicted, he would be put down.

The RAF had tried to distance themselves from the story of the hero dog, but now they had to speak up for him. An officer was sent to confirm accounts of Antis's bravery with 311 (Czechoslovak) Squadron—and how, though he was gravely injured, he never distracted anyone from their duties. Antis escaped with a fine. The RAF now recognized the propaganda value of the dog. The Battle of Britain had given Fighter Command its heroes. Now Bomber Command had a hero of its own.

Bozděch was sent around the UK to show Antis off. But all the attention went to the dog's head. He would go off with anyone who was friendly to him. On one occasion, he got on the wrong bus and ended up so far away from home that Bozděch had to arrange for a transport plane to fly him back to base. Then he disappeared for five days and was found in town badly injured. It appeared that he had tried to jump over a spiked fence, but had misjudged the height and had torn his belly. Cadets took him to a veterinarian in Inverness. He was returned four days later, but it was two months before he made a full recovery.

In 1944, Bozděch and Antis were returned to 311 (Czechoslovak) Squadron, who had been posted to RAF Tain in the north of Scotland. They now had Liberators and were assigned to Coastal Command on U-boat-hunting duties. So Antis returned to the skies, at the feet of his master, the air gunner.

At first they patrolled over the Atlantic, but after D-Day, the Germans lost their U-boat bases in France and moved their operations to Norway, so the Liberators patrolled out over the North Sea. Patrols lasted up to twelve hours and they suffered the most severe weather conditions. Bozděch thought that it was not a good idea to subject Antis to this and tried to leave him with friends. Given the flying conditions, patrols did not always make it back to RAF Tain. When they were diverted, Antis pined terribly for his missing master and refused to eat when he was away.

On one occasion, after returning from a long flight, Bozděch found that Antis had retired to his bed and was barely strong enough to raise his head. Bozděch took him straight to the veterinarian, who diagnosed kidney disease. Antis was now to be grounded permanently. Flying again would risk his life.

On May 5, 1945, a Liberator from 311 (Czechoslovak) Squadron made its last anti-submarine patrol. It dropped five depth charges. The U-boat exploded and sank. Two days later the war in Europe was over, but it was not until August 1945 that the Czechoslovak airmen were allowed to fly home. Antis would go with them on a permit signed by Air Vice Marshall Janousěk. He was now officially a military dog.

The Liberators of 311 (Czechoslovak) Squadron flew back to Prague, flanked by fifteen new Spitfires that the British government had given to Czechoslovakia to start a new Air Force. The airmen were given a hero's welcome. But a government official called Bozděch aside and told him that, while he had been away, his parents and his uncle had been arrested and interrogated by the Gestapo. His mother and uncle had been released after three weeks, but his father had been sent to an internment camp. When he went to see his parents—for the first time in six years—they had visibly aged. Although he had been fighting for his country, Bozděch felt guilty that his family had suffered for his actions.

Bozděch was promoted to captain and became influential in the Ministry of Defense. He married and, though Antis was not allowed in the church for the ceremony, the dog managed to dominate the wedding photographs. Bozděch and his bride moved into a spacious apartment in Prague, a wedding present from the Minister of Foreign Affairs, Jan Masaryk, whom Bozděch and Antis had met when Masaryk was with the Czechoslovak government in exile in London. Bozděch named his first son Jan after Masaryk.

The veteran air gunner then began writing *Gentlemen of the Dusk*, his memoir of flying with 311 (Czechoslovak) Squadron. To help with this, he needed various official documents that were supplied by the British Attaché in Prague. However, it was dangerous for him to be seen interacting with Western countries in the changing political climate of Czechoslovakia.

In February 1948, the Communists seized power in Prague. A few weeks later, Jan Masaryk was found dead. The official story was that he had committed suicide by jumping out of a window at the Foreign Office. Most people believed that he had been thrown out. Clearly, Bozděch was in danger. He had to flee the country, but he could not tell his wife of his plans as that would put her in danger. He would send for her and their son, Jan, later. But Antis would be going with him.

To avert any suspicion, they left the apartment one morning together as if Bozděch were taking Antis for a walk on the way to work. Later Bozděch left the office, saying he was going to a meeting, but he did not return. Bozděch had arranged to escape with two other men who were worried by the idea of taking a dog along with them. But Bozděch insisted that Antis would be helpful. He would be able to smell and sense danger before they could see or hear it. When they left the city, Antis was sent ahead to scout the route, once again proving himself to be invaluable.

The escapees were heading through the forest toward the border when night fell. By then they would have been missed, and people would be out looking for them. They were just approaching a stretch of open ground when Antis went on the alert. They held back. Suddenly the area in front of them was lit up by searchlights, and they heard machine-gun fire. Truckloads of border guards and tracker dogs were soon on the scene. But it soon seemed clear that they were looking for another band of escapees.

Bozděch's group then found they had to cross a river. Bozděch held onto Antis's collar, but as they crossed the three men drifted apart. When Bozděch and Antis arrived on the opposite bank alone, Bozděch knelt down and whispered the word "seek" in Antis's ear. The dog launched himself back into the water and returned with one of the other men clinging to his collar. Then he went back to find the third man, who had been swept downstream.

That night, in their wet clothes, the men almost froze to death, but they kept warm by hugging Antis. As they approached the border, Antis started to growl, then disappeared into the morning mist. When they caught up with him they found he had a border guard pinned to the ground. Calling the dog off, they tied the hapless guard to a tree.

From the top of a hill, they could see a bend in the river and a line of stones that marked the German border. There was a sentry's hut nearby. They had no idea if it was occupied. But Antis could tell. He went up and scratched at the door. The hut was empty. Then they waded across the river to freedom.

They were now in the American Zone of Occupation and had to complete various formalities to become, officially, refugees. Then they were taken to the American air base at

Straubing, where Bozděch met other Czechoslovaks he had served with during the war. His countrymen had also fled, because anyone who had served with the British or French during the war was now under suspicion in Czechoslovakia. Everyone was concerned about the loved ones they had left behind. News came that Bozděch's wife had taken their son to stay with her parents where they would be safe.

Bozděch's priority was then to rejoin the RAF. Others were doing the same. First they had to naturalize as British subjects. Meanwhile, they were confined to a camp, which Antis hated. The dog began to refuse food again and had to be force-fed by Bozděch. After three months, the refugees were taken to the RAF Headquarters in Wiesbaden to officially enlist, then on to the British Embassy in Frankfurt where their new passports were waiting for them.

The British government promised to arrange visas for Bozděch's wife and son, but told him that he would not be able to take Antis to England with him. Bozděch refused to go without him. While he appealed to the Air Ministry, he was shifted around to several camps in Germany and saw some of the devastation that he and the rest of 311 (Czechoslovak) Squadron had wrought. Eventually, he convinced the RAF that, because of Antis's fame and his wartime service, he should be registered as an official war dog. In return, the RAF insisted that Bozděch present himself for duty in Britain while the documentation was sorted out.

Bozděch was to leave Antis in the care of Corporal Hughes, who would handle the paperwork. Bozděch inspected his quarters and decided to trust Hughes with his precious dog. He stayed with Antis in Hughes' quarters until the time came for him to catch the train that would take him to England via The Hague and Harwich.

A few days after Bozděch arrived in RAF Cardington in Bedfordshire, he received a letter from Corporal Hughes, saying that Antis was pining slightly, but was otherwise fine. Antis arrived in England two weeks later. However, he was taken direct to kennels in Hackbridge, Surrey, where he would have to sit out his quarantine.

Bozděch got a pass to see him though. After that, he visited twice a week. But then Bozděch injured his leg in a sporting accident and was sent to a hospital in Plymouth. While he was convalescing, he was refused permission to visit the kennels. When Bozděch did not turn up for his regular visits, Antis tried to escape to find him. Then he began refusing his food and his health went into decline.

Because of the publicity surrounding Antis, the kennels appealed to the authorities. Within twenty-four hours, Bozděch was transferred to a hospital in Surrey and went to visit Antis, but the dog was almost too weak to raise his head. The veterinarian's prognosis was bad. There was nothing he could do for Antis medically, he said. It seemed as if he had lost the will to live.

Despite the pain his leg, Bozděch spent a long time kneeling down beside Antis with the dog's head in his hands. When he got up to leave, Antis began trembling. Then Bozděch remembered an old trick. Back at the air base, when he had been forced to leave Antis, he would leave a glove by the dog's pillow—a token that he would return.

Instead of returning directly to the hospital, Bozděch went to church and prayed for Antis. The following morning, there was a phone call from the kennels. Bozděch feared the worst. But when he arrived, he found Antis had started to eat and barked a greeting. Bozděch then visited every day, and quickly Antis returned to health.

When Antis completed his period of quarantine, Bozděch was presented with a bill for the kennels that he could not afford to pay. The PDSA picked up the tab. That March, Antis was awarded the Dickin Medal.

Bozděch and Antis were posted to RAF Dalcross, not far from the now-decommissioned RAF Evanton. When they visited their former home, they could still see the scratch marks Antis had made with his claws on the bottom of the door of their old room.

By Christmas Antis was having difficulty walking. His appetite declined, and his eyesight and hearing grew worse. Despite the pain he was obviously suffering, however, the dog could not be dissuaded from waiting outside in the cold while his master went about his duties. By summer, it was clear the end of the dog's life was in sight. That August they went for one last walk together. The following day, they took the train to London. At the PDSA sanatorium in Ilford, Antis was put down. He was fourteen years old.

The PDSA had already prepared a grave for him in their pet cemetery where other Dickin Medal winners from World War II are laid to rest. On the granite headstone are inscribed the words "VÈRNÝ AŽ SMRTI"—"*Loyal unto death*."

Recon

Recon was a ten-month-old Scottish terrier owned by a waist gunner, a staff sergeant from Texas. The dog assumed a similar rank and had a sergeant's chevrons and a single rocker clipped in the fur of his left foreleg.

"He's bucking for tech now," said his owner.

Recon had completed five missions over occupied Europe and would have been in line for the Air Medal if he had been human. But his sixth mission ran into trouble. The Flying Fortress's engines caught fire over the English Channel, and they had to ditch the plane. With Recon under one arm, the sergeant inflated his life vest and jumped into the sea. He said that Recon did not move a muscle and simply clung onto his shoulder as he swam for a dingy. However, the dingy was already so full that there was not room for both of them. So he hoisted Recon aboard, and stayed in the water himself, clinging to the edge of the vessel until Air-Sea Rescue arrived. After they were rescued, the crew made Recon an insignia— silver wings with the Scottie's head in the middle.

Propwash

Though one commanding officer complained that his air base was beginning to resemble a dog pound, authorities recognized that having dogs around was good for morale. The dogs with the Eighth Air Force were immensely loyal. Propwash belonged to a captain in the Eighth Fighter Command. She was not a big dog, but there was no room for her in a fighter plane. She had to stay on the ground when his master took to the air, but would not be moved from the ready room until the captain returned.

Then one day, the squadron had been out on a sweep over France. Shortly before they were due back, Propwash jumped up, bolted through the door, and disappeared. Twenty minutes later, news came that her owner's plane had crashed. The captain had managed to bale out, but he broke his leg. When he was found, Propwash was sitting beside him, licking his face.

Slipstream

Another fixture on one US air base in England was Slipstream, who was described by journalist Corey Ford as "part collie, part police dog, part Scottie, and the rest GI floor mop. His left ear lops over, and his right one sticks straight out; he has a corkscrew tail, a protruding lower lip like Mayor La Guardia's, and one brown and one yellow eye." He belonged to an airman named Chad, who would write home to his wife in Oklahoma City about him. His letters would say, "Slips enjoyed the crackers you sent" and conclude, "Slips send his bests regards," or "P.S. Would write more but Slips upset the ink."

But one day before Chad was scheduled on a mission over Hamburg, he wrote to his wife saying, "Don't worry, if anything ever happens, Slips will take care of you okay." Chad did not return from the mission to Hamburg. His plane was shot down. From then on, Slipstream met every plane that landed back at the air base, just in case. Eventually, the crewmen built a crate for Slipstream so a pilot from Transport Command could smuggle him back to Oklahoma City.

Dootik

The Russian Air Force also had a famous dog in its ranks named Dootik. His log book listed more than fifty operational flights. One afternoon when his plane was returning from a sortie it crashed. The crew were badly injured, but one of them managed to open the door. Dootik, who was a little shaken up by the crash himself, jumped out. Some hours later, the pilot was awoken by a large canine tongue licking his face. Help was at hand. Dootik had found his way back to the air base and had brought help.

Bamse

Dogs also played their part in the war at sea during World War II. The most famous sea dog was Bamse, a St. Bernard who served with the Royal Norwegian Navy. He was born in 1936 in Oslo and was brought up in Honningsvåg, at the northernmost tip of Norway, which is at about the same latitude as Point Barrow, the most northerly tip of Alaska. As a puppy, Bamse belonged to Captain Erling Hafto, a former naval officer and Honningsvåg's harbormaster.

At the age of two, Bamse—which means "teddy bear" in Norwegian—showed his remarkable loyalty when he kept a twelve-day vigil with the daughter of the house. She was desperately ill, and he stayed with her, only allowing the doctor and her mother into the room. The girl, who was also two, survived.

Although Norway had remained neutral in World War I, as World War II approached, the Royal Norwegian Navy needed to expand rapidly and it looked to the country's large fishing fleet and merchant navy for suitable recruits. Honningsvåg was the home port to the whaler *Thorodd*. Originally named *Fleuris*, she was built in the US as an escort for the French Navy, but the ship was never delivered as she was completed in 1919, too late for World War I. She had served as a cargo and passenger vessel between the Falkland Islands and the whaling stations on South Georgia, before becoming a whaler at Honningsvåg. Converted back into a naval vessel, she was commissioned by the Norwegian Navy on October 19, 1939, and was fitted out as a coastal patrol vessel with 20mm anti-aircraft cannon as her main armament. Her command was given to Captain Hafto, and Bamse officially joined the crew on February 9, 1940.

The *Thorodd*'s main role was to escort convoys in and out of Narvik. Bamse was furnished with a large wicker basket on the upper deck, where he could rest during the day, weather permitting. In high seas, he retreated to a boom cupboard that had been cleared out to serve as his own personal cabin. Despite his thick coat, in the bitter winter of 1939–40, Bamse would wake crewmen by crawling into bed with them on stormy nights. He disliked rough seas and suffered badly from seasickness.

Once again, Norway tried to stay neutral, but the Allies wanted to deny Germany Norwegian iron ore for their war effort, while the Germans wanted to use Norwegian ports and airfields to dominate the north Atlantic. On April 9, 1940, the Germans occupied both Denmark and Norway. British, French, and Polish troops were sent to Narvik, and *Thorodd* was involved in a number of naval engagements to support the landings. She was also used to house German prisoners of war, whom Bamse guarded. When German planes attacked the ship, they would see a large St. Bernard standing on the bow, on the gun platform, baring his teeth. He would not be moved, but as he faced real danger, the crew fitted him with a steel helmet. Photographs of Bamse at the time show him to be a real dog of war. There is no doubt that he boosted the morale of the rest of the crew, who were getting their first taste of modern warfare.

On June 9, 1940, the Allies were forced to evacuate Navik, due to the fall of France. Fighting continued on land, but the Royal Norwegian Navy were ordered to sail for Britain. Of the 130 vessels in the Norwegian Navy in 1939, only thirteen got away. *Thorodd* was one of them. The rest were captured, sunk, or otherwise rendered unseaworthy.

Carrying extra men who wanted to join the Free Norwegian Forces in Britain, the *Thorodd* joined a British convoy headed for Scotland. The passage was stormy, but on June 12 the *Thorodd* sailed into the port of Lerwick on the Shetland Islands. Bamse felt at home there. There was plenty of fresh fish, his favorite food back home in Honningsvåg. After announcing her arrival to the British authorities, the *Thorodd* sailed on to Port Edgar, near Edinburgh on the Scottish mainland. This became the headquarters for the Royal Norwegian Navy. His courage during the fighting in Norway was already well-known and respected among the Norwegian sailors, and he became the mascot, not just of the *Thorodd*, but also the entire Norwegian Navy.

There, for the first time, Bamse traveled on trains and buses. He also developed a taste for beer. Although he liked pubs, Bamse was well-known for herding his shipmates out at closing time and escorting them back to the ship. He could not abide the brawling of drunken sailors in pubs and bars. It was said that he had been hit over the head by a bottle in a fight. When a fight broke out, he would intervene by putting his front paws up on the shoulders of one of the combatants.

While the *Thorodd* was being refitted, Bamse stood guard. One night when a crewman named Anders Petterøe, who was supposed to be standing guard, slipped off to the pub, Captain Hafto tried to climb the gangplank. Bamse would not let him pass until Petterøe returned.

Captain Hafto was given command of the Norwegian patrol vessel *Nordkapp* based in Hvalfordhur in Iceland. It was assumed that, after taking Norway, Hitler would set his sights set on Iceland. From there, the Atlantic convoys would make easy pickings. Naturally, Captain Hafto wanted to take his dog with him on his new post. But the crew of the *Thorodd* were adamant that Bamse should stay with the ship. They got their way.

The *Thorodd* had been converted into a minesweeper and moved up the coast to Dundee. Her command was given to Lieutenant Reidar Cook Thovsen who was surprised to find a large St. Bernard among his crew. Britain was now fighting for its life, and the *Thorodd*, with crewman Bamse, went on patrol in the North Sea. Because of the constant danger from mines, Bamse was not allowed on the aft deck among the minesweeping gear. He had to take pride of place on the fore deck, keeping a lookout for floating mines.

On shore he was equally vigilant. When Norwegian seaman Olav Nilsen was attacked on the dockside at Dundee by a robber brandishing a knife, Bamse came to the rescue. He ran at the man, then sprung up on his hind legs. His weight and momentum pushed the man backward until he fell off the quayside into the water.

Bamse had no fear of the sea. When the crew of the *Thorodd* played informal games of football on deck, the ball, which was made of rolled-up cloth, sometimes went over the side and Bamse would leap overboard to retrieve it.

When a hapless, and probably drunken, sailor fell into the River Tay, Bamse barked loudly to raise the alarm, then dived in to rescue him. The tide was going out and Bamse leapt twelve feet down into the water, grabbed the man's clothing with his teeth, and pulled him to safety.

Bamse was also fearless when it came to fighting other dogs. He once took on and beat a bulldog, despite the fact that the latter was the wartime symbol of Bamse's British hosts. Other dogs were chased from the *Thorodd*.

On June 1, 1944, Bamse was enrolled as a member the Allied Forces Mascot Club. On the afternoon of July 22,

1944, Bamse died in Montrose. He was buried with full military honors in front of the crews of six Norwegian Navy ships. The grave is on the property of the pharmaceutical company GlaxoSmithKline, which maintains it. It is visited regularly by parties from the Royal Norwegian Navy. In 1984, Bamse was awarded the *Norges Hundeorden* medal and, in 2006, the PDSA Gold Medal. A life-size bronze statue of Bamse was also unveiled in Montrose that year. A duplicate now stands on the harbor front in Honningsvåg.

Irma

London suffered a ceaseless blitz from September 7, 1940, to May 10, 1941, when the German Luftwaffe bombed the city. It came under attack again from June 13, 1944, until March 1945 by V-1 flying bombs and V-2 ballistic missiles. By this time, Londoners had learned the usefulness of dogs in rescuing survivors from bombed buildings, and finding dead bodies among the rubble.

A German shepherd dog named Irma was awarded the Dickin medal for her rescue work. She was one of two Alsatians owned by Margaret Griffin, who worked with London's Civil Defense Services during World War II. Mrs. Griffin kept a diary meticulously recording her dogs' dedication and heroism.

At 12:15 a.m. on the night of October 10, 1944, the dogs were called out. Irma went to work searching a collapsed house in Ilford in the east of London. Rescue personnel began digging where she indicated and found the body of a woman. In the next house, a woman was trapped, and Irma found three women buried about fourteen feet down. In the next house, the dog found nothing, though a woman was missing. The next morning her body was located in a garden fifty yards from the blast.

That afternoon at 12:17, a V-2 rocket hit Leytonstone in East London. Mrs. Griffin arrived with Irma and the other dog, Psyche. They found three bodies.

At 1:20 a.m. on October 30, Mrs. Griffin and her dogs were called to Maryland Point in West Ham, East London. Irma found three children trapped in a cellar, but one of the children died before the rescue team could dig them out. The dogs were called back the next day to continue searching the rubble and found the bodies of three women.

At 4:00 p.m. on November 2, they arrived in Deptford, southeast London, where a flying bomb had hit a railway line and demolished five houses on either side. The dust was so bad that both dogs were sneezing. Irma made a violent indication toward the entrance to a cellar. It took two hours to dig through the debris. By that time, the man inside was dead.

A V-1 rocket hit an ambulance depot, two offices, and a pub in Shooter's Hill, southeast London, on November 11. Most of the casualties were in the bar and billiard room of the pub. Irma made a strong indication to a mound of debris on the edge of the site. The bodies of two women were found under seven feet of rubble. Irma made other indications to the site of the office. Tons of debris had to be removed before they found the bodies of two women. The dogs indicated that there was another body there, but they left before the rescue team found it.

At 1:30 a.m. on November 20, they were in East Ham where a large chimney had come down and was resting precariously on two mounds of earth thrown from the crater. The dogs took an interest in this. A rescue worker used a crane to move the chimney. Underneath was a void. With a flashlight, they could see some clothes. Digging down, they found a woman who was alive and conscious, but terribly crushed.

The following day, a rocket hit Walthamstow in northeast London about 12:30 p.m. Arriving at the site an hour later, Mrs. Griffin found four houses that had been completely demolished and twelve more that had been badly damaged. The water pipes had burst, and the gas main was leaking. Despite the smell of gas that permeated the rubble, Irma made an indication toward the back of the pile of debris. She and Mrs. Griffin crawled under the floorboards on their stomachs and found the bodies of a woman and two children.

A number of rockets fell on December 1. At 11:40 p.m., the dogs were called to Black House Lane in Walthamstow. A rocket had blown up a concrete road, eighteen inches thick, and demolished fifteen houses. Psyche took Mrs. Griffin up over a broken wall and indicated the spot where a child, alive and relatively unhurt, was found. Irma indicated upward, toward a wrecked bedroom. Two more children were found in there. Irma then indicated a house across the road. They crawled in under the floor to find the body of a woman in a cavity. In the next house, smoke from a fire burning under the floors put the dogs off the scent, but other indications around the site led to more bodies being unearthed.

At 10:30 p.m. on January 14, 1945, they were called to London Road, Barking, where a three-story apartment block over a row of shops had collapsed. The dogs made a series of indications, but as the block was built out of steel and concrete, heavy lifting gear would be needed, and they did not stay around to see what happened. Mrs. Griffin heard later that one live person had been rescued and four bodies had been found. Months after that, she heard that, in all, seventeen casualties had been recovered from the places the dogs had indicated.

The dogs were called to Osborne Road in Tottenham, north London, at 9:00 p.m. on January 20. Irma found two live casualties in number 1. At number 2, she indicated one side of a large fire burning fiercely there. There was thick smoke. A family of five was found. She also made an indication at number 3, and a live cat was found. At Number Four, she found four adults and located two more, with possibly a third behind them. They moved on to investigate a voice that had been heard but no one could pinpoint. Back at number 3, Irma made another indication, but the debris was packed so tight the rescue workers were making slow progress and work was suspended until it was light the following day. Meanwhile, Irma went on to investigate the crater. She made an indication below two huge mounds of earth that had been blown out, but Mrs. Griffin could get no one to dig there, as they were all too busy. So she marked the spot and called the leader of the rescue squad. He helped dig down, and they found a woman trapped. She was alive, but badly crushed.

On January 27, they were back in West Ham where a rocket had hit one house and flattened six more. Two boys were found alive at 90 Gordon Road. The dogs looked around the perimeter of the debris and Irma indicated so keenly that Mrs. Griffin felt sure that the victim was alive. She called the rescue officer, who brought three or four men. They began digging and soon they found a small boy and a young woman wrapped in their blankets and bedding. They had been blown out of their bedroom on the mattress and landed among the falling debris. Some boards that were sticking up had prevented them from being crushed. When Irma and Mrs.

Griffin arrived, the rescue team had actually been walking over the top of them. Both were conscious.

"But the girl was very much shocked and exhausted," Mrs. Griffin said.

Two days later, the dogs returned to Gordon Road. It was snowing and bitterly cold. Mrs. Griffin went under the floor cavity that ran under numbers 90 and 92. Psyche whined and lay down. Irma scratched at the rubble and found bed-clothes there. On Mrs. Griffin's recommendation, the rescue team started digging. They dug up the bodies of a man and a woman. Irma had made an indication number 94 two days before, but then they had been called away. They returned there and Irma went back to the little cavity she had indicated before. She again indicated that someone was there. Taking the wind into account, Mrs. Griffin advised that the rescue workers dig back from that point. After about four feet, they found the body of a woman.

At 3:00 a.m. on February 1, they were called to Barnaby Road, West Ham. Some live casualties were trapped there. The dogs gave an indication to a large mound of debris at the back of the house. Mrs. Griffin was told that the area had already been cleared, but she heard later that the body of an adult had been found there. Farther down the road, she got an indication from both dogs. A man and a woman were found there, alive. The dogs searched around the perimeter to no avail. Under a mountain of bricks and earth that had once been a house, Irma made an indication. An adult was found there.

Later that day, the dogs were searching either side of another crater. Both dogs made an indication, even though Mrs. Griffin had been told that the area had been cleared. While the rescue workers began digging, Mrs. Griffin went around the perimeter where a dead dog was discovered. In the other house that was supposed to have been cleared, Psyche gave an indication. Mrs. Griffin began digging, then heard a whine. Under the debris of a collapsed floor and smashed furniture, she found a setter. It took them some time to get the dog out. By then, he was so exhausted that Mrs. Griffin feared he was going to die. But after being given some hot tea, the injured weakened animal was wrapped in a blanket and left to lie outside in the fresh air. Then he revived a bit. They called the PDSA, who sent a van for him.

Mrs. Griffin was called again at 2:30 a.m. on February 6. A rocket had hit Chingford in northeast London. It had gone right through one house, and gas was leaking badly. Irma indicated upward and toward the dividing wall of two semi-detached houses, thirty feet of which was still standing. The dogs climbed up on a twenty-foot pile of rubble, and Irma indicated downward. Behind a bath, they found a cavity. Rescue workers began digging. After fifteen minutes, they called for silence and heard a baby cry. The rescue workers resumed digging, tunneling into the debris as fast at they could. They found a Morrison shelter, a heavy steel box used as an indoor air-raid shelter. One side was made from wire mesh and could be opened to accommodate two or three people. These shelters usually stood in the living room, where they doubled as a table.

The Morrison shelter in Chingford showed its worth that February. Inside, there was a woman with a baby and a small boy. It took an hour and forty-five minutes to dig though to it. During that time, the woman kept up a conversation with the rescue workers. But five minutes before they reached her, she fell silent. When they had made a hole big enough, they pulled out the children alive, but the woman was unconscious. By the time a doctor got through to her, she was dead from asphyxiation.

The dogs had made another indication to the huge pile of debris. The rescue team shifted much of it, but found nothing. Then, at the request of the team leader, Mrs. Griffin took the dogs back there. Psyche immediately indicated around the other side of the debris, where there was still a ridge around four feet high and four to five feet wide. The rescue workers resumed digging and found the dead woman's husband there. He was still alive and was rushed to the hospital.

On February 12, another rocket hit Leystonstone. It made a huge crater, breaking both the water and gas mains. Two houses had been demolished completely, and the cold wind was blowing around dust. Four live people were found. A woman who was trapped started screaming hysterically, which distracted the dogs. More live casualties were found at numbers 2 and 3. The dogs made another indication at number 2. They made a stronger indication at number 4. Part of the floor had been blown out, forming a cavity. In it, under two feet of debris, they found a seventeen-year-old girl. Eight people were found below the collapsed floors, and the leader of the rescue team said that Irma and Psyche had saved them hours of digging.

In all, the two dogs located 233 people, 21 of whom were found alive. But Irma was the star. She would bark differently, depending on whether the buried victim was alive or dead. On one occasion, Irma signaled with an "alive" bark and rescuers dug out a victim who was apparently dead. But Irma was proved right as the man, who was merely unconscious, eventually stirred. On another occasion, Irma refused to give up on two girls who had been trapped under a fallen building for two days.

On January 12, 1945, Irma was presented with her Dickin Medal. The citation read, "Irma. For being responsible for the rescue of persons trapped under blitzed buildings while serving with the Civil Defence Services in London."

At the same ceremony, Dickin Medals were presented to two other remarkable dogs. One was Beauty, who is considered to be the first rescue dog. A wire-haired terrier, she was owned by the veterinary officer of the PDSA, Bill Barnet, who led the rescue squads for animals in London during the blitz. One day in 1940, Beauty began digging among rubble alongside the rescue teams. She found a cat. This was the first of sixty-three animals she rescued during the war.

The other dog to receive the Dickin medal that day was a German shepherd named Jet. Training in antisabotage work at the War Dogs School in Gloucester, he had worked on airfields. He then retrained as a rescue dog and was the first to be used officially in that capacity. He was responsible for the rescue of 150 people trapped beneath blitzed buildings.

CHAPTER FOUR
WAR IN THE PACIFIC

THE US MARINE CORPS was no better prepared to utilize dogs than the Army was, but they were about to learn a bitter lesson. The battle for Guadalcanal, which lasted from August 7, 1942, to February 9, 1943, showed them how useful dogs could be. During the nighttime in the jungle, the Japanese had infiltrated American lines and killed marines who were sleeping in their foxholes. If the marines had had dogs with them, the barking would have warned them that the enemy was approaching.

They needed scout dogs as well as guard dogs. When the marines were out on patrol, the Japanese would often let the point man pass, then ambush the rest of the patrol. A scout might walk past an ambush, but a trained dog would not. So a dog-training program was inaugurated at Camp Lejeune on December 20, 1942. One officer and nineteen enlisted men were sent to for training at the Army dog-training unit at Fort Robinson, Nebraska. By the end of the month, they were expected back with thirty-eight dogs, mostly German shepherds, to set up the War Dog Training School. Its graduates would see action across the Pacific.

Caesar

Caesar was a three-year-old German shepherd belonging to the Glazer family. They had already made sacrifices for their country. The two oldest Glazer boys were in the army; the youngest was headed for the Merchant Marine. But when Mr. and Mrs. Glazer read the appeal from Dogs for Defense, they knew that an intelligent dog like Caesar might save the life of someone else's son, and they willingly gave him up. They expected him to serve with the army. Instead Caesar was to become a marine.

At Camp Lejeune in North Carolina, Caesar was assigned to Private Rufus Mayo of Montgomery, Alabama, and Private John Kleeman of Philadelphia, Pennsylvania. Trained as a messenger dog, Caesar was to carry dispatches between his two handlers. Both young men were crazy about Caesar. Mayo wrote home that the dog had more sense than most men, and he would "not give up Caesar for a general's commission." The dog sent his regards by applying a paw print to the bottom right-hand corner of every letter he sent home.

Kleeman even promised to bring Caesar when he came home on furlough to show him off. But he never got the chance. Before his next leave, the 1st Marine Dog Platoon was posted to Camp Pendleton in California, then on into the South Pacific. Caesar was with the landing party that hit the beaches of Bougainville in the Solomon Islands on November 1, 1943. He was with M Company of the 3rd Raider Battalion, who were holding a roadblock on the Piva Trail. Their walkie-talkies would not work in the dense jungle, so Caesar became the link between the front line and the battalion command post. He made several trips in the failing light, under enemy fire.

The following day, the marines laid a phone line, but this was cut by the Japanese and Caesar came into his own again. In all he made nine trips between the roadblock and the command post in the rear, braving heavy sniper fire.

On the second night, PFC Mayo was assigned to a foxhole several hundred yards in front of the rest of the company, and Caesar was sent with him as a canine sentry. He was a lifesaver. Caesar woke in time to catch a Japanese soldier in the act of dropping a grenade into the foxhole and chased him off. Mayo awoke and called Caesar back, but as he turned the Japanese soldier shot him.

"During the confusion of the battle, Caesar disappeared," said Lieutenant Clyde Henderson, commander of the 1st Marine Dog Platoon. "Mayo was frantic. He called me to learn whether I had seen him. He was half shouting and half crying. I hadn't seen Caesar. Soon we found a trail of blood through the jungle."

They followed it. It led back to the command post, down the trail Caesar had taken many times carrying messages. They found him in some bushes near where PFC Kleeman was usually waiting. Caesar was barely conscious. Wounded and in pain, he had tried to make his way back to his other handler.

When he saw Caesar lying there, Lieutenant Henderson said, Mayo "ran and lay down beside him and hugged him gently." Henderson, Mayo, and Kleeman quickly cut down two saplings and fashioned a stretcher out of the two poles and a blanket. There was no shortage of marines volunteering to carry the stretcher with the wounded dog on it to the first-aid station. When they heard what Caesar had done, other marines along the way stood at attention and saluted the fallen dog.

At the field hospital, Caesar was rushed into surgery. Mayo and Kleeman waited anxiously outside the hospital tent. After twenty minutes, the surgeon emerged. Caesar had been hit twice. The surgeon had been able to remove one bullet, but the other was too close to his heart. But Caesar was a strong dog, and the surgeon was hopeful that he would pull through.

Caesar made a full recovery and, after just three weeks, returned to active service. The commandant of the Marine Corps, General Thomas Holcomb, wrote to the Glazers, thanking them for volunteering Caesar and praising him for "saving the lives of many marines." However, the dog lived the rest of his life with a chunk of lead lodged behind his left shoulder.

Andy

A Doberman named Andy also landed on Bougainville. He was one of the "Devil Dogs," the name the US Marine Corps adopted for their war dogs during World War II. The marines themselves were named "Devil Dogs" during World War I, a title possibly ascribed to them by the German soldiers they fought against.

With his two handlers, Private Robert E. Lansley and Private Jack B. Mahoney, Andy led 250 men up the Piva Trail. His job was to search for snipers and Japanese ambushes that could be easily concealed in the dense jungle. They may have been hidden to the eye, but they could not fool Andy's sensitive nose and ears.

Andy was one of the few dogs in the platoon that could work off the leash. He walked about twenty-five yards ahead of the column. If the dog got too far in front, Lansley would make a clucking sound to attract his attention, then motion for him to fall back.

During the march, Andy would happily run ahead. But when he sensed danger, he would freeze with the hair on his back and neck standing on end. The marines then knew to throw themselves to the ground—and quick. On one occasion, he had come across a Japanese machine-gun post. Bullets missed Lansley and Mahoney by a couple of feet. They had no doubt that, without Andy's warning, they and many of the marines following them would have been dead.

That day, the company led by Andy advanced further than any other unit in the invasion force. They took the only signification position to be taken by US forces. And during the advance under the auspices of Andy, no marine was killed or wounded. Due to his aristocratic demeanor, the marines started calling Andy "Gentleman Jim."

On the night of November 7, the Japanese landed reinforcements and Andy was back in action again. On November 14, the American advance was held up by heavy machine-gun fire, but the marines could not determine where it was coming from. Privates Lansley and Mahoney volunteered to take the point with Andy and take out the machine-gun nests.

With Andy in the lead, the two marines headed into the jungle. Then Andy froze. They hit the earth. The enemy was ahead, but Andy's gestures were hard to read. He looked to the left; then to the right. With Mahoney covering him, Lansley crawled up to Andy's position. Peering through the undergrowth he could see two banyan trees—one to the left of the trail, one to the right. When he took a closer look, he noticed that the leaves looked odd. There was something wrong with the roots, too. The trees had been converted into two camouflaged machine-gun nests, one on either side of the trail to catch the advancing marines in lethal cross fire.

Lansley and Mahoney opened up on the trees, then lobbed grenades into the dugouts that lay beneath them. When it was all over, eight Japanese soldiers lay dead and the line could resume its advance.

Rollo

The Japanese got wise to the Americans' use of dogs and sought to target them. One of the first to lose his life was Rollo, one of the first six dogs to join the Marine Corps. With his handlers, Private Russell T. Frierich and Private James M. White, Rollo, a Doberman, led a number of successful patrols and was trusted to work off the leash.

However, Rollo and his handlers were assigned to an Army unit temporarily attached to the marines. Rollo and Friedrich were a good way ahead of the patrol when Rollo went on the alert. But the commander of the Army unit did not take Rollo's alert seriously and ordered them to go on. A little farther into the jungle, they walked into an ambush.

White was with the patrol some distance behind. He said, "We could hear the Japs hollering, 'Doggie, doggie!' and then chattering something in Japanese we took to mean 'dog.' They were intent on getting the dog."

In an effort to keep him safe, Friedrich sent Rollo back to White. But the gunfire grew more intense, much of it aimed at Rollo.

"The bullets as they crossfired kept coming close to us," said White. "I was debating how to get out. Friedrich was only eight feet from me, but behind a tree. I sent Rollo to him as the bullets came closer. Just as Rollo got to Friedrich, he was hit. Rollo whined a minute and then died."

Friedrich was also shot during the battle, while a Japanese bullet tore through White's helmet and grazed his scalp. The patrol was forced to retreat. When they fought their way back to that position, they found Rollo's body. Friedrich had disappeared and it was thought that he was taken as a prisoner of war.

Wolf

Another casualty of the Pacific war was Wolf, a German shepherd who led an infantry patrol though the Corabello Mountains on Luzon in the Philippines. He caught the scent of a Japanese formation that was about to attack. They were still 150 yards away, so the Americans had time to take cover.

During the battle, a piece of shrapnel from a shell tore through Wolf's coat. But he made no sound and those around him did not even know that he had been hurt. The Americans soon found that they were outnumbered and being encircled. Just in time, they pulled out. Fighting their way through enemy lines, Wolf and his handler took the lead again. Thanks to Wolf's alerts, they managed to make it back to headquarters without suffering a single human casualty.

It was only then that Wolf's injuries were discovered. A veterinarian performed an emergency operation, but was unable to save his life. The 25th Division's casualty list included the entry, "WOLF, US Army War Dog, T121, Died of Wounds—Wounded in Action."

Smoky

In February 1944, a jeep driven by American GI Ed Downey broke down in the jungles of New Guinea. When the engine died, Downey heard the whimpering of a dog. Searching the undergrowth by the roadside, he found a small Yorkshire terrier in a foxhole. He rescued the little dog and, when he got the jeep going again, he returned both the vehicle and the Yorkie to the motor pool of the 5212th Photographic Wing at Nadzab airfield, a forward air base on the eastern end of the island.

Downey did not like dogs and left the mutt with Sergeant Dare, a mechanic at the motor pool. Dare was a busy man, but took the time to feed and water the little dog, whose thick coat was ill-suited to the climate on New Guinea. She seemed to be on the verge of heat exhaustion, so he took a pair of shears and hacked away much of her fur. This left her fur gingery brown with smoky tips, so Dare called her Smokums.

No one knew whom the dog belonged to or where she had come from. She paced anxiously as if she had suffered some trauma, and it was feared that she would not survive the night.

Corporal Bill Wynne, an aerial photographer with the 26th Photographic Reconnaissance Squadron, shared a tent with Ed Downey. He heard about the dog and went to visit. She immediately took to Wynne and licked his face. A bond was formed. Wynne bought the dog for two Australian pounds—$6.44—money Sergeant Dare needed to return to a poker game. Wynne renamed his new pet Smoky.

She did survive the night. Corporal Wynne soon nursed her back to health and, against Downey's objections, moved her into their tent. She even shared Wynne's cot—after he had used his helmet to give her a bath. Her bath time became a daily routine, as Smoky was the perfect host for chiggers and other parasites that carry "scrub typhus," which is almost always fatal if untreated. There was no effective treatment for it until the development of antibiotics. When he bathed her, Wynne checked for the parasite, always hoping that he would not find one. If he did and she fell ill, he would have no alternative but to put her down. On his jungle air base there was no veterinary service.

Because of the danger of disease, some of Wynne's colleagues wanted Smoky to be tethered to his bed. But Smoky loved to disappear into the undergrowth and chase the humpback chickens in nearby villages, even though she would only be one mouthful for one of the pythons that inhabited the forest. Wynne was from Cleveland, Ohio, and was a little wary of the jungle. He did not want to chase after her, so he used the knowledge he had gleaned from prewar dog-training classes to get her to come back when he called. This was not as easy as he anticipated. Smoky was not a puppy, but a full-grown dog—though she weighed only four pounds. She did not understand commands in English and, when he took her to a nearby prisoner-of-war camp, he discovered that she did not understand Japanese either, so her provenance proved even more puzzling.

Wynne had been a dog-lover from an early age, though his relationship with his pets had caused him heartache. When his parents split when he was three, he spent a short time in an orphanage, where the children had an Airedale terrier called Rags. However, one of the older and more troubled children poured acid over it. He never forgot Rags's anguished yelps.

When Wynne returned home, he learned that his mother had bought a large white collie named Skippy. The dog was troublesome, though; he was always running away and his barking disturbed nearby residents. But one night, some neighbors were awakened and discovered that their house was on fire. Overnight, Skippy turned from neighborhood nuisance into local hero.

Wynne's best friend, George Hansa, had a Great Dane named Big Boy. The two pals and the dog were inseparable. Then a mongrel named Queenie found refuge in the Wynne household. But after she gave birth to a litter of puppies, Queenie was killed in a road traffic accident. The family found consolation in one of her pups, who was named Pal. Wynne taught him all manner of tricks. He could jump up and take the hat off someone's head, then hand it back to them. Or, after riding downhill on a sled with Wynne, Pal could tow the sled back up to the top of the hill for him.

Mindful of Queenie's fate, Wynne taught Pal to jump into his arms so that he could carry him safely across busy streets. Pal also leapt into his arms if a hostile dog came along. Without being taught, Pal found his way to Wynne's school and would wait outside the gate at 3:30 p.m. everyday. But one day, Pal did not turn up. Wynne never saw him again; he was heartbroken.

During the Great Depression, the Wynne family had no money to keep dogs. Wynne's mother lost her job, and they moved ten times as she looked for work. But with the beginning of the war in Europe in 1939, the economy began to pick up and life became more settled. When Wynne was just seventeen, he met Margaret Roberts and fell in love with her. The couple hoped to marry. Wynne found work in a local factory and began working two shifts a day to save money.

On his twentieth birthday, Margaret bought him a six-week-old Doberman–German shepherd cross named Toby. The dog would accompany him to work and sleep on the warm brick floor of the factory. Wynne and Toby also attended class at the Cleveland All Breeds Training School. The training there was approved by the American Kennel Club and incorporated techniques then being used by the army to train patrol and guard dogs. All of this set Wynne in good stead when it came to training Smoky.

Bill Wynne was drafted in 1943. After taking a laboratory technician course, he qualified for air reconnaissance duties and was sent to New Guinea, where he met Smoky, who soon began accompanying Wynne on his twelve-hour shifts in the photo lab. During his free time, Wynne taught Smoky new tricks. Her party piece was to fall on her side and play dead when Wynne aimed a finger at her and shouted, "Bang!" She would not move, no matter what anyone did to her, until Wynne said, "Okay." Then she would jump her feet again. Wynne taught her lots of new tricks to entertain the children in local villages.

Smoky also proved her worth to the war effort. She could tell when a tropical storm was approaching. Typhoons made photo-reconnaissance impossible and flying dangerous, resulting in huge aerial losses. So her forecasts made Smoky enormously popular with the fliers. They wanted to enter into a competition that the forces' magazine *Yank Down Under* was holding for mascots—even though the squadron had already entered its official mascot, a monkey named Colonel Turbo.

Turbo and Smoky had long been rivals. The monkey was known for its destructive ways after the pilot who had brought him from a zoo in New Mexico had died in a plane crash. When Smoky first joined the squadron's strength, it was feared that she could fall foul of the aggressive primate. In an effort to introduce them on friendly terms, Wynne put Smoky down at the full extent of Turbo's leash. They sniffed each other suspiciously at a distance. Then Turbo launched himself at Smoky, biting her nose. The Yorkie yelped and fled, but then returned to deliver a sweeping scratch across the monkey's snout. Turbo was shocked and he ran up a tree to tend his wounds. Convinced that he could get the better of a small terrier, Turbo came back down the tree and returned to the fray. But Smoky bested him again. After that Smoky would tease Turbo, then run out of range of the tethered creature. Eventually, Turbo became so bad tempered and destructive that he had to be shot.

Wynne took pictures of Smoky sitting in his helmet, but decided that would not be good enough to win the magazine's competition. Then he thought of photographing her descending by parachute. He took a pilot's parachute and tailored it for Smoky, using belts to make a harness. Wynne swung Smoky around in this rig to get her used to the sensation.

It was not considered a good idea to throw her out of an airplane. Instead she was to be dropped from the top of a thirty-foot tree. First her supporters had to trim off all the branches on one side so they could not snag her fall. She was carried up the tree, while a bunch of GIs were stationed at the foot holding out a blanket to break her fall if anything went wrong. Then with the cry, "Geronimo!" Smoky was released from the uppermost branches.

The drop was successful and photographs were taken. And Smoky appeared to enjoy the parachute jump so much that they took her up a couple more times—until, finally, the parachute was caught by a gust of wind. Smoky and her parachute were swept away, out of the range of the GIs and their blanket. Hitting the ground, she bounced twice, before lying still. Wynne rushed to her, consumed with guilt. But Smoky was just a little dazed and soon made a full recovery.

Not that Smoky was not able to put get in harm's way all by her self. While watching a softball game, she leapt from Wynne's lap and ran for third base, where the fielder, mistaking her for the ball, picked her up and was about to throw her to second until he was alerted by the cries of the spectators. Such diversions were a blessed relief for the men at Nadzab airfield, which suffered regular Japanese air raids.

Smoky won the magazine's competition, and *Yank Down Under* announced that she was the champion mascot of the South West Pacific Area. By this time, Wynne had come down with dengue fever. He was sent to a field hospital that was also caring for the wounded sent back from fighting the Japanese. Smoky was allowed to visit. Her presence proved such a tonic for the battle-scarred soldiers that the medical staff let her sleep on Wynne's bed.

"I never forgot the effect Smoky had on those men fresh from the conflict," said Wynne years later.

The Red Cross nurses borrowed her to take her around to other field hospitals.

When Wynne recovered, he was sent on leave to Australia. Smoky went with him, but Wynne was so afraid that the authorities would take her away from him that he taught her to stay quiet and remain still, and then carried her hidden inside a canvas bag.

When they landed in Brisbane, it was fearfully cold, especially for a dog that was used to the heat of the tropics. Wynne needed to find her a coat—not an easy task. He visited a hobby shop and bought some of the green baize that is typically used to cover a card table. A Red Cross helper volunteered to fashion this material into a coat. As Smoky was now a military dog, it was emblazoned with the US insignia, a 5th Army Air Force patch, a 26th Photo Recon emblem, a small brass button with a propeller on it as worn by enlisted men, two "six-months overseas" bars, an Asia Pacific ribbon, and a Good Conduct ribbon. She was a highly decorated dog, and her war had only just begun. Meanwhile, Wynne and Smoky spent their leave entertaining the wounded in the hospitals in Brisbane.

By the time Wynne and Smoky were to return to their unit, the 26th Photo Recon had been moved to Biak Island. From there they were flying reconnaissance missions over the Philippines. Nearer the equator, the temperature rose to 130°F inside their tent. Now the problem was to stay cool. The men could cool off in the ocean, but the waves were too big for little Smoky. So instead she went swimming in a bomb crater.

Smoky had no problem surviving on C-rations with the occasional can of SPAM, instead of the specially formulated canine rations given to official war dogs. There was no veterinarian help, should she need it, and scampering across the coral gave her feet none of the problems other dogs suffered in the Pacific.

Wynne taught Smoky new tricks. She perfected walking a tightrope, blindfolded. But when trying to master walking on a barrel, she kept falling off. It was only when Smoky took a little rest on Wynne's cot and he noticed something black next to her on the blanket that he realized she was whelping. Her puppy was christened Topper and the birth was toasted with "Coke" made from syrup water, and given a sparkle from the oxygen tanks. John Henbury, whose terrier Duke was thought to be the father, was also informed and his camp joined in the celebration. Topper was given to Wynne's friend Frank Petrilak, who had looked after Smoky when Wynne had first come down with dengue fever.

News came that Wynne had been certified for airborne duty. While he was away on his first photo-reconnaissance mission, his buddies discussed who would inherit Smoky if he was shot down. When Wynne heard about this, he decided that he was not going to leave Smoky behind again. He strapped Smoky's canvas bag around his waist, rigging it so that it would not interfere with his parachute. From then on, Smoky would fly with him.

The Catalina flying boat they flew had a maximum altitude of 13,000 feet, so no oxygen was necessary. Once onboard, Wynne told the rest of the crew that he had a dog with him. They had heard about Smoky and agreed she could come. But they decided that she would be more comfortable if her canvas bag was hung from the top bunk, where she would be near Wynne if anything untoward happened.

Their first outing was a search-and-rescue mission. They were looking for a downed pilot—a man Wynne knew and had flown with. But when they entered the search area, they suddenly found themselves in the middle of a tropical storm. Smoky had not been able to warn them because she had been taught to be quiet and lie still when she was in her canvas bag. It was touch-and-go, but after four hours they returned safely to Biak.

Smoky had acquitted herself admirably, and crews on subsequent flights had no objection to flying with her. On long flights, she was even allowed out of her canvas bag to stretch her legs on the bunk. Although the hum of the engines usually soothed her, sometimes the sheer volume of the noise made her bark back at them. Otherwise, she would sit swathed in blankets against the cold at high altitudes.

On tough missions, where they faced the very real possibility of being attacked by enemy fighters and shot down,

Smoky's presence broke the tension. She became a talisman, their good-luck charm. However, when on one occasion before a long and dangerous flight, she seized the opportunity to scamper around the airfield, her fellow crew members saw her reluctance to get onboard as an omen. Were they going to be shot down? Or face another tropical storm? But they survived that trip, too. Back on the ground, Wynne made Smoky a scooter from a wooden orange crate, pulleys, and roller bearings, and taught her to ride it. The other men on the base were so impressed, they painted her scooter red and spelled out her name along the footplate.

While the decisive Battle of Leyte Gulf, which finished off the Japanese fleet, was under way, Wynne and Smoky were on leave in Australia again—this time in Sydney. By the time they returned to their squadron, the invasion of the Philippines was in progress, and Wynne and Smoky were put on a tank landing ship bound for Luzon. Though it was cramped and noisy, and they had to survive on dehydrated rations, Smoky made new friends, including the ship's mascot, a Dalmatian who wore a life preserver, just in case he fell overboard.

As they approached the Philippines, they prepared the ship as best they could for kamikaze attack. Then general quarters sounded. The soldiers below were sealed in their compartments, behind watertight doors in case the ship was hit. Wynne and Smoky stayed on the loading deck, which was soon scattered with shrapnel. Wynne held onto Smoky, who was quaking with fear at the din from the guns. They saw enemy planes coming in for the attack, and a nearby Liberty ship was hit by a kamikaze. When the all-clear sounded and damage to the ship was assessed, Wynne discovered that they had escaped death by a matter of inches when a shell had struck a ventilator and flown over their heads, hitting eight men standing next to them. Wynne credited Smoky with saving his life, getting him to duck at the crucial moment, and called her his "angel from a foxhole."

After the assault force landed and established a bridgehead, Wynne waded ashore carrying Smoky. Soon they were ducking for cover again when an ammunition dump was hit. A jeep took them to the site of a hastily repaired airfield, where the 26th Photo Recon had commandeered an office block. Wynne and Smoky made themselves at home in an abandoned house nearby, though Smoky was in constant danger of slipping a foot through the slats of the bamboo floor, so they soon went back under the canvas.

By now, Smoky was getting very nervous and Wynne had to put his hands over her ears every time the alert sounded to warn them of incoming fire. But Smoky still provided much-needed entertainment to distract everyone from the growing pressures of warfare.

Then came Smoky's really big chance to aid the war effort. Telephone wires had to be run under the airstrip. To do that, engineers would have to dig up the runway, pull up the steel matting that underpinned it, dig a trench, lay the wires, then cover them over again. This would take three days. During that time, with its fighters grounded, the airfield would have been vulnerable to attack.

But Sergeant Bob Gapp from the Communications Section had seen a newsreel in which a cat in Alaska had run cables through a culvert, and he reckoned that an intelligent dog like Smoky could do the same. There was a series of three drainage pipes running under the runway. They were seventy feet long and eight inches in diameter, but soil had leaked into the pipes through the joints. In places, dirt half filled the pipes, giving Smoky only four inches of headroom.

Wynne was not sure that Smoky would go down such a narrow pipe. He wanted to know whether she would be able to see light at the other end of the tunnel. Wynne checked, and in the middle one light was clearly visible. Sergeant Gapp assured Wynne that, if she got stuck, his men would dig her out.

Wynne tied a thin string to Smoky's collar, so it would break easily if it got caught. Leaving Smoky with Sergeant Gapp, he ran to the other end of the culvert and called his dog. Just at that moment a P-51 Mustang fighter aircraft rolled down the runway over the culvert. The noise terrified Smoky. Gapp did his best to calm her down. But her mission could not be abandoned. Men's lives were at stake.

After about twenty minutes, Smoky had stopped shaking and was calm enough to make another attempt. Gapp took her to the entrance of the culvert, and Wynne called her again. This time, she made a few steps down the pipe, then scrambled back.

"Come, Smoky," Wynne called, and she started through again.

She was about ten feet in when the string snagged and she looked over her shoulder as if to say, "What's holding us up there?"

When the string was freed, she moved forward again. As she crawled through the dirt, her paws kicked up clouds of dust, and Wynne lost sight of her. But he kept on calling her, not knowing for certain whether she was coming or not. At the other end, though, the string was still being fed in so Sergeant Gapp knew progress was being made. At last, Wynne heard whimpering sound and saw two little amber eyes about twenty feet away. At fifteen feet, she broke into a run.

"We were so happy at Smoky's success that we patted and praised her for a full five minutes," said Wynne.

Sergeant Gapp hurried over and pulled more of the string out before detaching it from Smoky's collar. With the string running through the culvert, they could now pull the wires through. Then he hurried away to get the steak that had been Smoky's promised reward. She had done her bit and was now officially a war dog.

But still she had her duties as an entertainer to fill. Wynne got permission to use one of the abandoned houses nearby as a rehearsal hall and lay down sheets of plywood to stop her from paws getting caught between the bamboo slats of the floor. He taught her new tricks there in the early morning, before the heat of the day set in.

Wynne's buddies helped build a small stage from bamboo and palm leaves. A local carpenter made more props. These were decorated with the insignia of the 26th Photo Recon Squadron, which featured Donald Duck, replete with a yellow scarf and red flying helmet, a design donated to the squadron by Walt Disney. It showed Donald standing on a cloud, holding an air-reconnaissance camera.

A local seamstress further embellished Smoky's coat with a patch saying, "Smoky Champion Yank Mascot SWPA." Another patch was left blank for further honors. And the remnants of her parachute were fashioned into a clown's outfit. She drew big crowds, performing in the camp's movie theater after the main feature. She continued entertaining the patients in field hospitals, and entertained recently released American and European civilians who had been held in Santo Tomas internment camp outside Manila and suffered terrible privations at the hands of their Japanese captors. Smoky's picture appeared in the newspapers, and she was even interviewed on the radio.

Smoky's fame helped her become more self-reliant. When she was thirsty, she didn't need to bother Wynne, but could go over to the bags of drinking water in the center of the squadron area and stop a passerby. By scampering back and forth between the man and the water, and barking, she would let the person know what she wanted, and he would give her a drink. Wynne prevented others from teaching her tricks though. He thought it would confuse her if she had more than one master.

Though the air raids abated, there were still dangers. Smoky was dashing across a road after another dog when Wynne cried out, "Smoky, stand! Stay!" She stopped in her tracks and a truck missed her by six inches.

And there was the ever-present danger of disease. Frank Petrilak had to bury Smoky's puppy, Topper, who was just six months old when she died. Out of thirty dogs in the squadron, only four survived. One of them was Smoky.

As American forces advanced on Japan, the 26th Photo Recon Squadron were posted to Okinawa. This was now the front line, and the men were told to leave their personal possessions behind.

"No animals will be permitted to go," said their commanding officer. Wynne's heart sank. "Except Smoky. She has been with us a long time as squadron mascot and does not take up much space."

However, others managed to smuggle their pets aboard the troop ships.

More than twelve thousand Americans had been killed during the battle for Okinawa. The mood there was somber, but Smoky still managed to raise a smile as long as bully beef was on the menu. Then came the news that atomic bombs had been dropped on Hiroshima and Nagasaki—and Japan surrendered. The war was over. But instead of going home, Wynne and Smoky—now both billed as "Corporal Smoky"— were posted to Korea.

Instead of undergoing another long sea voyage, they waited for air transport. Meanwhile, Smoky came down with a sinus problem. The 4th Marine War Dog Platoon was based less than a mile away, so Wynne walked down there with Smoky. The veterinarian prescribed fresh eggs and milk. The mess only had powdered egg and milk, but it did the trick anyway. She also survived a typhoon that carried her and her cot spiraling high into the air. Wynne caught them when they came down. With their tent blown away, they were lashed with rain. They took refuge in caves, but remained soaked for days while the locals entombed their dead.

Stationed out in the countryside in Korea, Smoky again suffered from the intense cold after the heat of the tropics. She spent most of the day swathed in blankets. But she did manage to learn a new trick. Using cards with the letters S, M, O, K, and Y on them, she learned to spell out her own name.

The time approached when Wynne would be shipped home. He would not be able to take Smoky with him—officially. Army regulations stated clearly, "No dog or mascot will go back to the US on a War Department ship."

Wynne taught Smoky to hide inside his gas-mask bag, but there was no way he could ship her circus props with her. They would have to be left behind. Other men were also trying to smuggle pets onboard, and Wynne heard terrible rumors that animals that had been found were thrown overboard. He packed photographs of Smoky entertaining injured men and internees to bolster his case if she was caught.

It would be cold on the voyage, so Wynne adapted a turtleneck sweater for Smoky to wear. On the day they were to depart—November 1, 1945—they got up at 3:30 a.m., and ate a breakfast of bacon and pancakes before heading out on the twenty-five-mile journey to the harbor. They were taken out to the troopships by landing craft. Wynne's friend Piwarski had hurt his back and could not carry his barracks bag, so Wynne took it, while Piwarski carried his gas-mask bag with Smoky in it.

As they reached the side of the USS *General W.M.H. Gordon,* the officer in charge shouted at Wynne, but Wynne did not hear what he said and feared the worst. Then the officer gestured for Shorty Randall, who was carrying his terrier Duke hidden in a bag, to board. As Piwarski followed, Wynne dropped his bag, creating a diversion while Smoky was carried onboard unmolested.

Once Wynne was onboard, he took Smoky back, then went to find a bunk in the remotest part of the ship, three decks down in the bowels of the vessel. There he felt it was safe enough to let Smoky out to take some exercise on his bed.

Randall was caught with Duke and ordered to hand over the dog. Instead of being thrown overboard, the stowaway dogs that had been discovered were kept below decks, though the monkeys that had been found were put to sleep. Orders came that all men who had smuggled animals onboard were to report to the ship's office. The ship had hit a patch of bad weather. Wynne was suffering badly with seasickness and was too ill to go. Then Smoky was spotted by a Navy lieutenant, who wanted to see her master and her papers. But all Wynne had to do was pay a bond and sign a document absolving the *General Gordon* of any responsibility for the dog.

After twelve days at sea, they entered the Puget Sound. This time, Smoky was returned to her canvas bag, but when they disembarked no one checked their bags or their papers.

They were simply assigned a bed in a barracks at Fort Lewis, where they awaited transport home. The rest of the 26th Photo Recon Squadron were delighted to see that Smoky had made it through the red tape. The bad news was that, although Duke had made it to Fort Lewis, he had then gone missing.

While the men went through medical checks and processing, Smoky enjoyed an enriched diet of fresh milk and meat. Along with the other members of the 26th Photo Recon Squadron, Wynne was awarded the Asiatic-Pacific Campaign Medal and eight battle stars, the Philippine Liberation Medal with battle star, the Good Conduct Medal, and a Presidential Unit Citation with Oak Leaf Cluster, accompanied by silver crewman wings. These were added to Smoky's coat.

Then, after a stopover in a Camp Atterbury near Indianapolis, Wynne went home to Cleveland, where he turned up outside Margaret's house with Smoky under his arm. They made friends immediately. Smoky even got along with Toby, Wynne's Doberman–German shepherd cross.

Once the press in Cleveland heard that Wynne had returned home, Smoky was splashed over the front page. They resumed making hospital visits. Then Hollywood beckoned Smoky to show off her tricks, and Wynne became a member of the Hollywood Animals Handlers' Association. Smoky appeared in the TV show *Castles in the Air*, and Wynne performed with her as a song-and-dance act called "Mr. Pokie and His Dog Called Smoky." Then they appeared for thirty weeks in the show *How to Train your Dog with Bill and Smoky*.

Smoky died at home by the fireside in 1957. She was buried in Cleveland Metroparks, Rocky River Reservation in Lakewood, Ohio, where there is a memorial. Bill Wynne commemorated her in his book *Yorkie Doodle Dandy: Or, the Other Woman Was a Real Dog*. In it, he wrote, "After I lost my dog...

I felt so heartsick and vowed never again to get that close to anyone, animal or human, again. But Smoky, the little tyke who shared so much with me, who unquestioning and courageously responded to my every command, had become my truest friend."

Teddy

In October 1943, Teddy, brand number T115, was assigned to a Marine Raider Regiment of the 6th Army and sent by plane to Finschafen on Papua New Guinea, ready to take part in the Cape Gloucester operations on New Britain. The entire dog detachment went ashore with the first wave and figured prominently in the invasion. From December until March, Teddy was used continuously for patrol and messenger work. Lines were gradually extended to join up with the army forces near Gilnit. During these operations, there was not a single instance where a dog failed to accomplish a mission. Nor was there an instance when a patrol led by a war dog was fired upon first, or suffered casualties. In contrast, patrols without dogs suffered casualties, usually as a result of ambush or surprise attacks. During the campaign, the patrols led by dogs were officially credited with 180 Japanese casualties and taking twenty prisoners.

Sandy

Trained as a messenger dog, Sandy, brand number B11, also took part in the Cape Gloucester campaign on New Britain with his handlers, Sergeant Menzo J. Brown and Sergeant Guy C. Sheldon. The advance units were held up near Turzi Point by Japanese pillboxes and fortifications. They needed the support of artillery, but their walkie-talkies were temporarily out of commission. So Sergeant Brown sent Sandy back with a message for the battalion command post. The dog had last seen Sergeant Sheldon the night before. Since then he had moved, but Sandy found his way unerringly to his foxhole. The dog had to make his way through the tall Kunai grass and swim a river. For part of the distance, he had to travel beneath a curtain of mortar and shell-fire. Finally he had to jump a barbed wire fence that surrounded Sergeant Sheldon's position. But the message got through. As a result, artillery fire was directed on the Japanese defenses, pulverizing them and allowing the American forward units to resume their advance.

Dick

With his handler, Sergeant Herman H. Boude, Dick, brand number T127, went out on patrol for forty-eight days out of the fifty-three-day campaign. Scarcely a day passed without him alerting Sergeant Boude to the Japanese, varying in strength from single stragglers to entire platoons. Not once was his patrol the victim of a surprise attack. On each occasion, Dick alerted them in time to kill or capture the enemy. Once while on patrol, the scouting party discovered five camouflaged huts. But Dick indicated that only one was inhabited. They attacked, killing four Japanese without a single casualty.

Buster

While operating as a messenger dog with F Company of the 155th Infantry Regiment on Morotai Island, Buster, brand number A684, was directly responsible for saving the lives of an entire patrol of seventeen men. As a messenger dog, he ran through heavy enemy machine-gun and mortar fire twice, bringing instructions for the patrol to hold its position at all costs. Eventually, reinforcements arrived and destroyed an entire enemy force.

Bruce

During a banzai attack that occurred in Northern Luzon at 3:15 a.m. on February 17, 1945, against E Company of the 27th Infantry, Bruce attacked three Japanese infantrymen who were advancing with fixed bayonets toward a foxhole containing two wounded American soldiers. He saved their lives and, by discouraging the advance of the Japanese, averted more American casualties.

Duchess

Brand number 7H74, Duchess, and his handler, Sergeant Knight, were members of the 39th Infantry Scout Dog Platoon. On April 30, 1945, they were on patrol with the 3rd Battalion of the 123rd Infantry on the island of Luzon in the Philippines. Duchess was sent to inspect some enemy cave installations. On approaching a large one, the dog alerted at the entrance. Thirty-three Japanese were later found dead in the cave. On another occasion, Duchess alerted toward some Filipino huts eight hundred yards away. The enemy was concealed there. Mortar and machine-gun fire on the position killed nine Japanese.

Blackie

While out on reconnaissance patrol with F Company of the 123rd Infantry on April 12 and 13, 1945, Blackie, brand number H24, and his handler, Corporal Technician Kido, located a position where five hundred Japanese were bivouacked, and man and dog escaped without being detected.

The War Dogs of Guam

Dogs played a key part in the Battle of Guam, when the US retook the Pacific island between July 21 and August 10, 1944. Among the 1,462 US dead were twenty-five dogs, specially trained to serve as sentries, messengers, and scouts. They explored caves, detected mines and booby traps, and warned their fellow marines when the enemy was approaching. The canine dead now lie in an honored place at the War Dog Cemetery, a section of the Marine Cemetery near the landing beach at Asan.

Captain William W. Putney commanded the seventy-two dogs and 110 men of the 3rd War Dog Platoon on Guam. He had arrived at the Marine Corps War Dog Training School at Camp Lejeune on June 1, 1943. He was twenty-three years old and was fresh out of veterinary school. There had been problems with 1st War Dog Platoon, which had been commanded by a retired schoolmaster and amateur dog trainer with no military experience. It had been sent on to Camp Pendleton in California where Carl Spitz, a German soldier in World War I who had become a professional dog trainer in Hollywood, had been hired to knock the unit into shape before it was sent overseas.

To prevent further problems, it was decided that what the War Dog Training School needed was a line officer—that is, an officer trained for combat, rather than some other specialty. Putney had served as a private in the infantry before the war, but had returned to college. While studying veterinary science at Auburn University, he joined the field artillery

ROTC. Then, when he graduated, he was accepted into the Marine Corps as a second lieutenant. After three months' infantry training, he expected to be sent to the artillery. Instead he was destined for the War Dog Training School. His job there was to train two war dog platoons—the 2nd and the 3rd—one of which he would command overseas.

The dogs had to be trained in various disciplines: There were to be messenger dogs, who would carry ammunition, medicines, and other supplies, as well as messages, under enemy fire. Mine dogs would detect mines and other explosives, while scout dogs would search out the enemy, guard prisoners, and provide security at night in areas vulnerable to attack. Their handlers would, of course, have to be trained, too. The training was to be completed by July 15, 1943—just six weeks away.

Putney was to be assisted by Sergeant Raymond Barnowsky, who had been trained at the Army Dog Training Unit at Fort Robinson. The recruits were mostly teenagers who were just out of boot camp. They had volunteered to be marines and fight the Japanese. Like Putney himself, they were less than thrilled to be in the dog corps.

The dogs the marines had inherited from the army were largely German shepherds. But then the Doberman Pinscher Club of America had volunteered to provide as many dogs at the Corps needed for the duration of the war. Although the Doberman never actually became the official Marine Corps dog, it was believed that short-haired Dobermans would perform better in tropical climates than long-haired breeds. So Doberman pinschers became closely associated with the Corps, though Putney noted that the sign announcing the "War Dog Training Company" had a picture of a Great Dane on it. But then, the Doberman pinscher was a relatively new dog, only recognized as a breed in 1900.

The problem was that the members of the Doberman Pinscher Club were sending their most aggressive dogs, thinking that's what the Marine Corps was looking for. But the War Dog Training School was not training attack dogs. They needed dogs with good hearing, a good sense of smell, intelligence, obedience, and, above all, loyalty.

One particularly vicious beast named Herman arrived from Chicago. When two marines picked up his crate to load it on to a truck, he charged the door so hard that they dropped the crate and fled. But the chief veterinarian, First Lieutenant James A. B. Stewart, was not disheartened. He told them that they should never make sudden movements when approaching a new dog and they should call out his name. This did no good.

When they finally got Herman to Camp Lejeune, Stewart had his crate carried into the quarantine compound where dogs were kept for ten days to see if they were incubating any disease. Once the gate was closed, he opened the crate using a long rope tied to the door latch. Herman came bursting out, frothing at the mouth. Determined to attack the men who stood outside the compound, he sprang in their direction and locked his teeth on the chain-link fence. Stewart ordered that the gate should be padlocked, and the dog's food and water was to be slid in under it. To emphasize the danger, Stewart opened his jacket to reveal his armpit. Three months before, a Doberman had attacked him. He had put up his arm to protect his face and the dog had bitten him under the arm. Another man had managed to beat the dog off with the handle of a mop. At the hospital it took fifty-seven switches to sew up the wound.

Of the twenty-five dogs that had come in on the shipment from Chicago, four had to be sent back for health reasons. Herman remained locked in a compound for a week until he calmed down enough for the veterinarian to examine him.

Each dog was then tested with firecrackers to see if it would be afraid of gunfire. Then they were goaded by a man in a padded suit to see if they were too aggressive, or too cowardly. After these tests, another three were rejected.

After a week, when Lieutenants Putney and Stewart went to check on Herman, they found a marine named Mike Pappas singing a Greek folk song outside his compound. He stopped when the officers neared, and Herman immediately resumed his aggressive behavior. But Pappas told him to stop, in Greek, and he immediately backed down. Stewart ordered that, from then on, only Pappas was to feed and water Herman. After four days, Pappas had the dog eating out of his hand. On the fifth day, Pappas entered the compound, put the dog's food out of reach, then walked Herman around on the leash before feeding him. The next day, the two of them went for a walk around the camp. The day after that, Herman went for his medical exam and had his War Dog number—178—tattooed in his ear. It had taken just seven days to turn Herman into a good marine.

The men were then assigned their dogs, though they then slyly exchanged them for ones that they felt better suited them. Then the training got underway. A trainer took teams of twelve out to a nearby field and ran through the basic commands. These were repeated over and over until the dogs responded automatically. They learned both voice commands and hand signals. These would be vital when they were within earshot of the enemy. The dogs were also taught not to bark.

At the same time, the men learned how the dogs reacted to a danger or something of interest—how each of them would look, sniff the air, prick his ears.

The dogs were taught to jump through barrels, jump over fences, and scale walls. One dog, Lucky, could scale a wall nine feet eight inches high. They ran up inclines and crossed a narrow bridge made out of a railroad tie to improve their balance.

With their handlers, they had to crawl under a mesh of barbed wire while machine guns filled with blanks were fired over the heads. They had to crawl down flooded ditches and jump over ponds twelve feet wide. They also had to practice their swimming. These dogs were bound for the Pacific, so a mock-up of a ship was made and the dogs were lowered over the side in a harness.

The flora and fauna of Camp Lejeune made it an excellent place to train for the tropics. There were chiggers, snakes, scorpions, though the mosquitoes only bothered the humans. A dog named Peppy was bitten on the upper lip by a cottonmouth snake. Butch, the dog behind him, grabbed the snake and twirled it around until it was dead, despite being told not to.

Peppy's head began to swell up, and Putney administered first aid. He opened his medical kit and gave the dog a shot of morphine. Then he cut open his lip and tried to squeeze out the venom. As he applied a tourniquet to the dog's snout, two men fashioned a makeshift stretcher by cutting down two saplings and threading them through the arms of their two jackets. Then they rushed him to the veterinarian, who cut a hole in his throat moments before the swelling cut off the dog's breathing. It was touch and go, but Peppy was back in training three weeks later.

A trail was made in the forest, complete with concealed weapon pits, foxholes, bunkers, and ambushes. The ambushers worn padded suits and attacked the dogs with burlap sacks. One dog at a time was taken down the trail with the other handlers following behind, as if they were the riflemen on a patrol.

The first dog to be sent down the trail was a German shepherd named Pal, with his handler, PFC Benjamin A. Dickerson, directly behind. Dickerson removed Pal's choke chain and put on a leather collar. This told the dog that he was going to work. He was off the leash. Dickerson then made a gesture as if he was throwing something off down the trail, and Pal would head off to investigate. When he found nothing, Dickerson would make the gesture again and repeat the exercise.

Around fifty yards down the trail, Pal went on the alert and stopped. He pricked his ears and looked fixedly ahead. Dickerson made a low whistle that could not be heard by a human more than a few feet way. Pal heard it though, and turned back toward Dickerson who raised his arm and slowly let it fall. Pal followed it to the ground. Then Dickerson held up the flat of his palm, telling Pal to stay. Gunner Sergeant Holdren, who had constructed the trail, then explained that there was an ambush up ahead and told the men how to deal with it.

Pal was then sent ahead again, but he missed the next ambush. Practice grenades came flying over and a man in a padded suit leaped from the bushes and began flailing at him. Dickerson ordered Pal to attack. The man fended him off, but Pal pushed him to the ground and was attacking the man's throat when Dickerson ordered him to stop. He pulled back but stayed on guard, ready to attack again if need be. Pal was then praised and came to heel.

Pal and the handlers were then taught how to deal with bends in the road, and the other obstacles and dangers that hid in the forest. Pal went on to discover a machine gun next, moving left and right at Dickerson's unspoken command.

A series of foxholes and small caves had been dug. A dog had to tell which contained a man and which did not. To train a dog, a stick was thrown in. Pal emerged from the first foxhole with the stick between his teeth. From the second hole a man emerged, carrying the stick and flailing at Pal again. After that he approached the caves and foxholes more gingerly, stopping outside one that was occupied and raising the hackles on his neck.

Each dog was taken down the trail five times. Fresh features were added and fresh trails were laid. Then the roles were reversed. The dog was put in a concealed position, and attempts were made to approach them undetected. They also practiced this at night with the dogs alerting their handlers without barking, so that an intruder would not know that he had been spotted.

The Japanese had developed mines cased in ceramics or clay, which could not be detected by magnetic mine detectors. So dogs were taught to find them instead. They could sniff out booby traps, trip wires, and mines—both metallic and nonmetallic—almost anything that was buried. They would stop three paces in front of the object and refuse to move. But this had its limitations. If an area had been shelled, they also went on the alert over buried shrapnel, making them next to useless in those circumstances. Only later were dogs trained to sniff out explosives.

The handlers of mine dogs were also sent on an engineering course to learn about the construction and laying of mines. A small metal trap with rubber jaws was used to train the dogs. They were walked over it so it clamped on their foot. The handler expressed fear and horror as he removed the trap and threw it away. The next time, the dog would be on the look out for a trap. The traps were then hidden under leaves and grass. Then they were buried. The dogs even learned to detect an object that had been buried for many months.

They were taught to a detect trip wire by running an electric current through it. After a dog had been shocked, he soon learned to look out for thin metal wires stretched across a trail. It is thought that their sensitive hearing could pick up the low singing note a wire made, even in the gentlest of breezes.

As the dogs were trained by fear—of a pinch on the foot or an electric shock—they were under considerable stress when they worked. After half an hour or so, they would have to rest; otherwise, they would start to make mistakes. It was found that training worked better when dogs were rewarded by praise and affection. Generally, the Americans' training of mine dogs during World War II was a failure. The Marine Corps only used six. All survived and were returned to their owners.

Messenger dogs fared better. They carried notes in a pouch on their collars. Each dog was assigned two handlers and would be sent from one to the other. Gradually, the distance between them would be increased until the handlers were out of sight. Then they would move, so that the messenger dog would have to track them. This was obviously vital at the front where a combat unit and the command post would constantly be on the move.

One of the Marine Corps messenger dogs, Missy, became famous after a film clip of her carrying messages and ammunition, recorded by Pathé News, was shown in movie theaters in the US, coast-to-coast. The Marine Corps used bitches as well as males, but the females could not be spayed as they had to be returned to their owners intact. So, bitches could not be used when they were in heat, and they occasionally produced a litter of puppies. Unfortunately, Missy was killed on Guam. By that time, radio technology had improved to the point where the use of messenger dogs was no longer necessary, but messenger dogs continued to be trained until the end of the war.

Twenty-five-year-old Second Lieutenant William T. Taylor arrived to take over the 2nd Dog Platoon, and after a parade they moved on to Camp Pendleton by train, with the dogs in crates in the baggage car. They made slow progress, as priority was given to trains carrying men and materiel, but when they were shunted into sidings for hours on end, handlers took the opportunity to exercise the dogs. The dogs were also taken out of their crates to be fed and to relieve themselves against an ersatz fire hydrant built by a police sergeant at Lejeune.

At Camp Pendleton, the dog handlers were mocked by the other marines until the handlers stood up to them in a mess hall. A fight was narrowly avoided when a gunnery sergeant intervened. After a nighttime confrontation with the dogs, there were no more catcalls. Paratroop marines were caught trying to sneak into the Dog Platoons' camp at night, and then acknowledged that there might be something in the use of dogs. After that they began coming around for demonstrations of just what the dogs were capable of. Soon they were losing money to PFC Arthur Spielman, from New York City's Hell's Kitchen, who took bets that his dog Bunkie could recover any particular stone they required from a collection scattered on the ground. The dogs further proved their worth in a night exercise in which the Paratroopers were pitted against the Raiders. The dog teams had no problem tracking the movements of the would-be enemy and catching them in the open.

One dog died; another became too aggressive. Replacements were recruited from Carl Spitz in Hollywood, but one of them, Lady, promptly deserted. The handlers were issued M-1 Carbines rather than the heavier Garand favored by the riflemen. And at Pendleton, the dog platoons acquired a fully equipped canine hospital.

On February 14, 1944, the unit shipped out from San Diego on a freighter that had been redesigned as a troopship. They were headed for Guadalcanal. The trip would take nearly two months. The men passed the time teaching their dogs new tricks, most of which had no military purpose. However, the most popular game was hide-and-seek in which, on command, the dogs had to search out objects hidden around the ship. The champion was Butch. With his handler, PFC Keith Schaible, he proved very useful on Guam, seeking out mines, explosives, and enemy soldiers hidden in caves. Sergeant Barnowsky spent his time training a puppy named Skeeter to perform intricate routines that were later used to entertain the troops in shows across the Pacific.

A tropical storm blew in, and the dogs began to get sore feet from the salt water that crashed over the decks. They were washed and treated, then wrapped in bandages, but the dogs would chew off the bands. Condoms, thoughtfully supplied by the Marine Corps for other purposes, were found to be more effective.

The dogs also suffered from the heat. The Dobermans acclimatized quite quickly, but the German shepherds had a harder time and had to be hosed down, while a sable-and-white collie named Tam had to been supplied with an electric fan. The possibility of shaving off his coat was suggested, but his exposed skin would be prey to sunburn. It had been foolish to send a collie to the tropics in the first place. Next to useless in the daytime on a tropical island, the only thing he would be good for was guard duty at night.

Dog platoons arrived on Guadalcanal fifty-seven days after leaving San Diego. The Japanese had departed by then, and the island was being used as staging area for US forces to island-hop across the Pacific. Men and dogs feasted on coconuts. The dog teams were then assigned to the units they would be supporting during the forthcoming campaign and began to go on maneuvers with them. On Guadalcanal, the dog handlers received no mockery from the other marines. They knew how well the 1st War Dog Platoon had performed on Bougainville.

Two dogs came down with a strange condition that paralyzed their rear legs. It was feared that this would spread to all of them. But Putney figured out that their rations were being supplemented with frozen carp from New Zealand, which deprived them of vitamin B1. After a ban on feeding the dogs carp was instituted and the animals were given B1 injections, they recovered.

The dogs then participated in a full-scale assault on the beach as a rehearsal for the landings on Guam. Offshore, they lowered the dogs from ship onto landing craft as they had practiced back at Camp Lejeune, but on the high seas, this took over an hour. They were not going to have that much time during the real invasion. With only four days to go, though, there would be no time for further practice.

Stopping at the atoll of Kwajalein on the way to Guam, they figured out that, if they lifted boats up to the ship's gunwales, they could load the dogs and men speedily, then lower the boats back down to the water. In a rehearsal, they were away in ten minutes.

After witnessing the fighting off Saipan, the unit was dumped on the Enewetok atoll, where there were no trees to shade the dogs from the tropical sun and no fresh water. Even a hole dug in the middle of the island filled with salt water, but they let the dogs play in it to keep cool. Fortunately, it rained and the handlers collected enough fresh water to slake the dogs' thirst and the humans'. But soon they ran out, and the dogs began drinking seawater again.

There was another island about a mile away with trees on it. They waded out, then swam across the channel to it. There were no coconuts on the trees, so they could not give the dogs the milk to drink. But some of the halves of coconuts that had been harvested had collected water from the downpour. It was enough to save them from dehydration. But Tam, who had taken in a lot of seawater, lay coughing in the shade. He died soon after and had to be buried at sea.

Boats came to carry them back to the troopship. Putney received notification that he had been promoted to First Lieutenant. Then they headed for Guam.

On the night of July 20, 1944, they were close enough to Guam to see the naval bombardment under way. The landings began at 6 a.m. the following day. Guam was the first piece of American territory to be occupied by the Japanese in World War II; it was also the first piece of American territory to be liberated.

First the beaches were strafed and bombed. Then the 3rd Marines would go ashore on Red Beach, followed by the 3rd

War Dog Platoon. It would split in two. Half would move left to join up with main body of the 3rd Marines; the rest would move inland to deploy along the perimeter. Meanwhile, the 2nd War Dog Platoon would land with 9th Marines on Blue Beach and the 21st Marines on Green Beach. Their aim was to join up with the 1st Provision Brigade that was landing twelve miles to the south. With the pounding the beaches were taking, they did not expect much resistance.

The men felt a certain amount of trepidation. This was the first time they would be in action. But for the dogs, it was just another training exercise. They sprang eagerly into the boats, which were then lowered away.

As they neared the starting line, they could see the amphibious tanks were already ashore. The landing craft carrying infantry men were nearing the beaches, and the naval bombardment had lifted to pound the cliffs above the beaches. Then the signalman on the command boat ordered the dog platoons to go in.

Explosions splashed water into the landing craft and, as they approached the beach, they could see fierce fighting was under way. They hit the beaches at full speed and ran down the ramps as machine-gun bullets kicked up the water around them. Then a mortar landed, injuring two men.

Putney found one of the handlers, eighteen-year-old Tex Blalock, lying face down in the sand, paralyzed with fear, and kicked him. Blalock jumped up and ran up the beach, followed by his dog, Duchess, who bounded after him unafraid. Blalock's helmet fell off. He ran back to retrieve it, while Duchess sat and waited for him without a care.

One group reached the ditch on the far side of the road that ran along the top of the beach and began to crawl along it toward the 3rd Marines' command post. Another group began to dig in, in the dunes. Lieutenant Putney found that the map he had been given was out of date and he could not identify where he was from the aerial photographs. He decided to reconnoiter ahead. Taking Private Raymond Tomaszewski with him, he passed a number of dead marines, but reached the command post unscathed.

They were then ordered to bring the dogs up. Lieutenant Putney sent Tomaszewski back to get them. He was to follow a riverbed to the other side of the dunes and crawl up a ditch to fetch them. Then he was to bring them back the same way.

With the dogs tied up in the creek, the men were to dig a line of foxholes facing the jungle to protect the command post. They could sleep there that night with the dogs as a precaution against any nocturnal counterattack. But the command post moved off and, at dusk, Lieutenant Putney pulled his dog teams back, leaving the Japanese to mortar empty foxholes.

When the dog teams returned in the morning, they found the earth around their former position had been churned as if it had been freshly plowed. Nearby, a Doberman named Monty found a Japanese soldier asleep in a foxhole. When they woke him, they found he was drunk, having consumed one bottle of Suntory whiskey and two of sake. He was sent as a prisoner to the rear.

A Japanese position on the cliffs above the beaches had been strafed, but it was still feared that there were some up there. A dog team was needed. Nineteen-year-old PFC Carl Bliss and his quick-witted Doberman, Hobo, would lead the patrol. About two hundred yards inland, Hobo found an abandoned Japanese hospital in a cave. At the top of the cliff, they found a deserted machine-gun post. Then they headed on along the ridge. The trail led though thick jungle where they had to proceed single file.

When Hobo reached a clearing, Bliss gave a low whistle and motioned to Hobo to lie down. Then he crawled up to him. He was joined by Lieutenant Putney, who saw eight Japanese soldiers who appeared to be asleep. But when Gunnery Sergeant Symsanski, a veteran of Guadalcanal and Bougainville, reached them, he said that the men were dead—and that the dog had known it all along.

Lieutenant Putney then sent Hobo and Bliss to search the rest of the ridge, accompanied by PFC Donald Rydgig, who had volunteered to go along. As Rydgig entered a patch of sword grass, three shots rang out. Only two of them came from a carbine. Putney found Rydgig concussed and slightly injured. Men with machine guns were brought up to rake the grass with fire.

Meanwhile, PFC Allen Jacobson and his dog, Kurt, had been scouting in front of an advance unit of the 3rd Battalion, 21st Marines, when Kurt went on the alert. There was a Japanese soldier in the undergrowth. Jacobson crept forward and killed him, along with another soldier who had leaped out of the bush. But the two men had been the outpost of a larger force. In the firefight that ensued, 350 Japanese died. Jacobson was injured, but he refused to be evacuated until he was assured that Kurt, who had also been wounded, was cared for. If it had not been for Kurt's alert, there would have been a huge loss of American lives.

When Lieutenant Putney returned to the platoon's base at the bottom of the hill, he knocked Kurt out with half a grain of morphine, then patched him up as best he could. But Kurt died that night. Jacobson had been taken out to a hospital ship and survived.

Another patrol was to be sent up onto the ridge. This time it would be accompanied by PFC Leon Ashton, his Doberman, Ginger, and a flamethrower to torch the sword grass if need be. On the top of the ridge, Ginger went on the alert immediately before they reached the patch of grass. But the lieutenant leading the patrol was not convinced and told Ashton to get closer. When Ginger reached the grass, she growled. Two shots rang out. Ashton fell. The lieutenant could not tell if he was dead or seriously wounded, as Ginger would let no one near his body. Ashton sent a runner back to Lieutenant Putney.

Putney sent PFC Robert Johnson who had worked with Ginger before he had been assigned to Ashton. Ginger let Johnson lead her away. Ashton was dead. A bullet had hit him in the throat and come out through the back of his head, leaving a hole in his helmet. When the flamethrower torched the sword grass, they found the Japanese soldier no more than six feet from Ashton's body. He also was already dead, and it seemed that they had pulled the trigger simultaneously.

PFC Leon Ashton was awarded the Silver Star posthumously. Ginger was assigned to Rydgig, who was killed at Iwo Jima. Only Ginger survived the war.

Lucky, the dog that could scale a nine-foot wall, was found crouching unharmed near the body of his handler, PFC Edward Topka, who had been mortally wounded. He growled at the corpsman, but let him tend Topka's wound, though nothing could be done. PFC Topka was also posthumously decorated for gallantry. After his death, Lucky would not work with another handler and had to be returned to his owners in the States.

Another handler, PFC Raymond Rosinski also died. Two more were wounded, one severely.

These needless deaths convinced the dog handlers that the regular infantry had not been taught how to use the dogs properly, and it was decided that dog teams would not be sent out unless Putney, Taylor, or an NCO accompanied them. As it was, the marines were now engaging the Japanese at such close quarters that, for the moment, dogs were no longer needed to find them.

However, on July 25, 7,500 Japanese massed on the top of Mount Tenjo. They got drunk on sake, ready to make a suicidal attack on the F Company of the 9th Marines below. With them was PFC Ed Adamski and his Doberman, Big Boy. At around 10:00 p.m., Big Boy jumped up and pointed his nose at Mount Tenjo. Then he dropped down again and curled up. Adamski told the sergeant in charge that the Japanese were coming—but not right now.

Half an hour later, Big Boy was on his feet again, growling. The Japanese were on the move. An hour after that, Big Boy sprang to his feet once more. With his nose pointed toward Mount Tenjo, he strained at the leash. For the next thirty minutes it was a struggle to keep him down in the foxhole. Then the cry of "Banzai!" split the night. Big Boy grew frantic. The Japanese threw themselves at the marines' trenches. Adamski shot one man in the onslaught, but spent most of his time trying to restrain Big Boy, who would not understand why he could not savage the assailants like he had at Camp Lejeune.

Wave after wave of Japanese came crashing on the marines' position. All the officers of F Company were killed or wounded. The Japanese died by the thousand. Somehow Adamski and Big Boy survived the night to be relieved by tanks in the morning.

Farther down the line, Skipper, a messenger dog, had alerted the marines twelve minutes before the attack. Originally an Army dog from Nebraska, Skipper, a black Labrador retriever, was mild mannered and obedient. He stayed in the foxhole as he had been told. While his handler, PFC Dale Fetzer, was involved in hand-to-hand fighting above, the assailant dropped a grenade into the foxhole, killing Skipper.

As the line moved northward, there were marine scout dogs from the 2nd and 3rd War Dog Platoons in front of every unit in the advance. Twelve messenger dogs followed to provide security at night.

More dogs died. A German shepherd named Poncho, originally recruited though Carl Spitz in Hollywood, was on sentry duty when he alerted the outpost to the approach of twenty Japanese. In the firefight that followed, Poncho was killed by a grenade. Lieutenant Putney then had the unpleasant duty of writing to Poncho's owner, a young boy named Bobby.

Another casualty was Hobo. He and Private Bliss were scouting along a ridge in front of the 3rd Marines when they reached a clearing. Hobo was sent to scout the undergrowth on the far side. There was an enemy position there. They opened up, and Hobo fell. The marines quickly cleared the enemy outpost with machine-gun fire and mortars. Then Bliss ran forward. Hobo had been hit in the abdomen and was bleeding heavily.

The injured dog was rushed back to Lieutenant Putney, who immediately called for a red Doberman named Bebe. She had gone deaf after being too close to an explosion during an exercise at Camp Lejeune. Now useless in combat, she had been brought along as a blood donor. But Hobo's spleen had been macerated and he died. Bliss was devastated, but he was still proud that no enemy had ever gotten past his dog.

The Japanese began targeting dogs in the mistaken belief that without their dogs the marines would not find them. The death toll among dogs rose dramatically. Nevertheless, their handlers survived. Ashton was the last to die on Guam, though others were wounded, some several times.

One of the canine casualties was Tubby. He was a hero dog that had already saved numerous marine lives. On the second night ashore, he had alerted his handler, PFC Guy Mason Wachstetter, to two Japanese soldiers trying to infiltrate the command post. And on the night of the mass attack on July 25, he had gone on the alert long before the attack, and Wachstetter had killed four Japanese in front of his foxhole.

On another occasion, Wachstetter and Tubby had been stuck in an exposed position for two days with no rations. Wachstetter had to cut up a chocolate bar, which Tubby ate with some distaste. But still the dog did his duty, alerting Wachstetter to a Japanese soldier who, moments later, came screaming toward their foxhole. Wachstetter shot him twice in the chest.

But then Tubby was out with Wachstetter and PFC Vincent Salvaggio one night. As usual, he was lying in front of their foxhole. He was calm, and there was no sign of an attack, when suddenly he fell into the foxhole. There was a bullet hole in his chest and a bullet lodged in his heart. No gunshot had been heard, so Tubby must have been taken down from a distance by a sniper or a stray bullet.

PFC Marvin Corff was awarded a Silver Star for killing four Japanese on the night of July 25, thanks to his dog, Rocky's, alert. The dog and his handler did not get along well. Rocky was not an affectionate dog and did not like being touched very much. And when star shells lit up the skies, he would bite. Corff would have to muzzle him and put his arms around him until he calmed down. Battle fatigue made him even more aggressive, and Corff was savagely attacked at one outpost. But Rocky's alerts had saved his life on numerous occasions, and Corff never complained about the bites because he knew that if he did, there was a chance Rocky would be taken away from him. During the mopping up, they went out on more than fifty patrols together. Corff even visited Rocky after the war when the dog had been returned to his original owner. Corff himself went on to become a veterinarian.

Agana, the capital of Guam, was thought to have been cleared of ordnance. Down one road alone, thirteen mines had been found, but Lieutenant Putney asked Private Schaible and Butch to check it over once more. At an intersection, Butch stopped and would not move. A bulldozer had already scraped the surface, and nothing was visible. Lieutenant Putney reported this to his commanding officer, who replied that the engineers had already cleared that area. Later, a jeep carrying a high-ranking officer was blown up in that very spot, though the officer escaped with his life. Schaible and Butch were then put back on mine-hunting duty, and they moved down the road. Each time Butch halted, Schaible would plant a flag. Then the Engineer Corps would come along and clear the mine. By then Butch was the darling of the senior officers. They would try to pet him, but he would growl and Schaible would have to warn them off.

As messenger dogs were no longer needed, Missy was sent out with her handler, PFC Claude Sexton, as a scout dog. But when he let her off the leash, she went missing. It was thought that she had gone looking for her other handler, Earl Wright. She was found dead with seven .25-caliber bullets in her.

Wright was devastated. As a replacement he was given a black German shepherd that had been found guarding the Japanese headquarters. He called her Lady, after Lady Tokyo, as Tokyo Rose called herself in her propaganda broadcasts. Once she was taught the words of command in English, it was found that she had already been trained as a scout dog. She went to Saipan with the 2nd War Dog Platoon, and then served on Okinawa and in Japan. Lady returned home with Wright after the war and presented him with a litter of seven puppies.

Another casualty was Bobby, the War Dogs' mascot. Bobby was a small dog, about the size of a cocker spaniel, and he had been donated by Lieutenant Putney's brother Julian when they were back at Camp Lejeune. A happy dog, he scampered around freely until he was run over by a tank. As he was not a war dog, he was not buried in the War Dog Cemetery, but on his own under a palm tree.

When the fighting was over, the dogs still faced the danger of disease. Fortunately, Lieutenant Taylor had liberated a Japanese cave hospital. Along with a large array of vital medical supplies, he had also found a powerful Zeiss microscope. Using this, Putney discovered that all the dogs were suffering from hookworm, which infested the intestinal tract, and began a course of treatment. More than eighty percent of the dogs were also suffering from heartworm. Spielman's dog, Bunkie, died during the course of heartworm treatment.

The marine war dogs joined the Military Police to protect their patrol from Japanese stragglers who attacked at night. Dog teams would also go out on patrol to track the stragglers to their hiding places. When what amounted to a squad of Japanese soldiers was seen crossing the causeway onto the unoccupied Cabras Island, four dog teams were sent. They moved in a line down the narrow island, flanked by men with machine guns and followed by a marine with a flamethrower.

As PFC Stanley Terrell and his Doberman, Cappy, approached a pile of rocks, the dog froze. A shot rang out, and Cappy fell with a bullet through his chest. Terrell tried to rush to his dog's aid, but Putney tackled him and brought him down. A Japanese soldier was seen running between the rocks, so the marines held their fire. But then came another shot.

When the machine gunners opened up, Putney released Terrell and he ran to pick up his dog, but Cappy had been dead before he hit the ground. The others moved up. Two grenades were thrown over the rocks, and the position was raked by the flamethrower. One man came running out on fire. He was mown down.

The dogs gave no further indication that anyone was alive behind the rocks. Five dead were found. One survivor appeared from behind nearby rock with his hands up, wearing nothing but a loincloth. Rydgig gave him a cigarette.

For six weeks after the island of Guam was declared secure, the patrols continued until both dogs and men were exhausted. By the end of the war, they had conducted more than 550 patrols in the jungles of Guam. On forty percent of them, they encountered Japanese stragglers, resulting in the death or capture of hundreds of enemy soldiers. More than three hundred of them were accounted for by the dog handlers themselves. Even so, they did not round up all the stragglers. One Japanese soldier lived alone in a cave for the next twenty-seven years and was only discovered in January 1972.

After the end of the Guam campaign, no one doubted the war dog's worth. The 6th and 7th War Dog Platoons were sent to Iwo Jima, where they were used to seek out the numerous caves where the Japanese were hiding. Men from 3rd Platoon were also sent there, but as replacements in rifle companies. Eight men were killed, and more than twenty were wounded. Three men from the 2nd Platoon were killed trying to rescue the pilot of a crashed plane that blew up as they approached. The platoon went on to Okinawa, where they tracked down the Japanese in the cave and cane fields. No men or dogs were lost there. Of the 110 men in 2nd and 3rd War Dog Platoons, 16 were killed in action. Another forty were wounded. But only twenty-five of the original handlers were still with their units when they returned to Camp Lejeune.

When Putney returned to the War Dog School, he refused to sign any more death certificates for his dogs until efforts had been made to detrain them and return them to their owners. It was already too late for some. Peppy had already been put down after his handler, Benny Goldblatt, had been injured. A rehabilitation program was set up. There were 559 dogs still on duty with the Marine Corps at the end of the war. Putney was charged with making them safe so they could be handed back to the families that had donated them. To that end, female marines were brought in to get the dogs accustomed to being around women. Romance blossomed.

Some of the dogs were too ill to send home. Fifteen were destroyed for health reasons. Another four were put down because they were still a danger to the public. The remaining 540 were returned home to their original owners or sent to families prepared to adopt them, or they stayed with their handlers. A dog food company in Los Angeles offered the war dogs free food as long as they lived.

Putney retired from the service as a captain. He continued practicing as a veterinarian in civilian life. In 1989, he returned to Guam to find that the Marine War Dog Cemetery set up in 1944 had gone to wrack and ruin. Five years later, it was moved to the US Navy Base at Orote Point, where it could be maintained by the government. The War Dog Cemetery was rededicated there on July 21, 1994, the fiftieth anniversary of Guam's liberation. Four years later, a bronze statue of Kurt, the first of the 3rd Platoon's war dogs to be killed in action, was unveiled. He sits, ears cocked, on top of a plinth that bears the names of all twenty-five war dogs who gave the lives there. A replica sits in College of Veterinary Medicine at the University of Tennessee.

Captain William W. Putney's own memorial was the book *Always Faithful*—the English translation of the US Marine Corps's motto *Semper Fidelis*—published in 2001. It detailed the history and contribution of the K-9 Corps.

After the end of the war, the so-called K-9 Corps stopped recruiting mature dogs and began training them from puppies. Eventually, the marines' war dogs program was discontinued, though before long it would be needed again.

Lucky

There was another war dog on Guam called Lucky, but he did not arrive there until the late PFC Edward Topka's Lucky had been rotated home. The second Lucky belonged to Donald R. Walton, who had been given the German shepherd as an eight-week-old pup by his friend Doug Springer. Walton had taught Lucky to obey basic commands before he was called up into the Navy.

While he was in the service, Walton's wife and infant son were to live with her parents in Washington, D.C. City life was not going to suit Lucky, who was used to roaming free in Owl Creek, Pennsylvania. So Walton called the Marine

Corps, who were desperate for dogs at the time. They came right back to him, saying, "Yes, we want your dog."

Walton sent Lucky by train to Camp Lejeune in a crate marked "USMC Devil Dog." Lucky was then eighteen-months old.

The Marine Corps kept the Walton fully informed of Lucky's progress. After basic training, he was sent out to the Pacific Theater in 1945 as a replacement for a casualty. His job was to seek out Japanese soldiers still hiding out in the caves and tunnel complexes on Guam. He was then used in the amphibious assaults on other Pacific Islands as the marines pushed west across the Pacific.

Walton received letters both from the Marine Corps and from Lucky's handler. He could even write back. A letter addressed to Lucky, giving his serial number, 651, sent via an army post office number in San Francisco, would be forwarded to his handler.

In one of the handler's letters, he explained how useful Lucky was because he was never surprised by the enemy, always sensing their presence. Walton said:

> One of the favorite tactics of the Japanese was a
> night banzai attack to try to overrun a position of the
> marines—throw them into confusion and do a lot of
> damage to them. When the handler went to sleep, he
> slept with the palm of his hand under the throat of
> Lucky. Lucky had been taught never to bark or growl.
> But if he sensed anything out of the ordinary at night,
> his throat would vibrate in a silent growl, which would
> awaken the handler. And the handler then roused the
> other marines. And they were never, ever surprised
> by a banzai attack by the Japanese. And the presence
> of the dog was such an important matter to the other

marines that the handler threw away his own shovel. All the marines dug holes when they always took cover. But the handler never dug a hole, and neither did Lucky. The other marines dug two extra holes. They wanted Lucky right with them.

Lucky was with the marines when they made their first landing on mainland Japan. This was a full-scale amphibious landing because, though the Japanese had formally surrendered, no one was sure that the fighting was over. They had to be ready for anything. Lucky went on to serve with the postwar occupation forces.

Lucky's handler came home safely after the war and wanted to adopt Lucky, saying he was "a sweet dog you could do anything with." But Walton had to write and tell him that he wanted Lucky back.

"That was, perhaps, the toughest letter I have ever written," said Walton.

Lucky returned to the US and Camp Lejeune, where he was detrained. In April 1946, he was sent back to Walton, who was instructed to romp with the dog for thirty minutes a day to wear him out. He was also told never to give the command to attack, or the one used to get a dog to guard a prisoner. And Walton was told to feed Lucky three pounds of food a day, including two pounds of meat, which is what he had been fed in the Marine Corps. Unfortunately, at that time, the family ration of meat was just two pounds a week, so Lucky would have to get used to a civilian diet.

Lucky was returned in a crate, though now he was officially a War Dog, rather than a Devil Dog. Late one night, Walton picked him up at the station in Richmond, Virginia. When the crate was unloaded on the platform, Walton spoke Lucky's name. Though Lucky had been trained never to make a sound, when he recognized Walton's voice he made a very low quiet whining noise.

"As soon as he heard my voice, he couldn't resist that little whimper," said Walton. "And I opened the crate. He ran off to the bushes to take care of the necessary. And then he came roaring back, put both hands on my shoulders and wagging his tail violently. He recognized me."

Walton took Lucky to the family's new home, which he had never seen before. When he let Lucky in the front door and switched on the lights, "he pussy-footed every inch of that house," said Walton. "He was looking to see if there were any threats anywhere in that house. And then he came back and laid down at my feet." It was part of his training to make sure that they place was safe.

After he returned, Walton noticed that Lucky was more self-assured and more disciplined. But he was not rough or aggressive. He was never put on a leash and was free to run about. And he never got lost as he had when he was a puppy. The Waltons also found that they did not have to lock their doors or windows. Everything was perfectly safe as long as Lucky was there.

Lucky also looked after the Waltons' son and, when a second baby came along, made it his personal duty to keep tabs on the baby. From the time the elder boy was three, he was allowed to go out on expeditions into the surrounding countryside, as Walton knew that his son was perfectly safe as long as Lucky was with him.

Lucky would take on the toughest mongrel, but he did not like cap pistols. When the boys played with cap guns in the yard, Lucky would put his head in Walton's lap as if pleading with him not to let them shoot each other. Also, at the beach, he would swim out and try to herd the boys toward the shore. Plainly, this came from his Marine Corps training. Whenever he saw someone in uniform, he would go up to see who it was. It seemed he was hoping that someday he would meet his handler again.

The Marine Corps training had also improved Lucky's fitness. When Walton tried to leave him in a field with a high fence while he went to work, Lucky was back at the house within a matter of minutes. And when a neighbor's bitch was locked up in a windowless garage after coming into season, Lucky was seen emerging from a ventilation opening fourteen feet above the ground. As a result, there was a healthy litter of puppies.

Lucky lived to the age of fourteen, when he finally had to be put down.

CHAPTER FIVE
KOREA

THE US ARMY DECIDED TO RETAIN its infantry war dog platoon, but they were to be attached to infantry units for training and operations. By the time the Korean War flared up in June 1950, the 26th Infantry Scout Dog Platoon was the only scout dog platoon in the world.

In 1946, the Quartermaster Corps had stopped taking dogs on loan from civilians and began buying them directly from the breeders. Initially, individual breeders were brought into the Army Dog Association, Inc. The Army had already decided that it only wanted German shepherds, as they could work in both cold and hot climates. The initial breeding stock, acquired in Germany in 1945, consisted of one male puppy and five females. These were sold to breeders for $1 each. The Army could pick one male puppy, between twelve and fifteen months old, from the first three litters of any dog in the program. The breeders could make their money by selling the rest of the litters.

But as the Quartermasters Corps had no facilities to kennel or train these dogs, the program foundered. The responsibility for the purchase of war dogs was left with the 26th Infantry Scout Dog Platoon.

The Army maintained around a hundred sentry dogs in Korea, but most of them were killed or starved to death when North Korea invaded. By the time General Douglas MacArthur had pushed the North Koreans back to the Yalu River and the Chinese got involved, there were no American dogs in Korea. Then in May 1951, the entire 26th Infantry Scout Dog Platoon was ordered to prepare to embark for Korea. In actuality, only six dogs and seven handlers were sent.

On July 11, 1951, a new Army War Dog Receiving and Holding Station was established at Cameron Station, Alexandria, Virginia. The war dogs were processed and conditioned before being shipped to the Army Dog Training Center at Fort Carson, Colorado. The US Air Force supplied its own sentry dogs. Most of them were trained at the Sentry Dog Training Center at Showa Air Station on the main island of Honshu, Japan. The K-9 Sentry Dogs Handlers, who were all volunteers, trained with their dogs for several weeks before returning to Korea for deployment. The sentry dogs were used mostly at night, like the army, for patrolling the air base perimeters, and guarding fuel storage sites, bomb dumps, and supply areas.

The 26th Infantry Scout Dog Platoon saw plenty of combat action, and their success saving lives made them invaluable to ground operations in Korea. One regimental commander remarked that after using a scout dog team for a while, the infantry patrols did not want to go out without them. However, it was generally found that the dogs did not work well in the mountains. The winds there made the air swirl, and there were occasions when a dog could not scent the enemy until it was within thirty feet. Again there was the problem of the patrol leaders ignoring the dog's alerts. On occasion, a patrol leader ignored three alerts. The dog handler was awarded the Silver Star posthumously.

Members of the 26th Infantry Scout Dog Platoon were awarded three Silver Stars, six Bronze Stars of Valor, and thirty-five Bronze Stars for meritorious service. Then as the war drew to a close, the Army awarded a citation to the whole unit. It read:

General Orders 114

Headquarters, Eighth United States Army,

Korea, January 18, 1953

CITATION: "The 26th Infantry Scout Dog Platoon is cited for exceptionally meritorious conduct in the performance of outstanding services in direct support of combat operations in Korea during the period 12 June 1951 to 15 January 1953. The full value of the services rendered by the 26th Infantry Scout Dog Platoon is nowhere better understood and more highly recognized than among the members of the patrols with whom the scout dog handlers and their dogs have operated. Throughout its long period of difficult and hazardous service, the 26th Infantry Scout Dog Platoon has never failed those with whom it served; has consistently shown outstanding devotion to duty in the performance of all of its other duties, and has won on the battlefield a degree of respect and admiration which has established it as a unit of the greatest importance to the Eighth United States Army. The outstanding performance of duty proficiency, and esprit de corps invariably exhibited by the personnel of this platoon reflect the greatest credit on themselves and the military service of the United States."

York

There was one scout dog that stood out. His name was York, brand number O11X, and he was decorated for outstanding service while serving with the 26th Infantry Scout Dog Platoon in Korea. He was awarded the Distinguished Service Award by General Samuel T. Williams after performing 148 combat patrols between June 12, 1951, and June 26, 1953, and it was said that his silent alerts on enemy locations had saved many American lives.

York remained in the Far East until March 1957, when special permission was granted for him to return to the US. He was accompanied on the trip by a returning enlisted man and was delivered to the Army Dog Training Center in Fort Carson to be used as a member of a demonstration team. It was felt that York would help improve public relations and arouse more interest in the recruitment and procurement of dogs for military purposes. However, the Army Dog Training Center, Fort Carson, was deactivated on July 1, 1957, and York was transferred to Fort Benning, Georgia, to be attached to the 26th Infantry Scout Dog Platoon there.

CHAPTER SIX
VIETNAM

WHEN LIEUTENANT PAUL B. MORGAN went to Vietnam as a military adviser in 1965, he knew he needed a dog just to stay alive. He got lucky. He gave a set of silver rosary beads and a .38 caliber pistol to a village priest named Father Nguyen Cong Tu. In return, the priest gave him a German shepherd named Xa Xi, after the local soda the dog was very fond of. But Morgan called her Suzie.

As he was a staunch anti-Communist, there was a price on Father Nguyen's head, but Suzie had protected him. She would attack anyone who threatened her master. As a military adviser, Morgan was also a marked man. Suzie slept with him every night, tethered to his wrist by a piece of parachute cord. She saved his life on numerous occasions.

Bear

Morgan had a long association with military dogs. He had signed up at the age of nineteen after two years of college and serving in the ROTC. Most of the men in his family had served in the military. During basic training at Fort Benning, Georgia, he was to play an enemy soldier for an attack dog, but the handler dropped the leash and the dog savaged him.

The dog's name was Bear. He had served with distinction in Korea. His handler had been awarded the Bronze Star and the Purple Heart, which he handed on to Bear as the military had forbidden the presentation of medals to animals. But now Bear was old. They managed to get him off of Morgan before he did much more damage than shred his tunic. Despite this, Morgan liked Bear and asked how he could become a dog handler. Bear's handler told him to volunteer.

In the spring of 1957, Morgan became a guard at the K-9 unit. His job included feeding the dogs, cleaning out their kennels, and being the fall guy for Bear. Soon he was going out on training exercises with Bear. That Christmas, they went out on a real mission. A sergeant living off-post with his wife reported their five-year-old son had been kidnapped. The local police had no tracker dog, so Morgan and Bear were sent. They tracked the boy to a neighbor's house. They had left the child at home alone, and he had wandered over the neighbor's to play with their son. No harm had been done, but it was a dark and cold night. The child could easily have gotten lost, though Morgan has every confidence that Bear would have found him.

At Fort Gordon, Morgan was attached to military police reserve squad of dog handlers for Georgia and North Carolina. These were local police dog handlers and veterans of the Korean War. Morgan's sergeant had two German shepherds, Luger and Rommel. Morgan was assigned Luger, who was lazy, slow, and overweight. Nevertheless, during an exercise, they managed to capture four Green Berets—including two officers—who were playing enemy infiltrators.

Morgan joined the 82nd Airborne where he was trained as a paratrooper. There he was teamed up with Bear again. They made a parachute jump together. Bear wore a reserve parachute bag with holes cut for his legs and tail. This was attached under Morgan's own reserve chute. The arrangement did not suit Bear, who barked and snapped at those trying to attach him. Eventually he had to be muzzled. He also weighed eighty pounds so, with all his other equipment, Morgan had to kneel in the doorway with Bear's paws on the floor before they made the jump.

When Morgan's chute opened, Bear would hang down between his legs, making it impossible for Morgan to land properly with his legs together. On the way down, Bear struggled, so Morgan pulled off his muzzle and tried to put his ball in his mouth, but he dropped it. Then Morgan's helmet slipped of his eyes. On landing, Morgan was dragged along by his parachute with Bear under him. Eventually, he cut the dog free. But then Bear went running about the drop zone, barking until someone cut him out of his makeshift harness. It was on this exercise that Morgan learned to tie his dog to his wrist with a parachute cord. He could then sleep comfortably with the dog in his arms, confident that no one could approach him during the night.

In addition to proving his worth as a guide, Bear was also put through his paces as a scout dog. Morgan walked point with Bear out in front on a fifteen-foot leash. The dog could spot a hiding man from fifty yards and take him down if he ran. Morgan spent his time studying the dog. There was, after all, nothing Morgan could teach Bear, but he could learn from the dog. Bear kept them out of the hands of the troops playing the enemy, and Morgan and Bear passed the training exercise. Then Morgan was sent to Alaska where he got to work with sled dogs. During a blizzard, he slept with one in his sleeping bag to keep from freezing.

Suzie

In 1964, Morgan joined the 6th Special Forces at Fort Bragg, North Carolina, and became a Green Beret in April 1965. That June, now a lieutenant, he was sent to guard a bridge in Gia Dinh Province with South Vietnamese Rangers from the Army of the Republic of the Vietnam and the newly acquired Suzie. A former police dog, she could sniff out explosives and had once helped capture a Vietcong suspect when he had leapt from a taxi stopped at the roadblock and tried to make a run for it.

On August 15, 1965, the Rangers came under attack from the Vietcong. When the bridge they were guarding was hit by a rocket, Morgan and Suzie took cover on the south side. Suzie went on the alert as two Vietcong approached with a 57mm recoilless rifle. They fired at the bridge, but missed. Morgan and the ARVN (Army of the Republic of Vietnam) returned fire, killing one Vietcong and wounding two others. After another two hours of fighting, three more were dead. In his after-action report, Morgan gave Suzie the credit for alerting them to the attackers. The two of them became inseparable companions.

They were on convoy duty together picking up ammunition from Ton Son Nhut air base outside Saigon when one of the Rangers turned up with very red eyes. Morgan concluded that he had either been drinking or smoking marijuana. Suzie growled at him. The convoy then came under attack. Back at base, the Rangers' commander struck the man with the red eyes and had him arrested. He had gone AWOL a month earlier. It was suspected that he had joined the Vietcong and returned to the unit to organize the ambush.

The man with the red eyes was held in a tiny tiger cage too small to stand up or lie down in, but had to be released when he was wounded by a mortar shell. He then killed two Rangers and stole a uniform and their equipment.

Morgan and the Vietnamese Rangers were in an exposed position. On both sides, the local village had been infiltrated by the enemy. They needed the support of helicopter gunships. The gunships, in turn, needed parachute flares fired by mortar to see what they were shooting at. But the Rangers' mortar had fallen silent. Morgan and Suzie went to investigate; they were joined by Sergeant Nhan and Corporal Phung.

They found that the mortar pit had been hit by a grenade. One Ranger was dead, and three others were badly wounded. Lieutenant Morgan put down his M-14 and tried to help the injured men. Then he dropped two illuminating rounds down the mortar tube, one after the other.

Suzie began barking.

"Look out!" yelled Sergeant Nhan.

Lieutenant Morgan turned to see the man with the red eyes throwing a grenade. Sergeant Nhan grabbed Morgan's M-14 and shot at the attacker. Morgan pulled out his .45 and fired, too—but, stepping back, he fell over Suzie into the mortar pit. Corporal Phung flung himself on the grenade, killing himself, but saving Lieutenant Morgan, Sergeant Nhan, and Suzie from serious injury. Phung was the hero of the moment. Lieutenant Morgan and Sergeant Nhan also gave credit to Suzie, whose bark and sounded the alarm. But it was Morgan who was awarded the Army Commendation Medal.

The whole incident had shaken Morgan though. He realized that he was not safe, even from the AVRN Rangers he had come to advise, and he was convinced, now more than ever, that he should sleep with Suzie and his M-14 by his side, and with his sneakers on his feet.

Suzie came along when Morgan and the Rangers raided a French villa often used a headquarters building by the Vietcong. No VC were found, so they booby-trapped the place and, while most of the Rangers withdrew, Lieutenant Morgan and Suzie stayed behind with an ambush party. During the night, the VC approached. Suzie growled and bared her teeth. Morgan called in helicopter gunships to attack. At dawn, they went out to examine the scene. Suzie did not go on the alert. The enemy had gone, taking their dead with them, along with the Rangers' booby traps.

Lieutenant Morgan was a Catholic and went to take mass from Father Tu. He would bring Suzie with him, and both would receive the priest's blessing. According to Father Tu, dogs were protected from the knowledge of death so that they would be brave and serve man. As a reward for their selflessness and devotion, they would all go to a canine version of heaven.

When Morgan was hit by a sniper whose bullet gashed open his forearm, Suzie licked the blood away. Then she led the charge when they went out after the sniper. Morgan was afraid that she would get killed but, at the approach of helicopter gunships, she held back. Then she went out to find a couple of wounded Rangers who had gotten separated from the patrol.

No dogs were allowed in medevac choppers, so Lieutenant Morgan stayed behind with Suzie until another helicopter came to pick up the dead. The two of them scrambled onboard together. He thanked Suzie for saving his life again.

Suzie woke Lieutenant Morgan at 4:00 a.m. one day, in time to hear a helicopter being shot down just two miles from their position. Other helicopters were coming to pick up Morgan and his men to carry them to the search area where they were to look for the downed helicopter's crew. Of course, with Suzie's acute hearing, she alerted him when the helicopters were about to arrive.

At the landing zone, Suzie led Lieutenant Morgan to antiaircraft bunkers that had fired on the helicopter. Suzie alerted, indicating that there was an enemy soldier in the first bunker. Sergeant Nhan threw in a grenade. At a second bunker, Suzie threw herself flat behind some undergrowth before Lieutenant Morgan tossed in a grenade. She then checked that the enemy soldiers inside were dead before they moved on.

When they found the downed helicopter, they learned that none of the crew had survived the crash. But Suzie guarded the dead pilot's body until a helicopter came to pick it up. Onboard the Huey, Suzie sat next to the body, again guarding it. Once again, she had been the hero of the operation.

In December 1965, Lieutenant Morgan left the Rangers to take up an assignment as a military policeman in Saigon. He returned Suzie to Father Tu, knowing she would be well looked after.

Polar Bear

From 1967 through 1968, Lieutenant Morgan had the job of picking up deserters in New York City. He worked with a German shepherd named Styx. Then in 1970, Lieutenant Morgan returned to Vietnam and was to be posted to Fire Base Diana out on the border with Cambodia. On his way, he met a German shepherd dog named Polar Bear, who had been wounded in the shoulder and the face. Polar Bear's handler had been killed in the same incident that had wounded the dog two days before; they had been flushing out a VC bunker.

Since then the dog turned on anyone who tried to be-friend him. He even tried to attack Morgan, who made it clear that he would finish the dog off with his M-16 if he tried it again. But threats were of little help with a dog. Instead, Lieutenant Morgan tried the simple approach of giving Polar Bear straightforward obedience commands. The dog found this reassuring and did what he was told. Morgan then took off his helmet and filled it with water for the dog. Polar Bear growled suspiciously, but then lapped up the water.

After the death of his handler, Polar Bear had not been expected to survive, so his wounds had not been tended. Morgan held the dog down while a medic tried to patch him up, though he snapped, growled, and whined with the pain. Morgan got Polar Bear some food to sooth him. By default, he ended up adopting the dog, largely because everyone else wanted him out of the way. Polar Bear responded to his kind-ness with affection.

Morgan then tracked down the dog's unit, thinking he would return him. But they were surprised to see the dog; he was already listed as killed in action and it was plain that now that Polar Bear had no handler they intended to put him down. To prevent this, Morgan claimed that he was going to take the dog to Saigon to hand him into the kennels there. No one believed him, but they were glad to get rid of the dog and gave Morgan some dog food to feed him on the way. Instead, Morgan took him to Fire Base Diana, where the dog quickly made himself at home in Morgan's bunker.

Ostensibly on guard duty, Polar Bear slept on Morgan's bed and gulped down all the delicacies his new master gave him. Although he was not taken out on patrol, Polar Bear showed great courage when a North Vietnamese regiment tried to overrun the base. His barking drew attention to North

Vietnamese Army (NVA) soldiers who had come within thirty feet of the command bunker. During the engagement, eight Americans were killed and twelve were wounded. Morgan was one of the wounded. He had been hit when two mortar shells exploded near him. Polar Bear stayed with him until he passed out from the pain. Morgan was then medevaced out to a hospital in Saigon and never saw Polar Bear again. Two weeks later, the dog was hit by a mortar round and killed. He was buried with full military honors.

In 1971 Morgan was sent back to Fort Campbell, Kentucky, where he continued to work with K-9 sections. Five years later, he retired from the army and started his own K-9 security company.

Kaiser

Marine Lance Corporal Alfredo Salazar volunteered for duty as a dog handler in the newly formed 1st Marine Scout Dog Platoon at Camp Lejeune, North Carolina. On December 3, 1965, he was the transferred to Fort Benning, Georgia, where he met the eighty-five-pound German shepherd that would be his companion for the next seven months. He called him Kaiser.

"He came to me and licked my hand," Salazar said. "From then on we were a team."

The two of them then went through rigorous training with the Army's 26th Infantry Scout Dog Platoon. From there, they were sent to Camp Pendleton, California, for their final preparation before being sent to Vietnam.

In country, they took part in a dozen major operations and went out on more than thirty combat patrols. Out on a search-and-destroy mission with D Company of the 1st

Marines, 3rd Marine Division, Lance Corporal Salazar and Kaiser were leading a patrol through heavy brush toward a small village. As they broke through the undergrowth, they were raked by heavy automatic fire and hand grenades. Kaiser was downed almost immediately.

Salazar and the lead marines returned fire. Then, as the patrol moved in to attack the Vietcong, Salazar knelt by his wounded companion.

"He tried to lick my hand," Salazar said. "Then he died."

The men carried Kaiser back to the company area, where he was buried under the shade of a tree near their tents. Kaiser was the first marine scout dog killed in action in Vietnam. In his honor, they renamed their camp "Camp Kaiser."

Nemo, et al.

Nemo, an eighty-five-pound black-and-tan German shepherd dog, brand number A534, joined the US Air Force in 1964 when he was eighteen months old. After completing an eight-week training course at Lackland Sentry Dog Training School at San Antonio Texas, he was assigned to guard duties at an air base near Washington, D.C.

In January 1966, Nemo was shipped to Vietnam with a large group of dogs and was assigned to the 377th Security Police K-9 unit. With his handler, Airman Second Class Bob Thorneburg, he was to guard Tan Son Nhut, the largest air base in Vietnam, located just northwest of Saigon.

The facilities there had originally been designed for three thousand people. By then, there were 25,000 living on the base. During the day, when other people came to work there, the number swelled to 50,000.

The war was just hitting its stride and the Vietcong were beginning to target American air bases. That year there were three attacks on the air base at Pleiku. Other attacks followed on Bien Hoa and Tan Son Nhut. In each case, the attackers ran into trouble with the sentry dogs. They tried smearing their bodies with aromatic herbs to put the dogs off the scent. When that did not work, they began shelling the kennels, but that failed too.

On December 4, 1966, the Vietcong mounted an attack on Tan Son Nhut again. In the early hours, several dogs around the perimeter went on the alert. Some sixty or seventy VC were about a hundred yards outside the wire. Airman Second Class Leroy E. Marsh released his dog, Rebel. He was brought down in a hail of bullets, but Marsh had enough time to reach another sentry post several hundreds of yards away and call for help.

About an hour later, another sentry dog named Cubby went on the alert. When he was released, he was shot down, too. When a third sentry dog named Toby was shot just before dawn, his handler returned fire, killing a VC. Another handler chased a group of VC, who retreated and hid. By then, the Security Police were on the alert for an attack. Thirteen Vietcong were gunned down by a machine gun as they approached the main aircraft parking ramp. The security police then sealed the perimeter so no one could escape. But when they searched the base in daylight, they found nothing. However, it was assumed that some of the infiltrators were still hiding in the base, waiting for nightfall.

That night, Nemo and Thorneburg were assigned guard duty near an old Vietnamese cemetery about a quarter mile from the air base's runways. No sooner had they started their patrol when Nemo alerted on something in the graveyard.

But before Thorneburg could radio the central command post, they came under fire. Thorneburg released Nemo and he charged forward. Then Thorneburg heard the dog howl with pain. Thorneburg opened fire and killed one VC before he was shot in the shoulder and knocked to the ground.

Despite a serious head wound, Nemo was not done yet. He threw himself at the Vietcong. This gave Thorneburg the time he needed to call in backup forces.

A Quick Reaction Team arrived and swept the area but found no other Vietcong. However, security forces with sentry dog teams found and killed eight more Vietcong. Meanwhile, the wounded Nemo crawled over to Thorneburg and covered him with his body. When help arrived, Nemo would not allow anyone to touch his master. Ultimately, the dog was pulled off, and he and his master were taken back to the base for medical attention.

A bullet had entered under Nemo's right eye and exited through his mouth. The base veterinarian, Lieutenant Raymond T. Hutson, managed to save Nemo's life and made many skin grafts to restore his appearance. But Nemo remained blind in one eye.

However, the handler and the dog who saved his life had to say their final good-byes. Thorneburg was so badly injured that had to be evacuated to the hospital at Tachikawa Air Base in Japan to recuperate. When he had fully recovered, he returned home with full military honors.

Meanwhile, Nemo went back on perimeter duty, but then it was found that his wounds needed further treatment. On June 23, 1967, the air force ordered that Nemo also be returned to the United States with honors. He was the first sentry dog to be officially retired from active service. Nemo flew home in the care of returning airman Melvin W. Bryant.

During the twenty-four-hour flight, the plane touched down in Japan, Hawaii, and California. At each stop, air force vets examined Nemo for signs of discomfort, stress, and fatigue. He was to be treated as a war hero.

When the C-124 Globemaster touched down at Kelly Air Force Base, Texas, on July 22, 1967, Nemo was greeted by a welcoming committee headed by Captain Robert M. Sullivan, the officer in charge of the sentry dog training program at Lackland.

"I have to keep from getting involved with individual dogs in this program," Captain Sullivan explained, "but I can't help feeling a little emotional about this dog. He shows how valuable a dog is to his handler in staying alive."

Nemo then returned to Lackland Air Force Base, where he was given a kennel with his name on it. After settling in, Nemo and Captain Sullivan made a number of cross-country tours and television appearances as part of an air force drive to recruit more dogs.

Nemo spent the rest of his retirement at Lackland and died there in December 1972, aged eleven. An attempt was made to preserve his body, but his remains were finally laid to rest at the Department of Defense Dog Center on March 15, 1973.

Ebony

In the spring of 1969, baseball player Joseph J. White was hoping for a contract from the Pittsburgh Pirates. Instead, the mailman brought his draft papers. He faked a knee injury and got a letter from his family doctor. The army took no notice. They had their own doctor examine White and deemed him fit for service.

A reluctant soldier, White caused endless trouble during his eight weeks of basic training. Soon he was on his way to Vietnam, and before he knew it he was walking point with a patrol near the DMZ—the De-Militarized Zone that separated the Republic of Vietnam in the south from the communist north. After six months' fighting in the jungle, witnessing the increasing scale of the seemingly senseless slaughter, and suffering the privations of life on a firebase, White became convinced that, if he did not get out of the infantry, he would die. Then he met a dog handler who arranged his transfer to the Canine Corps.

White was assigned to the 47th Scout Dog Platoon. At the gate to their camp was a sign that read, "Stand Tall, You're Entering Scout Dog Country." On his first night there, White was told they had three dogs without handlers. He asked the other handlers which dog they would choose. They all said, "Ebony." So the following morning White and Ebony became a team. She was an all-black German shepherd and was already well-trained. She would do all basic commands off-leash and responded to hand-signals as well as verbal commands. They hit it off immediately. White was impressed by how friendly and happy she was, taking a genuine pleasure in her performance over the obstacle course. She had been a scout dog in Vietnam since 1967, so it was more a question of training White than of training Ebony.

After running through the basic commands of "sit," "down," "come," "stay," and "heel," and tackling the obstacle course, White was taken out on a practice trail where two other handlers were hiding. White missed the first one, not noticing that Ebony's ears had pricked; but the second time it happened, he spotted the alert.

The following morning, the trainer gave some Vietnamese children a few dollars to hide down the trail. This time,
White did not miss a single alert. He practiced again that
afternoon. Then he was sent on a mission. Although he was
still a rookie as a dog handler, a dog team had been requested
and all the others were already out in the field.

For White this would be on-the-job training. Veteran dog
handler Sergeant Ronnie McCrary was sent with him. Mc-
Crary was not keen to go. He had worked with the unit they
had been assigned to before; on that occasion, his dog, Sarge,
had indicated a strong alert in the direction of a stream at
the bottom of hill. McCrary assumed that the enemy must
be down there taking a drink. As they approached, Sarge
unexpectedly ran off. McCrary could not call him for fear
of alerting the enemy. He became concerned, as Sarge had
been unswervingly loyal and obedient for three months in
dog handling school at Fort Benning, Georgia, before they
came to Vietnam.

Eventually, they became convinced that there were no enemy around. McCrary went down to the stream and looked
for Sarge. There was no sign of him. McCrary called his
name. There was no response and, humiliated, McCrary had
to return with the patrol alone. Three days later, Sarge turned
up. He had made his way ten miles across hostile, moun-
tainous, jungle-covered territory without a scratch. Having
had his highly trained dog run out on him, McCrary was not
looking forward to going out with the same outfit again.

White was not used to going out on patrol with a dog.
He found that he had to leave a lot of his own personal kit
behind to make room for Ebony's food and water—because
she was black, he realized, she would need a lot more water.
Ebony had not been on a mission for two months, and the

preparations for going out into the field made her excited.
She wagged her tail so hard that her whole body shook.

Ebony and White went to the airstrip with two other dog
teams to await a chopper to fly them out on the mission. The
dogs, of course, were up and ready long before their handlers
even heard the helicopter coming. The dogs loved flying in
the open bay of a Huey. White feared that Ebony might slide
out of the open door when the helicopter turned, but she was
a veteran of flying and simply extended her claws, gripping
the grooves in the steel floor. She turned her head toward
the door, enjoying the feel of the rushing wind and panting
so that slobber ran from the side of her mouth. Her nose
twitched as if she were making a scent map of the terrain below. It was not uncommon for dogs who had gotten separated
from their handlers in the heat of combat to make their way
on their own all the way back to base, as Sarge had done.

The Huey landed at a forward operating base. White was
briefed at the command post by Captain Hunter. An enemy
regiment was in the area, and it was their job to locate them.
Ebony was on hand to sniff out the VC and to protect the
men against surprise attack.

On McCrary's recommendation, Ebony was let off the
leash so that she could get the scent of each man in the patrol.
When it was time to go, Ebony trotted across the landing
zone to the beginning of the trail, then looked back to make
sure the rest of them were following. White was used to walking point alone, and McCrary had to remind him to keep an
eye on Ebony. The two of them were supposed to be working
as a team. Ebony would scout ahead, but return to White to
remind him of her presence as if she were teaching him the
job of being a dog handler.

When they stopped for the night, Ebony and White were supposed to stay in the middle with the officers, so that Ebony could get some rest away from the distractions of the perimeter. But one of the enlisted men invited them to join him in his position. It would be more dangerous there, but White preferred the company of other enlisted men, and Ebony knew that they were more generous with their rations than the officers were. Ebony drew a daily ration of two three-ounce bags of doggie burger, the equivalent of two cans of horse meat, but that was supplemented by whatever her human companions would provide. Although the enlisted men had to share their rations, having White and Ebony with them on the perimeter had its advantages. It meant that there was an extra man to share the guard duty, and a dog's eyes and ears to alert them to the approach of the enemy when they were sleeping.

As they headed on into the jungle the next day, White watched Ebony closely for alerts. He was aware that new handlers often overinterpreted a dog's every move, reading an alert where there was none and slowing down the patrol. On the other hand, some new guys got themselves killed because they dismissed an alert and urged the dog onward when they had been warned that danger lay ahead. It was a difficult balance to strike.

On the fourth day, they headed onto a denser patch of jungle. Ebony suddenly stopped and turned her head. Then she crouched with one ear pointing ahead, the other to the side. Her nostrils flared. White turned to the other men, but they had already seen Ebony's reaction. When White turned back to Ebony, she had relaxed her stance. Nevertheless, McCrary and the platoon sergeant decided to send a squad to check out what dangers lay ahead.

While this was going on, Ebony and White hung back with the rest of the platoon. They heard a commotion up ahead, but no gunfire. The squad returned. What Ebony had alerted them to was not the enemy but a bunch of monkeys. True, she had alerted and then relaxed. White realized that he was going to have to learn to read her reactions better.

That night Ebony went on the alert again. This time a roar in the undergrowth indicated that a tiger was on the prowl. Ebony was eager to attack the large cat. White had to restrain her with all his might to prevent her from joining what he reckoned to be an unequal fight. However, they dared not shoot the tiger, even though it came within ten feet, for fear of giving away their position. Mercifully, the tiger eventually turned and wandered away. Once it was gone, Ebony quickly went to sleep. White bedded down beside her, finding her presence among the dangers of the forest a great comfort.

In a spare moment, McCrary showed White Ebony's antiwar trick. All you had to do was say, "Ebony, would you rather be in the army, or would you rather be a dead dog," and Ebony would roll over on her side and play dead. It always raised a smile.

After five days on patrol, Ebony had to be rested. She and White were airlifted back to camp where White could take a shower. This was one of the great advantages of being a dog handler. The rest of the men would continue on their patrol for another fifty or sixty days.

The 47th Scout Dog Platoon relocated to Phu Bai, just south of the ancient city of Hué. Ebony had an extra assignment there. She was to warn White and the other men who were smoking pot of any approaching officer. The unit also got a new commanding officer, who disliked seeing his men idle, so he visited combat units, asking if they needed dog teams. This did not go over well with the men, who responded by leaving a grenade in his bed, or shouting "Incoming!" at night and pelting the tin roof of his hooch with rocks.

There were fights between the male dogs. One particularly savage German shepherd named Bullet was often involved. When out on a mission, he would often jump from the chopper at the landing zone and bite the first man within reach. On one occasion, he sank his teeth into another dog's neck and the handlers had to beat him over the head with a shovel, then jam it between his jaws to make him let go. White grew so close to Ebony that he would take her with him when he visited the local massage girls. When another dog handler decided to do the same thing, the owner of the massage parlor objected. So the two of them tied their dogs up outside and left them there with the command "Watch." This meant they would allow no one to enter or leave the building, effectively closing the massage parlor down. The owner complained. Eventually the military police turned up and they were arrested.

The commander of the 47th Scout Dog Platoon had to come and bail them out. He gave them a lecture, but they weren't punished. After all, the dog handlers were vital to the war effort. As they were out ahead on patrol, they had a dangerous job, and few people volunteered for the position. As a result, dog handlers flaunted their invulnerability to discipline by growing their hair long and wearing love beads. One officer even refused to take White on a mission because of his appearance, saying that he doubted such an obviously undisciplined individual could do the job.

The strain of being out in front on patrol also took its toll on the men. One dog handler drew a gun on the other men and threatened to shoot them just days before he was due to go home.

But still the dog teams were in demand. A colonel who was attached to the South Vietnamese Army had heard about Ebony and White, and requested their services for a special mission. White was flattered. At first, being out ahead of Vietnamese troops confused Ebony, but she soon settled to the task.

Ebony had a reputation for giving 110 percent to her job. Once, while waiting to be airlifted out after the end of a mission, she kept going to the edge of the landing zone to give the alert. The patrol found NVA soldiers waiting thirty yards down the trail. Thanks to the alert, they got the drop on them and no American lives were lost.

However, the dog platoons did suffer their losses. The 47th lost one dog and his handler. Seven dogs from the 42nd had been killed and three were wounded in just two months, though no handler had been lost. But worse news came from White's old infantry unit. The point man who had replaced him had tripped a series of booby traps that killed the first seven men in the patrol and seriously wounded the next seven. The rest were badly shaken.

Out on patrol in the mountains, Ebony and White, along with another dog handler named Gibbs and his dog, got separated from their patrol and they decided to make for the lowlands of eastern Vietnam, where they were more likely to come across other Americans. Two hours down the trail, Ebony suddenly put her nose in the air in full alert. They froze. This was not her usual alert. A raised nose often meant that there was a dead body up ahead. However, it was best to be cautious. They edged their way forward and, after about twenty-five yards, they found themselves in an enemy bunker complex.

Fortunately, no one was at home. But they could tell that the enemy had been there recently and could well be coming back, so they took off into the hills, avoiding any trails that could have been used by returning troops. This was difficult as they had no machetes to hack their way through the jungle, and they shed their extraneous equipment to lighten their load.

From the top of the next hill they could see all the way across to the South China Sea. The lowlands and a highway were beneath them. They shared what remained of their food with the dogs and settled down for the night beneath the undergrowth. In the morning they plunged on downhill through the jungle. Soon they were out of water. As the day grew hotter, they began to dehydrate and realized that they were in danger of dying. The dogs got to the point where they could only walk three paces before collapsing.

Suddenly Ebony went on the alert. She seemed to revive her vigor. White had seen her act like this before and his hopes soared. They stumbled on for another twenty yards through the jungle and found the clear water of a mountain stream. Ebony had saved their lives.

After they had drunk their fill, they followed the stream downhill. It grew wide and, at one point, it ran through a ravine with a sheer wall on either side. There was no way around it. To continue their journey they would have to negotiate a fifteen-foot waterfall. For the men, this would be easy enough. At the bottom of a waterfall there is invariably a deep pool. But on either side there were jagged rocks. They could not risk the dogs falling on them.

Gibbs and White figured out that if they tied the two dogs' leashes together, they would be nearly twelve feet long. The dogs could safely drop the last three feet. First Gibbs jumped over the waterfall into the pool below. Then White let the dogs down one at a time before leaping over the waterfall himself.

Soon they were crossing the paddy fields in the lowlands below where they came across the squad of marines who had been sent out to look for them. Less than a mile farther on they reached the highway where they hitched a ride back to Phu Bai.

White had already served 365 days in Vietnam, but he extended his tour so that he could leave the army as soon as he got home. Their next mission was to investigate a trail used by the NVA for resupply. Their commanding officer on the mission was a second lieutenant who was known as "Sergeant Rock" because he had been promoted from the ranks after notable acts of bravery. On the map, he pointed out places where he thought they might be ambushed. Then, after Ebony had scrounged food from everyone, she and White took point, as always. They were followed closely by two grunts with M-16s and one with an M-79 grenade launcher. Behind them were the second lieutenant and his radio man, followed by the medic and the rest of the men. Way down the line was the machine gunner. This concerned White, who was now a veteran of some two hundred patrols.

When the commanding officer gave the signal to move out, Ebony was already ten yards ahead of White, awaiting his order to head off. She needed to hear one word—"Search!"—before she would move off. Otherwise she would stand there blocking the path. The trail descended so steeply that White had to grab onto trees to prevent himself from falling head-over-heels. But this did not seem to bother Ebony.

At the bottom, they found a broad trail that showed signs that it was being used frequently by large numbers of enemy troops. Ebony sniffed in both directions. Her ears scanned the area, then relaxed. White was confident that there was no one about.

Ebony awaited instructions and White pointed left, indicating that she should go that way. She pranced off, but then, after about five minutes, she went on the alert. However, White noticed that she assumed the same attitude she had adopted on their first mission together. This time it was not monkeys that she had spotted in the undergrowth, but a family of gibbons making their way through the jungle canopy above.

Around twenty minutes later, they reached one of the places where the commanding officer (CO) had indicated they could be ambushed. It was dark and the jungle was dense. As Ebony was black, it was easy to lose sight of her. Then, halfway around a bend, Ebony stood stock-still. Her level of concentration indicated that what she had spotted was not the local wildlife, and White threw himself to the ground. The men following him did the same.

Once they had heeded her warning, Ebony returned to White's side to take cover. The lieutenant moved up to join them and asked White what was happening. White had seen Ebony's head moving, alerting to several places in one area rather than a single position. He explained that there was a group of men up ahead, not just a lone sniper or trail watcher.

As all the things Ebony had alerted them to were in one small area, White assumed this was not a patrol that was on the move. He reckoned that the enemy were about fifty yards ahead. The lieutenant pulled out his map and pointed out another bend in the road. It would the perfect site for a bunker that could house a hundred men—and there were only twenty-five in the patrol. On the other hand, there might just be a small party of ambushers that they could take on.

To find out, the lieutenant decided to fire a gas grenade through an opening in the trees. This would provoke a re-action without giving their position away. The man with the grenade launcher loaded a gas round, while the rest of the patrol readied themselves with their M-16s.

As the gas canister sailed through the trees, there was silence. Then they could hear the low hiss as the gas escaped. After what seemed like interminable seconds, there was the sound of movement. This turned into a stampede. Then it fell quiet again, and when the gas dispersed the patrol gingerly edged forward.

Ebony bounded ahead. White had to whistle to recall her. He knew from her attitude that there were no enemy soldiers ahead, but he was afraid that she might step on a mine or trip a booby trap. When they reached the next corner, Ebony peered around it and, excited, indicated that there was some-thing she wanted White to see. He knew that, in Vietnam, curiosity could be a death sentence, but Ebony indicated the way ahead was safe.

When he caught up with her, Ebony indicated a place where the brush had been squashed flat. From what he could make out, when they heard the Americans coming, an enemy patrol had taken up position in the undergrowth, ready to ambush them. The trail was straight and wide at that point. They could easily have wiped the American patrol out. But when the gas grenade came flying over, the ambushers took flight. With their eyes stinging and throats choking, they ran for it. Single-handedly, Ebony had saved the lives of twenty-five men.

When the base at Phu Bai got a new air-conditioned hamburger and ice cream parlor, Ebony was not allowed in—even though White protested that she was a better soldier than anyone in there. However, by then, Ebony had something of a reputation, and it was not hard to find a party of guys willing to smuggle her in past the man guarding the door. After White had finished eating and Ebony that taken full advantage of the air-conditioning, they left, walking unapologetically past the doorman.

It was a hot day, and back at the kennels, bad news awaited them. Gretchen, a dog who no longer had a handler, had died of heat exhaustion because no one had filled her water bowl. White vowed that this would never happen to Ebony.

But White was due to go home and Ebony was to stay in Vietnam. As Ebony had saved his life on numerous occasions, White was determined to save hers. He would pamper her to the point where she would be no good as a working dog. Even though he was repeatedly ordered not to, he let her sleep in his hooch with him and took her everywhere he went. When Ebony was assigned a new handler, White whistled to distract her. And when the new handler took her on the practice trail, White would call her and ruin the exercise. Eventually, the new handler was assigned another dog and White was told that Ebony would now become the company pet and never have to go out in the field again. Nevertheless, they had to say their good-byes and White flew back to the States.

Back home, White never forgot Ebony and kept her picture on his desk. He even considered joining the Police Department as a K-9 officer after hearing that some dog handlers had managed to get their former dogs returned from Vietnam that way. But the police would only employ male dogs, and Ebony was a bitch. Later White heard that some two thousand American military dogs had been designated "surplus equipment" and been handed over to the South Vietnamese Army. He believed that Ebony died chained to her kennel in the confusion that followed the fall of the south to communism.

Hans

John Burnam was just eighteen in 1966 when he found himself on his way to Vietnam. He had been in the army for just five months, having volunteered for the 1st Air Cavalry in September 1965 after graduating from high school. He was landing on a hilltop LZ when he jumped from the helicopter onto a punji stake, one of the sharpened spears of bamboo the Vietcong placed among the elephant grass to lance the unwary. Usually they were smeared with excrement to give the victim blood poisoning. The stake had gone in below Burnham's kneecap and come out the other side. The patrol were under fire before a medic could get to him.

When the firefight was over, Burnam was medevaced out to a field hospital at Qui Nhom. Then he was moved to a US Army Hospital in Yokohama for reconstructive surgery on his knee. He was hoping for a one-way ticket back to his hometown, Littleton, Colorado, but the doctor said his injury was not severe enough for that.

When he was discharged from the hospital, Burnam was sent to Okinawa, where he was to serve out the rest of his tour in southeast Asia. As there was no needed for combat troops there, he was assigned to the 267th Chemical Company as a dog handler–sentry at the huge supply depot on the island. He was given a large German shepherd named Hans who, when he stood on his hind legs, was taller than Burnam.

Hans was ferocious and Burnam was afraid of him, but he knew that to master the dog he must first master his fear. This was hard enough when the dog was in his cage. However, Hans's attitude gradually mellowed and he stopped growling when Burnam approached. Then came the day that Burnam had to take Hans out of his cage. To Burnam's surprise, instead of attacking him when the cage door was open, Hans eagerly consented to wearing a choke chain and leash.

Once in the open ground behind the kennels, Hans strained on the leash, pulling Burnam along. But eventually he got tired. Then Burnam gave a tug on the leash and said, "Heel." Again to Burnam's surprise, the dog obeyed. And gradually, with the help of a military dog-handling manual, Burnam learned about grooming, voice and hand commands, deployment, and first aid.

They joined the rest of the platoon for regular group training sessions. Burnam was at a disadvantage there, as the others had been on a twelve-week course at a dog-training school in the States. But eventually Burnam became Hans's master. After a month of training, Burnam could get Hans to attack and to stop on command. A leather collar, like those worn on guard duty, was substituted for the choke chain and the dogs were set on a handler who was wearing a heavy burlap protective suit. The dog would knock the man down, then go for his throat, biting deep into the burlap before he was called off. Hans sank his teeth in so deep that, afterward, his gums were bleeding. Burnam had no doubt that the dog could kill a man. While he learned to love Hans, Burnam never lost his fear of him.

In February 1967, Burnam was given his security clearance, and he and Hans went to work guarding a stockpile of chemical weapons. In his spare time, Burnam visited in the local bars. In one called the Texas Club, he met a beautiful Japanese girl named Kiko. She wanted to marry him, but Burnam did not want to stay in Okinawa and did not think that she would be happy back in Colorado. He also missed his girlfriend back there. At the time Burnam was only nineteen, and to take Kiko back to the States would require reams of paperwork. But there was no easy out for him. To complete his tour, Burnam would have had to stay on Okinawa for another year. So to break off his relationship with Kiko, Burnam volunteered to go back to Vietnam. Everyone thought he had gone out of his head.

Timber

To return to the 1st Air Cavalry would have taken time. It was quicker to reenlist with the 173rd Airborne Division, an elite parachute outfit. And in March 1967, Burnam was on his way back to South Vietnam. But when he arrived in Saigon, he found that he had not been assigned to the 173rd Airborne, but rather to a regular infantry regiment, and he was sent out to a base at Dau Tieng in hostile territory out near the Cambodian border.

During a fresh round of training, two dog handlers from the 44th Infantry Platoon Scout Dogs turned up to make a presentation geared toward recruiting more dog handlers. When they finished, Burnam volunteered. He missed Hans and was eager to work with another German shepherd.

The other recruits were put off being dog handlers because they were daunted to learn that the handlers always walked point. However, Burnam ascertained that, so far during the Vietnam War, no dog handler had been killed, though a few had been wounded. Burnam was the only volunteer and, as he already had experience with dogs, he was eagerly accepted.

Walking over to the K-9 compound, Burnam was greeted by the familiar smell of dogs. The Army Corps of Engineers had built a line of dog kennels among the rubber trees. There were forty dogs in runs that were separated by metal fences and protected from shrapnel and small-arms fire by sandbags. After one of the sandbags exploded, the Vietnamese were banned from the area and the handlers had to fill the sandbags themselves.

Burnam noticed the relationship that scout-dog handlers had with their dogs was different from the relationship the handlers had with sentry dogs. Handlers of scout dogs would talk to them as if they were human; handlers could even be seen sitting under a tree reading a letter or a book to their dogs. Along with their scout dogs, the 44th Scout Dog Platoon also had a mascot: a small black mongrel named Forty-Four that they had brought from the States. When Forty-Four was run over, he was replaced by a Vietnamese puppy named Hardcore. But the puppy also perished when he was attacked by one of the more aggressive scout dogs.

A two-year-old black-and-tan German shepherd named Timber was assigned to Burnam. He was as aggressive as Hans. At first he failed to respond to Burnam's commands and bit him a few times, but slowly they began to work together. Training involved an obstacle course. The dogs had to learn to balance in the middle of a seesaw. They also had to negotiate a walkway made out of a ladder that had been laid down horizontally, jump through a window, and crawl down a tunnel made of fifty-gallon drums laid end to end. The dogs and their handlers had to tackle this obstacle course over and over again. It was forbidden to encourage the dogs by giving them treats. Out on patrol, the handler could run out of treats, and then the dog would be useless. The scout dog had to obey his handler's commands without question. Fortunately, a German shepherd's intelligence and love of human companionship makes the breed easy to train to give unconditional obedience.

The other handlers taught Burnam to watch Timber and interpret what he was seeing, hearing, or smelling, or what type of danger he was sensing. Soon they were ready for their first mission. With B Company of the 2nd Battalion, 22nd Mechanized Infantry, they were to go out into the forest in a convoy of APC, set up a temporary base, then go out on foot to find the Vietcong, who were working in the area.

Timber was not happy in the APC. He growled at the rest of the platoon. The other men felt the same about Timber and could not see the point of bringing a dog team along.

It was hot and when they set up in a jungle clearing, Burnam poured water into his helmet for Timber to drink. He had brought four canteens: three for the dog and one for himself. He was also carrying plenty of dog food. Timber always got fed first after Burnam had checked his food for the bugs that got everywhere in Vietnam.

Then suddenly there was a call. An NVA formation had been spotted nearby. They jumped back in the APCs and headed out across the rough terrain. Then Burnam's APC was hit by an RPG and caught on fire. The men began to jump out, but Timber's leash was caught in the door. Burnam had to cut his leash. Timber was now in a panic. Bullets flew, and there were explosions all around him, and Burnam found it difficult to keep him under control with just the ten inches of leash he had left.

Burnam crawled off into the jungle, dragging Timber behind him. He was certain that, if the dog ran off, he would be killed. Timber continued to cause trouble, nipping at him while Burnam tried to tend a wounded man. Eventually, Burnam lost his temper and hit him on the snout. This only made him behave worse.

Then the APC blew up. Timber was hit and fell over on his side. Burnam also felt the sting of shrapnel on his face, but he had no bandages so there was little he could do for the dog and he was surrounded by men who were wounded and dying.

The platoon leader, though badly injured, had called for support, and soon artillery shells and bombs were falling near their position. Timber panicked again and Burnam had to pin him to the ground.

Then suddenly, they were being relieved. Another dog handler turned up and, despite Burnam's protests, took Timber away. Burnam was on his way to the hospital. He was not badly injured, but was suffering from combat fatigue. Back at Dau Tieng, he found that Timber had been patched up, too. But, though he loved Timber, he had found it impossible to control the dog under fire. So he asked to be assigned another dog.

Clipper

Burnam's new partner was another eighty-pound German shepherd named Clipper. But unlike Timber, Clipper was docile and would let anyone stroke him.

Booby traps along jungle trails were a constant threat in Vietnam, and Burnam and a handler from Kenosha, Wisconsin, named Oliver Whetstone set about teaching Clipper and

Ollie's dog, Erik, to spot trip wires. Again this was as much a training session for Burnam and Whetstone, who had to learn how to interpret their dog's reactions. The training had to be confined to the camp though, as all the terrain outside the wire at Dau Tieng was considered hostile.

As always, the scout dog and his handler were on point, because a dog's eyesight, hearing, and sense of smell are so much more acute than a human's. If Clipper went on the alert, soldiers were sent up to check out the situation. If they made contact with the enemy, Clipper and Burnam would fall back into the main body of the patrol. If not, they would continue on point. That was standard operating procedure.

One night the kennels came under attack. The men took shelter in a bunker, but were concerned about the dogs' safety. If the enemy breached the camp's defensive perimeter, the dogs were unprotected. They were caged in their runs and could easily be killed without a chance to flee or fight back. But the handlers were reassured by the dogs' continued barking.

Then several 82mm mortar rounds hit the tin roof of the kennel block. The handlers made for the door of the bunker, but were ordered to stay where they were by their commanding officer. One of the handlers rushed back from another part of the base that was not under attack, only to be peppered with shrapnel from a mortar round.

Despite the danger, the handlers rushed out to the kennels to make sure the dogs were all right. The dogs grew excited to hear them coming. Several had been hit and were wounded. Clipper's paws were covered with blood, but he had not been wounded. He had cut himself frantically clawing at the kennel door. But Ollie's dog, Erik, had been hit in both lungs, and another man had to shoot the dog to relieve his suffering. Other dogs also had to be put out of their misery.

The dogs were given a proper burial, and the commanding general visited to express his condolences. It was clear that the Vietcong acknowledged the advantage that the dogs gave the Americans and they had decided to target them.

Next, Burnam and Clipper were choppered out to lead a sweep along the Cambodian border. Like other dogs, when riding in a helicopter, Clipper liked to stick his head out the open door and enjoy the wind rushing through the fur on his face. He liked to stand up, and Burnam had to keep a firm grip on his leash. But on one occasion Burnam gave Clipper a little scare by releasing the leash just enough to give the dog the impression that he was falling out. Clipper dropped on his belly and clung to the floor. Reassured, he scooted back to Burnam and they made up with a big hug. Clipper had learned his lesson. After that, he no longer stood up or leaned out the open door.

The helicopters put down at the landing zone, and the passengers leapt out. This was always a dangerous time. The helicopters' rotors made a lot of noise and blew away any airborne scent, so a scout dog's special talents were useless.

The dog team were to have two men with them, providing security. Burnam told them to stay well back so that Clipper could pick up the scent of an enemy from all around him. Although they were in hostile territory, Clipper went a long time without giving an alert, and Burnam wondered whether the noise of the helicopter was still ringing in his ears. Then there was a slight pricking of the ears. Burnam got down on one knee and the patrol behind stopped. But Burnam could see nothing and told Clipper to go on.

A hundred yards farther on, Clipper gave a strong alert, his ears rigid. Two men were sent to circle ahead. Forty yards farther on, they found footprints. When Clipper reached the prints he wanted to follow them, so a small squad was sent to see where they led. The squad returned to say that they had found the footprints of a lot more people. The information was radioed in. Orders came back that they were not to be distracted by what they had found and were to continue the mission as planned. After each alert, Burnam lavished praise on Clipper.

A few hours later, Clipper gave another alert. Again Burnam could neither see nor hear anything unusual. Nevertheless, he passed the message back that Clipper sensed something was ahead of them. A squad went ahead and, seventy-five yards up the trail, they found a large clearing, though there was no sign of the enemy.

When they reached the clearing, the men hung in the trees while the platoon leader assessed the situation. Clipper took an interest in some bamboo shavings. It seemed the VC had been sharpening some punji stakes there. Then Clipper went on full alert. Burnam turned to see a tall man in clean fatigues with two stars on his helmet. It was the commanding general who had visited after the mortar attack. At Burnam's command, Clipper raised his paw to shake hands with the general.

After the general left in a chopper, the patrol, led by Burnam and Clipper, headed on. Farther up the trail, Clipper alerted again, more strongly than ever. Burnam fell to one knee. The platoon commander came up to assess the situation and sent a squad forward to investigate. They returned to report that there was a wide trail up ahead that had been used recently; there were fresh footprints and cart tracks along it. It ran toward the Cambodian border and the Ho Chi Minh trail, which was used to bring men, equipment, and supplies down from North Vietnam.

As they crossed the trail, Clipper suddenly alerted again, but the men behind motioned for him to go ahead. Burnam was told to ignore Clipper's alert, but the dog refused to go forward. At that moment, shots rang out. Burnam and Clipper threw themselves to the ground. The platoon loosed off a fusillade into the trees ahead. But when they got up to move on toward the tree line, more shots were aimed at them. Burnam wanted to keep Clipper on the ground, fearing that the sniper in the trees might be tempted to single the dog out for a bullet, but he was ordered by the company commander, who had now turned up on the scene, to get up and head for the tree line.

They reached the trees with no more shots being fired. A bunker had been found nearby, and the platoon commander asked Burnam to have Clipper check it out. Burnam knew that Clipper did not like going down tunnels or into bunkers, and he said he would not force him to. However, he would go up to the bunker and see if Clipper gave an alert.

The two of them followed the lieutenant up a trail. Clipper suddenly alerted, but there were so many men about that Burnam did not think the alert was significant and ignored it. Suddenly there was a muzzle flash and a lieutenant's helmet came flying off his head. His body slammed back into Burnam, knocking him down. Man and dog took cover under the trunk of a downed tree while a firefight developed between the VC up ahead and the grunts behind. Burnam and Clipper were pinned down by the intense crossfire. The enemy were in entrenched positions only fifteen feet away, but there was little Burnam could do; he had lost his helmet. He had no grenades, and the barrel of his rifle was blocked up with mud. He was only grateful that Clipper, unlike Timber, did not panic under fire—though he was frightened. Burnam could feel him shivering.

An artillery barrage had been called in and walked closer to the enemy position. Then a grunt came up to get Burnam and Clipper, and they crawled to safety. Both were, miraculously, unscathed. But Burnam felt a twinge of guilt. He had ignored Clipper's alert and several men had paid with their lives.

As if to reinforce what a dangerous position they were in, news came that another dog handler had been killed. Ed Hughes had plainly been targeted because he was a dog handler. When his body was recovered, his dog patch was missing. His dog, Sergeant, had been shot, then hacked to death with a machete. The dog's ear was missing, taken as a souvenir. While Ed Hughes's body had been flown home, Sergeant's was sent for an autopsy in Saigon.

There were more casualties. Randy Cox and his dog were in an armored personnel carrier (APC) when it was hit by a rocket. The dog died. Cox was badly injured and had to be sent to a special burn unit in the States. Mike Phillips and his German shepherd, Beau, who had trained together at the Scout Dog Training School in Fort Benning, Georgia, were out scouting for the infantry when Beau alerted, preventing the patrol from walking into an ambush. But Beau was hit in the leg by a 7.62mm bullet. Phillips sheltered the dog with his body while he returned fire. Beau was patched up and returned to duty. On their next mission they came under heavy mortar fire. Phillips was wounded in the arm by shell fragments, while a piece of shrapnel sliced through Beau's belly and broke his back. The dog was flown out to a hospital in Saigon. His chances of survival were so slim that his death certificate was filled out at the scout-dog unit. But after surgery, he made a full recovery. After a month, Beau returned to the 44th and the death certificate had to be thrown away. However, another dog, Prince, died after being sent out on a long training march in 110°F heat, and he joined the other dogs in the camp's canine cemetery.

Back at the base, Burnam continued training Clipper to avoid trip wires. At first, though he gave a mild alert, Clipper would duck under a trip wire and keep going. A "no" did not seem to make any impression on him, so Burnam began attaching a blasting cap to the end of the wire. When it went off, it scared Clipper. After that, he avoided trip wires, or sat down in front of them. Soon he would avoid multiple trip wires that Burnam would lay out for him.

Clipper put what he had learned to good use. He and Burnam had been out on a combat mission hunting for VC hideouts. They were on their way back to camp at Dau Tieng when they were ordered to wait beside some rubber trees until the rest of the platoon caught up. When they moved off again, the platoon spread out. Burnam and Clipper were walking between two rows of rubber trees when there was an explosion to their right. Burnam hit the deck, dragging Clipper down with him. Between the next rows of trees a soldier lay injured. Burnam crawled over to him. His legs were covered with blood. Burnam called for a medic. When he arrived, Burnam looked around and saw a trip wire that had detonated the booby trap. If he had been just one row over, it could have been him that hit the trip wire, and he wondered whether Clipper would have spotted it. Although Clipper had been trained to spot trip wires, he had never been put to the test. Now was his chance.

After the wounded man had been choppered out, Burnam asked to go on point with the rest of the platoon following in a column behind him. They were still half a mile from Dau Tieng. The intervening terrain was knee-high with grass and weeds. There could be booby traps and trip wires anywhere. As they headed off, Clipper gave a glance to the left, then moved to the right. Later, he glanced to the right and moved to the left. The maneuver was repeated on numerous occasions. Every so often the order came for the column to halt, then move off again. Burnam did not know why. He simply did as he was told.

Burnam assumed that Clipper was spotting booby traps and was simply moving around them, as he had been taught in training. His handler could see nothing in the tall vegetation. When they reached Dau Tieng safely, the platoon leader came up and knelt down to hug Clipper, thanking him and Burnam for steering them past all the other booby traps.

"What other booby traps?" asked Burnam. Though he assumed they had been there, he had seen nothing.

The lieutenant explained that after Clipper had first moved to the right, one of the men following had spotted a grenade tied to the bottom of a tree to the left. After that, every time Clipper changed directions, they stopped to mark the booby trap so that they could be detonated later. They had come the rest of the way across very dangerous ground without casualties, and the lieutenant said that he was going to recommend Burnam and Clipper for a Bronze Star. But even Clipper was not faultless. On another occasion, he got his paw caught in an animal snare.

The jungle was full of other hazards for man and dog alike. While Clipper had little exposed skin to be attacked by mosquitoes, his paws were plagued by bugs. When he was groomed, Burnam found ticks in his fur. Out on patrol, Burnam used a lighted cigarette to burn them off, though normally Burnam avoided smoking around Clipper lest it dull his sense of smell. When they got back to the base, Burnam bathed Clipper in disinfectant.

Clipper became a favorite with the men of the 2nd Battalion of the 12th Infantry Brigade. When they were searching a deserted VC base, Clipper sniffed out a huge stash of marijuana. The men filled their pockets before the order came through to destroy the grass.

Assigned to capture an NVA courier, Clipper waited in an ambush until the man came by. Then, when given the order, he sprang out and knocked the man to the ground. Told to watch him, he bared his teeth and stood guard while the man was searched.

The old injury to Burnam's knee began troubling him again, preventing him from going out on any further missions. He was sent for medical treatment in the hospital at Cu Chi. Then the Tet Offensive that began on January 31, 1968, kept him from returning to see Clipper. By then he was a "short-timer." With less than thirty days to go before he was rotated home to the States, he would not be returned to his unit.

However, Burnam volunteered to ride shotgun on a convoy to Saigon in return for a helicopter ride to Dau Tieng to say good-bye to Clipper. Then he left the dog and returned to the US in the certain knowledge that Clipper, his closest companion, would die in Vietnam.

Stormy

Ron Aiello was a US Marine Corps scout-dog handler in Vietnam in 1967–68. He had teamed up with a German shepherd bitch named Stormy in December 1966 at the Scout Dog Training School at Fort Benning, Georgia. After completing the twelve-week training course there, they were shipped out to South Vietnam on a Hercules cargo plane along with the other scout-dog teams.

During his thirteen-month tour, Aiello went on a number of search-and-destroy missions with Stormy. On one he teamed up with Dave Gradeless and his dog, Devil. Flying out to join the patrol, Aiello put a muzzle on Stormy. Although she was friendly, he found that helicopter pilots were nervous around marine dogs.

According to marine intelligence, there was a large unit of heavily armed North Vietnamese regulars in the area they were to search. Several units had gone ahead to set up blocking positions. The dog teams were to lead a platoon to flush out the NVA. They were to set out at 6:00 a.m. the following morning. Aiello and Stormy were to take point, with a rifleman close behind as a bodyguard. Gradeless, Devil, and their bodyguard were fifty yards to their flank. Aiello did not let Stormy run free, but kept him on a six-foot leash attached to a body harness.

They had only gone about a hundred yards when Stormy stopped and looked away to the left. Gradeless and Devil had also stopped, and Devil was looking in the same direction. But neither of the handlers could see anything in the undergrowth there. Word came from the platoon commander for them to proceed in the direction of the alert and find out what the dogs had spotted. In the undergrowth they found some old fortifications, left by the French, which had become overgrown. However, some of the vegetation there had been flattened as if someone had recently abandoned the position in a hurry. Aiello reasoned that the fortifications had been used as a look-out post. When the guards there had seen the dogs, they knew that they were about to be discovered and got out fast. The enemy knew they were coming.

Aiello and Gradeless praised their dogs, then set off in the direction they thought the enemy were traveling. After about an hour, Devil went on the alert. Gradeless got down on one knee and the platoon halted behind him. Suddenly an NVA soldier in a khaki uniform leapt out of a bush in front of Devil, brandishing an AK-47, and ran away. Gradeless's bodyguard raised his rifle, took aim, and fired, hitting the fleeing man in the head. They took his Kalashnikov, searched his body, and moved on.

Stormy then went on the alert, looking to the right. A woman soldier leapt from the undergrowth, wielding a machete. She ran screaming straight at the dog team. Aiello was mesmerized, but then pulled out his .45 and shot her, hitting her in the arm, but this did not slow her frenzied attack. Stormy was ready for her though. She lunged, hitting the woman on the side and knocking the machete from her hand. The bodyguard then clubbed the woman with the butt of his rifle. She was knocked out cold. Once she had been disarmed and searched, a medic took care of her wounds. Blindfolded and tied up, she was now a prisoner of war.

The platoon took a short break in the shade. Aiello fussed over Stormy again and gave her some water to drink in his helmet. Then they started out again. They had not gone far when Stormy stopped, looking at the ground. Devil did the same. When the platoon commander came up to find out what was happening, the dog handlers told him that they thought the dogs had spotted mines or booby traps ahead.

To check, the marines cleared the patch of ground that had caught Stormy's attention. They found a small air vent. This meant they were standing on top of an underground complex. The job now was to find its entrance. As the search continued, they found more air vents. They were spread out over a wide area, indicating that there was a large series of bunkers under the ground there.

In the middle of the afternoon, both Stormy and Devil took an interest in a bushy ridge on the left flank. A path ran along the top of the ridge, and a squad of marines were sent to check it out, but they found nothing. The leader of the search party then suggested that one of the dog teams take a second look. This was not standard operating procedure. After a dog alerted its handler to something of interest, the dog team stayed with the main body of the platoon for protection, while a fire team went to take a closer look. Nevertheless, Aiello volunteered to take Stormy to have a second look. He was confident in her ability.

They followed the path along the ridge until Stormy made an alert toward a patch of thick vegetation. When a marine checked it out, he found the tunnel entrance. The platoon engineer then blew it up with explosives. After that the platoon returned to camp, where the dog teams were widely praised. They had flushed out the NVA and, when they fled, they ran directly into the blocking force. Finding themselves outnumbered and surrounded, they surrendered without firing a shot. Everyone agreed that this was all the dogs' doing.

As a reward, the platoon commander gave them new quarters on the second story of a French colonial house that served as his headquarters. The trouble was, he said, that the only entrance was by way of a ladder—that might be a problem for the dogs. But these were marine dogs. Learning to climb a ladder was part of their training. On the command "Hup, girl!" Stormy and Devil effortlessly scaled the ladder to their new home.

Aiello left the Marine Corps in 1968 and went into business. In the year 2000, he founded the US War Dogs Association, Inc. With other former dog handlers and their supporters, he raised the money to have a bronze statue of a war dog and his handler placed on the grounds of the New Jersey Vietnam Veterans Memorial and Educational Center in Holmdel, New Jersey. The memorial was dedicated on June 10, 2006.

The Vietnam War Dog Handlers Association raised a million dollars to erect a bronze statue of a German shepherd and his handler as a memorial to the war dogs of all wars at March Field Air Museum in Riverside, California. It was dedicated on February 21, 2000.

Caesar

The Australians also had dogs in Vietnam. Their Combat Tracker Teams were based on the dog teams that the British had used in Malaya. They were trained at the Tracker Wing of the Infantry Training Centre in Ingleburn, New South Wales. When eighteen-year-old Peter Haran went there in the spring of 1966 after six months of basic training, he saw a black Labrador cross being put through its paces. It was a dog he instantly admired. There seemed to be an instant rapport between then. When the dog trotted back to the kennel block at the heel of his handler, he looked back at Haran with his big brown eyes.

Haran had been a dog lover since his childhood in Zimbabwe, which was then still called Rhodesia. When he joined the army he wanted to work with dogs and had applied to the Tracking Wing. He had been told to report for duty the following day. He was on a three-week trial. This was his big chance.

The first week was spent in a classroom where Haran and eight other trainees learned about the capabilities of dogs. The point that was brought home to them was that, working with a tracker dog was not just about handling the dog physically. The important part was to learn to read the dog's reactions.

After a week in the classroom, they were sent out to act as quarry. After being issued a rifle, blank ammunition, a map, a compass, a day's rations, and some dirty clothes taken from the Vietcong, they were dropped off in a forest south of Sydney. Their task was to reach their allocated designation ahead of the tracker dog and his handler. A human tracker, also trained in the Tracking Wing, would join the dog team to look for physical signs of Haran and the other prey.

They ran for several hours without seeing any sign of their pursuers. But when they were in sight of their objective, the human tracker appeared to tell them that a dog had been on their scent for some time and was "pointing" at them from a clearing nearby. The dog was Caesar, the Labrador mix Haran had seen on this first day. This was the dog Haran wanted to work with.

Instead, Haran was given another dog named Damien. He would not do what he was told and would take any opportunity to get into a fight with another dog. It soon became apparent that Damien could not be trained as a tracker. In the end, he was shot.

Now Haran had no dog. But then came the news that Caesar's handler, Phil Little, had been assigned to other duties. It was a dream come true. Caesar—service number D6NO3—already had a reputation for being obedient and diligent, the qualities needed to be a good tracker.

A mixture of pedigree Labrador and Australian kelpie, Caesar was intelligent and athletic. He had come to the Army from a home for stray dogs and would have been put down if the military dog recruiters had not come by that day. There was one thing that was notably odd about him. One of his ears had a piece missing and stuck out sideways; the other was always erect.

Haran and Caesar were on the list to go to Vietnam, along with Haran's friend Denis Ferguson and his canine partner, Marcus, a champion dog who had formerly belonged to the governor of New South Wales. They were to join the 2nd Battalion of the Royal Australian Regiment, or 2 RAR. On May 7, 1967, Caesar and Marcus were packed in special dog crates in the belly of a C-130 Hercules transport plane filled with supplies. Haran and Ferguson also flew in the cargo bay so that they would be within view of the dogs.

They flew to Saigon, then on to the Australian Task Force base at Nui Dat, where they would be part of the first Australian tracker dog team in Vietnam. The conditions there were primitive—for the men at least. They lived in tents. But the dogs lived in solidly built kennels constructed by the Royal Engineers. They also had plenty of room to play in the adjoining rubber plantation. Two weeks later, the rest of 2 RAR, who had come by sea, began to arrive.

Caesar did not adjust well to Vietnam. He did not like the monsoon rains, especially when he was out on guard duty. And he did not take to helicopters, but they were a fact of life in Vietnam. The dog teams were put on Ready Reaction status. That meant they had to be prepared to chopper out to any place where they were needed with ten minutes' notice. But the noise of a Huey's rotor blades made Caesar jumpy. He frothed at the mouth. But he found a small space inside where he was comfortable and always sought out the same spot.

On their first mission, Caesar and Haran were flown out to a patch of jungle where the Vietcong were known to operate. But 2 RAR were new to Vietnam and did not know whether they would be facing trained soldiers armed with Kalashnikovs and RPGs, or peasants wielding machetes.

Caesar's first mission was hardly taxing. When told to "seek 'em out," all he had to do was follow a trail of blood. Haran concentrated so hard on Caesar—looking for him to "point," indicating that the enemy was near—that he fell into a weapons pit. When he climbed out again, he found Caesar pointing. They were in no danger though. The dog was pointing at a dead VC fifty yards up the trail.

They had stumbled into a bunker complex that then had to be searched, along with the surrounding villages. Caesar found this so exciting that he did not sleep. That night there were also explosions to keep him awake. Then, in the morning, the helicopters came to take them back to Nui Dat. Only then would he sleep.

One day, when out on patrol, they stopped to eat lunch and found themselves in the middle of a minefield. Caesar had already wandered off to relieve himself. If he stepped on a mine on his way back, he would kill them all. Haran commanded him to sit and stay. Much to everyone's relief, the dog did what he was told. The men then prodded the ground with their knives to find the mines. While the others were finding their way out of the minefield, Haran had to clear a path out to Caesar who was sitting and staying some twenty meters away. While he was doing this, a Huey came in. Haran was terrified that Caesar would jump up and bark at it to chase it away and set off a mine. Fortunately, he was tired and sat there and did what he was told.

In the end, after a harrowing afternoon in the tropical sun, they made it to safety. It was a lucky escape, and Caesar's obedience won praise all around. That very afternoon, another tracker dog, Cassius, had suffered heatstroke. His handler, Norman Cameron, had seen the dog's eyes roll. He foamed at the mouth, then collapsed. But no transport was available to take him to the hospital. Cameron wrapped Cassius in wet towels and was carrying him in his arms to the hospital, but on the way they were ambushed. There was a firefight, and four Vietcong were killed before they could continue on their way. They eventually got to the hospital five hours after Cassius had collapsed. He lived only another thirty minutes. The tropical heat had simply been too much for him. An autopsy revealed that his internal organs had simply been cooked.

That evening, Caesar and Haran were just settling down when they were called out again. An Australian patrol had engaged the Vietcong, who had then escaped into the undergrowth. It was Caesar's job to find them. Again, there was a trail of blood to follow and the prints of heavy army boots, not the soft shoes the villagers wore. Caesar kept his nose glued to the track; then, at a junction, he stopped. When Haran urged him on, he turned back and sat on Haran's foot. There was something wrong.

Suddenly the air was filled with explosions and cries of "I'm hit, I'm hit." They had walked into another minefield. Haran berated himself for not keeping a close enough eye on his dog. In fact, it could have been much worse. Where Caesar had refused to go on, there were two M16 "jumping jack" antipersonnel mines. Sometimes known as "Bouncing Betties," they sprang up about three feet in the air before detonating the main charge, cutting down anyone around them. These two were contacted to a huge bomb buried under the junction. If that had gone off, the entire platoon would have been wiped out. Again, Caesar was praised for saving the men from a larger catastrophe.

But it was not all work and no play for the handlers and their dogs. Haran and Ferguson purloined a forty-four-gallon oil drum to use as a dog bath. After their bath, Caesar and Marcus frolicked like puppies.

The Australian Task Force had eleven tracker dogs in all. Sometimes they would be sent out with US troops when one of their own scout-dog teams was not available. Then in January 1968, the Australian Task Force was moved from Phuoc Tay province, southeast of Saigon, north to Bien Hoa and Long Khanh. The move coincided with the Tet Offensive. When the base came under mortar fire, Caesar was terrified and Haran had to comfort him—it was usually the other way around, with the dog comforting the man.

The Trackers were moved back to Nui Dat when 3 RAR moved in. With just two months left of his tour, Haran was moved to the huge base at Bearcat, east of Saigon, where he hoped to have a quiet time after the Tet Offensive. There was little to do there, though one night Haran and Ferguson took Caesar and Marcus swimming in what they thought was a swimming pool. It turned out to be the camp's main water supply. On one particularly hot day, Caesar was sent out to the perimeter. Like Cassius before him, Caesar collapsed in the heat. But Haran got him to the vet in time and he survived.

Once the date of Haran's return to Australia was fixed, he was told that handlers could not take their dogs with them. Instead, they were to prepare them for being taken over by new handlers. This was devastating news; Haran went to visit Caesar in the kennels one last time. When he turned away, he heard Caesar pick up his bowl and drop it in his own familiar way.

Of the eleven tracker dogs employed by the Australians in Vietnam, none returned home. Caesar was handed over to 4 RAR, then served with 5 RAR, 7 RAR, and 9 RAR before being retired to the British Embassy in Saigon in July 1970.

Denis Ferguson returned to Vietnam for a second tour in 1970 and teamed up with Marcus again. He offered to pay $2,000 for the administration and quarantine fees to take the dog back to Australia. His request was denied. Marcus was then transferred to 4 RAR in 1971. By then the dog's sight was failing, and his fate is unknown.

Back in Australia, Peter Haran went on to become a journalist. When he settled down in Adelaide with his wife and two children, he bought a dog, an Irish setter that he named Caesar.

CHAPTER SEVEN
WAR ON TERROR

No BOOK ON CANINE COURAGE would be complete without a chapter on the dogs of 9/11. The dogs employed in the aftermath of the terrorist attacks were trained to military standards and found themselves in the middle of an undeclared war. Between 250 and 300 dogs went to work at the World Trade Center and the Pentagon—first in a desperate search for any survivors, then looking for cadavers. Local police forces used their own K-9 units and recruited other Federal Emergency Management Agency–certified Urban Search and Rescue dogs from across the country.

America was under attack, and these brave dogs were sent into the danger zone to search crumbling buildings. Nobody knew whether there were going to be more explosions. There was only one documented canine fatality: a four-year yellow Labrador retriever named Sirius who worked for the New York and New Jersey Port Authority. He was stationed in the basement of the South Tower. When his handler, Port Authority Police Officer David Lim, heard the first plane hitting the north tower, he put Sirius back into his kennel and told him to "stay."

Officer Lim then went into action, racing up forty-three flights of stairs to assist fleeing office workers. He was on the fourth or fifth floor, helping to carry a woman down to safety, when the tower collapsed. Lim himself was buried, but was rescued at three o'clock that afternoon. He made several attempts to get back down to the basement kennel area to find Sirius, but the Fire Department were trying to secure the area and would not let him though. Doctors even prevented him searching the rubble, fearful of the emotional toll it would take on him.

It was not until the following year that Sirius's body was discovered. Investigators said that Sirius died instantly when the building crushed his kennel. On January 24, 2002, the dog was removed in a body bag, complete with a salute and a prayer.

"There was a flag over his bag, and I carried him out with another officer, John Martin," says Officer Lim. "Everyone saluted. All the machinery was stopped—the same thing that is done for human police officers and firefighters. I thought it was very nice."

Sirius was honored at a memorial ceremony at Liberty State Park in Jersey City on April 24, 2002, where Officer Lim was presented with Sirius's old bowl that was found at the site.

Like the human rescuers, some dogs that survived the initial incident may have suffered long-term health problems. Indeed, within five years, thirty percent of the search-and-rescue dogs were already dead—including the German shepherd Git Anders from Plainfield, New Jersey. He had searched the rubble of the Twin Towers with Sergeant John Gillespie as part of the Union Country Sheriff's Department K-9 Unit. On September 30, 2001—less than three weeks after 9/11—they were with other officers giving chase to a stolen car. When the suspects abandoned the vehicle,

Sergeant Gillespie chased after the driver and apprehended him. Git Anders chased after a twelve-year-old girl also fleeing the car. He brought her down by biting her leg. Officers Ronald Fusco and Craig Montgomery then arrived on the scene and—despite the police badge on Git Anders's collar—mistook the dog for a stray. They could not call him off as he only responded to Sergeant Gillespie's commands. So they tried to pry the dog forcibly from the girl's leg, but Fusco was bitten in the process. The officers then shot Git Anders eleven times, wounding the animal fatally. Sergeant Gillespie returned just as his dog was dying.

Other 9/11 rescue dogs have been lost in the line of duty, such as the black Labrador retriever Kinsey. The World Trade Center was Kinsey's first mission. After being found playing dodge ball with the kids on the playground of an elementary school in the Dallas–Fort Worth area, she had been taken to a shelter and was scheduled for euthanasia in 2000 when she was rescued by Bob Deeds, a rookie with Texas Task Force One. He trained her in search and rescue, and by 2001 she had earned her Type I–Advanced Disaster Dog certification.

Kinsey spent eleven days on the night shift at Ground Zero. "She wanted to find someone alive," said Deeds, "and she would bark and nip at me in frustration."

The dog worked tirelessly, despite being treated several times for cut pads. In appreciation of her effort, she was inducted into the Tarrant County Veterinary Medical Association's Hall of Fame.

In all, Kinsey went out on seven Federal disaster missions. Then in January 2008, she was on an exercise at Disaster City—the world's largest search-and-rescue training facility, built after the Oklahoma City bombing. She slipped and fell some twenty feet from a training structure. A veterinarian at Texas A&M said she would never walk again. The accident left Kinsey in pain and, reluctantly, Deeds had her put down.

"She remained brave to the end," said Deeds. "When it was time, she kissed my hand, closed her eyes, and went to sleep. She didn't fight it. She was on to the next adventure."

Among the other brave dogs at the World Trade Center were guide dogs Salty and Roselle; they led their blind owners down more than seventy flights of stairs. The two Labradors were awarded the Dickin Medal. One was also presented to police dog Appollo, who received it on behalf of all the search-and-rescue dogs of 9/11.

A German shepherd, Appollo was with the K-9 unit of the New York Police Department. In 1994, he had graduated from the NYPD Canine Special Operations Division, and was one of the first dogs specifically trained in search and rescue. Appollo passed Type-II (Basic) training in Florida in 1997, and Type-I (Advanced) in Indianapolis in 1999. He was also part of the first qualified NYPD K-9 teams to join the Urban Search and Rescue New York Task Force 1.

On September 11, 2001, Appollo and his handler Peter Davies were the first search-and-rescue dog team to arrive at the World Trade Center. At one point, Appollo was almost killed by falling debris and flames; he was saved only because his coat was drenched after he had fallen in a pool of water. But as soon as the debris was cleared, he was back at work again.

The citation for his medal reads: "For tireless courage in the service of humanity during the search and rescue operations in New York and Washington on and after 11 September 2001. Faithful to words of command and undaunted by the task, the dogs' work and unstinting devotion to duty stand as a testament to those lost or injured."

Appollo also received the American Kennel Club Ace award in 2001 and was honored at the Westminster Kennel Club Dog Show in Madison Square Garden in 2002. He and Officer Davies later worked in the Dominican Republic after a hurricane. Appollo died in November 2006.

The German shepherd Storm was also with the NYPD K-9 unit. With his handler, David Sanabria, he was at a Canine Search Specialist course in Seattle on 9/11. Thanks to a private jet loaned by the General Electric company, they reached Ground Zero on September 14. The first thing Sanabria noticed was people shouting out, "K-9! K-9!" Within a quarter of an hour of their arrival, the NYPD K-9 unit had found six bodies.

Sanabria started by sending Storm out with the instruction "locate." This meant he was to look for a living person. He came back with nothing. Then Sanabria said, "Body," meaning that Storm should look for a corpse. They worked twenty-hour shifts. On one occasion, Storm found seven bodies in one place, crushed under a beam.

Storm climbed the mountains of rubble fearlessly, but Sanabria had to recall him from one cavern when he saw the beams supporting the roof glowing with heat. Later, Storm found two cops. One of them, Joe, was a guy they used to work with. His father, who had lost two sons at 9/11, gave Storm Joe's badge to wear on his collar.

As time went on, Storm was locating bodies that were up to seven feet below the surface. Sanabria and Storm worked at Ground Zero for eight months before they were released back to regular patrol duty. A life-size picture of the two of them was featured in "Faces of Ground Zero," a photographic exhibition held at Grand Central Terminal in January 2002.

Within hours of the collapse of the Twin Towers, the golden retrievers Ana, Dusty, and Harley of California Task Force 7, along with handlers Rick Lee, Randy Gross, and Rob Cima, were on their way to New York. According to Lee, the dogs were like point men in Vietnam; they determined whether someone was alive, and consequently whether they would have to go in. It was hard to keep Ana from injuring herself on the twisted steel, but she would make her way through thick debris and disappear down deep holes for minutes on end. In some places, the debris was still hot and smoke was billowing off it. Lee had to pick her up to prevent her going too near.

The German shepherd dog Anna arrived with her owner Sarah Atlas on the afternoon of the attack. Anna was a "live find" dog with New Jersey Task Force 1 and went about her work frenetically on the first day. She had little training in cadaver work. However, she found two bodies in a stairwell. They were identified as FDNY firefighters.

While they were working, Building Seven of the World Trade Center collapsed. Atlas admitted to being very scared, but Anna worked on. On their first night, they slept on the sidewalk. After that they moved into the Jacob K. Javits Convention Center, where they were served Army rations. Anna pulled ligaments in her back and legs and was burned from melting plastic. She also had very sore paws. Nevertheless, they stayed on the job for ten days.

"We'd already stayed two days longer than a normal shift," said Atlas. "People were still coming up to us begging us to keep looking. It was very hard; they still had hope and we knew there was none."

Atlas was diagnosed with posttraumatic stress syndrome and pneumonia. She also risked her own health by taking off the mask she had been given to prevent inhalation of debris because Anna could not understand her.

Two months later, Anna fell ill and died, though her death was unrelated to her rescue work at Ground Zero. On October 1, 2011, the flag on the Capitol building in Washington, D.C., was flown at half-mast in honor of Anna. A certificate was presented commending Anna on "the bravery and courage displayed while serving as a rescue dog at the World Trade Center after the terrorist attacks on September 11."

Another early arrival at Ground Zero was Bear and his owner, John Gilkey of Pennsylvania Task Force 1. He got the call on his pager at work at the Lear Corporation in Carlisle, Pennsylvania, and drove home to pick up his eight-year-old chocolate-brown Labrador retriever, who was trained for cadaver search. They teamed up with Roseann Keller and her seven-year-old German shepherd, and the rest of the FEMA team, and headed for New York. At Ground Zero, Bear tripped lightly over the debris, only suffering two minor scratches the entire time he was there. He indicated a cadaver at forty or so different sites, meaning perhaps that there were body parts there. He died two years after 9/11 at the age of eleven.

Belgian Malinois DJ had been a police narcotics-detection dog before being trained as a tracker dog and a cadaver hunter. He was known to be fearless. At Ground Zero, his handler, Tim Swan, of the New York Federation of Search and Rescue Dogs, had to tie a long rope around him, fearing that he would slip from one of the twisted I-beams and disappear down a deep hole below. After three days, DJ's group of police dogs moved on to Fresh Kills on Staten Island, the landfill site where the debris from the World Trade Center was taken. There they were presented with the nearly impossible task of finding human remains among the rubble. DJ worked himself so hard that he almost collapsed from dehydration and had to be rushed to a veterinary team that was on hand for just such emergencies.

Duke, a Labrador retriever with California Task Force 8, was asked to search one of the caverns in the rubble a hundred feet from the entrance to the site. His handler, Howard Orr of the Santa Barbara County Fire Department, said that thousands of rescuers had already been over that spot. But Duke quickly indicated that there was something there. The bodies of three firefighters were found there the next day. Duke had already been a search dog for two years and proved his worth at the Echo Park Building collapse in 2000, and would go on to serve in California at the Paso Robles Earthquake of 2003 and the La Conchita mudslide of January 2005, and in the aftermath of hurricanes Katrina and Rita in August and September of that year. Duke died on August 8, 2011.

Dutch should not have been much use at Ground Zero. The only FEMA-certified Portuguese water dog in the USAR system, he had been trained by Missouri Task Force 1 to hunt for corpses in the wilderness, not in urban situations. Nevertheless, he was happy enough searching The Pile, as the rescuers began to call the mound of rubble left on the site. He did not even cut his feet on the glass-strewn floors of the World Financial Center in the Dow Jones–Oppenheimer building, whose top twenty-one floors he had been tasked to search. He was even lowered down large holes with his owner, Connie Millard. At one point, a firefighter singled him out for special praise. The day before, Dutch had found the body of his brother.

Hawk was also with Missouri Task Force 1. An Australian shepherd dog, he was trained to find live victims. As it was, he had to content himself with finding the remains of dozens of the dead. On one occasion, firefighters said that there were no victims in the place Hawk indicated. But his owner, Cathy Schiltz, and a teammate convinced them to carry on digging. Eventually, they unearthed a police car with two officers in it.

Ann Wichmann of Colorado Task Force 1 was terrified when she saw her Labrador retriever, Jenner, walking along a steel beam over a pit. Sometimes she felt he was simply overwhelmed by the scent of dead bodies. But Jenner was an experienced disaster dog and kept on going. At one point he followed his nose behind a pile of rubble and found the body of a firefighter, intact. Like the other dogs at Ground Zero, his presence was a comfort to bereaved rescue workers. At one point, a firefighter dropped to his knees to confide that he had lost fifteen friends at the World Trade Center. Jenner died of cancer in 2004. Wichmann then quit FEMA, but continued to train dogs on her Colorado farm, which she named "Jenner," after her beloved dog.

A border collie named Lucy had worked on site of the Oklahoma City bombing and after the crash of the Space Shuttle *Columbia*, and had found a victim of drowning as well as two murder victims, all before she arrived at Ground Zero. She was part of a second wave of search-and-rescue dogs that turned up on September 27. Even so, she found human remains within minutes of arriving on West Street. She also found the body of a firefighter in the ruins of the Marriott Hotel.

An image of the golden retriever name Riley became world famous when he was transported over a canyon some seventy feet deep in a basket strung beneath a line rigged up by Pennsylvania Task Force 1. He seemed a little dubious about getting into the basket at first, but eventually he settled down and did as he was told. His picture appeared in newspapers and magazines across the world. On another day, Riley kept going back to the same spot. The rescue workers told his handler, Chris Selfridge, that they had already checked there and found nothing. By then, Riley was hot and frustrated. He disappeared under an I-beam and lay down in a shady cavern. Selfridge called him, but the dog would not come out. Selfridge then crawled down to get him. He put him on a leash and tried to pull him out, but Riley would not budge. Eventually there was nothing else to do: Selfridge called the firefighters and told them to search again. After ten minutes, they found human remains.

Both Cholo with Texas Task Force 1 and Sunny Boy with California Task Force 3 were trained as live-find dogs, and both found live firefighters. They were not victims but rescue workers who had not cleared the area that the dogs were supposed to search. Cholo, a German shepherd belonging to Joanne Reitz, died in 2004. Sunny Boy, a Doberman, quickly adapted to finding cadavers. He kept returning to one area and finally pawed a spot on the ground. Four firefighters who were cutting a beam nearby came to take a look. Later one of them came up to his handler, Shirley Hammond, put a hand on her shoulder and said, "It was our brother." Hammond had used Dobermans in search-and-rescue work for twenty-seven years and had found live victims as well as the dead.

While most dogs simply got on with their work, some suffered from stress or nervous disorders when confronted with the sheer scale of the destruction. And there was some criticism of the dog handlers for jeopardizing the health and safety of their dogs by subjecting them to the conditions faced at the 9/11 sites. But while the handlers insisted that their first priority was the safety and welfare of their canine partners, they still had their duty to do.

The canine search-and-rescue teams at the Pentagon faced another problem—security. There was a possibility that top-secret information rested among the ruins of the offices they were to search. For the first two days, dog teams searched the area for survivors. After that, the area officially became a crime scene controlled by the FBI and the Secret Service, while Officer Jim Lugaila, a search-dog handler from the DC Metropolitan Police K-9 unit, was put in charge of running the canine operation.

Again, dog teams from all over the US were called in. Heather Roche from Maryland's Bay Area Recovery Canines brought in three of her Labrador retrievers—Alley, Cassy, and Red—to work with DC's K-9 unit.

"They drove us to the hot zone in Gators, directed us to the piles, and looked after our safety as we worked," said Roche.

For weeks the dogs navigated the hazards of the rubble piles. Amid the clatter and chaos of the recovery work, they discovered dozens of bodies.

"They worked so hard and it was so hot and we were on a day shift, so it melted all of us," said Roche. "Just the work basically—twelve-hour shifts out in the sun."

The dogs were not allowed to drink while they were working for fear that they would be ingesting particles kicked up by the crash. They were rotated out every so often and washed thoroughly when they left the hot zone. Still, it was a long and tiring day.

"By the time we were done every day, they slept hard," said Roche. "They were sleeping like rocks, but they were willing the next morning. They were rejuvenated and pulling on the leash to go back to work."

Alley dragged Roche to the pile, where Roche had to unleash her. With her nose down, she would work her way over each pile in rows, then work on the larger items at the edge. This was nothing she had been taught, but by using this method she came across items that other dogs had missed among the debris, even though it had been raked and sorted repeatedly. She seemed to have an intense desire to find even the smallest item.

Cassy was the oldest of the three dogs Roche brought to the Pentagon. The noise of the machinery at the site did not faze her even when it came close. She had been trained in active indication, but knew not to touch anything she had found. She was twelve years old, and retired after her laborious duties following 9/11.

Red was the youngest of Roche's three dogs. She was just eighteen months old and Roche had little confidence in her at first.

"I never thought she would be a successful search dog," said Roche, "and actually at six months old I found a home for her and had found another dog. Her personality is not what is needed for a working dog."

But Roche took Red back.

"Then, no matter what I asked her to do—whether it was climbing up things, going somewhere I stayed far away, ladders, you name it—she did it every single time and she did it perfectly."

Searching the rubble at the Pentagon was Red's first real mission. Even so, she had no problem with noise and commotion, and she was just as good as her two more experienced teammates.

Dusty, another Labrador retriever, came in with the sixty-one members of New Mexico Task Force 1's Urban Search and Rescue team. He was not certified at finding human remains, but adapted well as there were few other distractions.

Nor was he afraid of the broken glass and twisted metal inside the damaged building, or put off by the smell of jet fuel.

Yellow Labrador retriever Gus went inside the building while construction workers were still tearing apart the damaged section. Every so often, during the demolition work, they would spot something that looked like clothing or fabric and Gus would be sent in. The dog would raise a howl at places where human remains were found. Gus had been a field-trial dog until his owner, Ed Apple, had him retrained for search work after the Oklahoma City bombing. He then joined Tennessee Task Force 1.

A German shepherd called Jake also ventured into the building when it was structurally unsound, and he burnt his feet searching areas that were still hot from the fire. "But that never stopped him from doing his job," said owner Sam Balsam of Maryland Task Force 1.

Nero, another German shepherd, had been deployed in Nairobi and Turkey before 9/11. He went into the building while it was still burning. He was not put off by the dense smoke. With his handler, Elizabeth Kreitler of Virginia Task Force 1, he searched hot, smoke-filled offices filled with waterlogged debris that in some places was two feet high. He was trained to find survivors, but soon learned to indicate unrecognizable human remains. However, after he had finished his search, specially trained cadaver dogs were sent in. Nero saw service again after Hurricane Katrina in 2005.

The five-year-old black Labrador retriever Smokey was injured while searching the rubble of the Pentagon. After he cut his paw on a piece of metal, a veterinarian cleaned the wound and prescribed antibiotics. He also said that Smokey should rest, but the search dog was eager to get back to work. As it was important that the wound did not get wet or contaminated, the vet suggested that Smokey wear a boot while searching. This did not sit well with Smokey, who had the boot off in minutes. So they bound his paw with duct tape instead. His handler, Fairfax County Deputy Sheriff George McMahon, checked it each time they went into the work zone.

"Smokey's drive never slowed down, even when he was hurt," said McMahon.

As the search of the building came to a conclusion, the debris was brought out onto the parking lot, where bulldozers spread it out across the asphalt. Then the K-9 teams had to search for pieces of human remains, avoiding glass, sharp protruding objects, aviation fluid, and the occasional fire. The German shepherd Thor and his handler, Fairfax County firefighter Blair Miller, continued this task for two-and-a-half weeks, finding pieces of human flesh as small as a quarter.

On December 15, 2001, the United States Police Canine Association held a ceremony in honor of the dogs, handlers, and support teams who undertook the K-9 search and recovery mission at the Pentagon. The ceremony was dedicated to those who had worked "to bring home to their families, those American heroes that were senselessly slaughtered during a terrorist attack on the United States of America at the Pentagon on September 11, 2001."

No search-and-rescue dogs were deployed at the crash site near Shanksville, Pennsylvania.

CHAPTER EIGHT
IRAQ

DOG TEAMS WERE IN DEMAND AGAIN during the wars in Iraq and Afghanistan. After the initial invasions, the IED—Improvised Explosive Device—became the weapon of choice for the insurgents, and dogs were needed to sniff them out.

During the height of the fighting in Iraq there were some two thousand working dogs deployed in the Middle East. Their numbers had been increasing by about twenty percent a year since 9/11. The dogs were given basic training at Lackland Air Force Base in San Antonio, Texas. There, they were familiarized with the crack of gunfire and the roar of a helicopter's engines. They were trained to sniff out explosives on command. When they found them, they were taught to freeze, staring at the explosive device.

Belgian Malinois and German shepherds predominated. Merely by baring their teeth, they could cow a hostile mob. They were also taught to attack. A big dog leaping can bring down even the strongest man. But other breeds were trained, too. Even small dogs, such as poodles or beagles, can be trained to detect explosives in submarines or other confined spaces.

As IEDs became more powerful, dogs were trained to wear backpacks carrying a radio receiver so that the handler could issue voice commands from a safe distance. Unfortunately, that left the dog in harm's way.

"As much as I love these dogs, their job is to take a bullet for me," said trainer Sergeant Douglas Timberlake.

The training took six months and the Department of Defense reckoned that it cost $25,000 to purchase, feed, raise, train, and care for the average military dog, though the cost can top $40,000 in some cases. The US Army also employed more than four hundred veterinarians worldwide. Each dog was given a thorough medical examination twice per year— more often than most people get a physical. The dogs' checkups include blood tests, X-rays, and electrocardiograms.

Attack dogs have such powerful bites that they often break their teeth, so military vets sometimes do root canals to save the teeth.

"Here, we treat them, because that's part of that dog's equipment: to use his teeth," said Dr. Lorraine Linn, a dog surgeon at Lackland.

The most common injury among military dogs working in Iraq or Afghanistan was a cut or grazed paw, but they were also bitten by spiders and stung by scorpions. Also, blowing sand irritated their eyes and ears, and the heat of the sun brought on a dangerous stomach condition called "bloat," where the buildup of gas in the stomach causes the dog acute distress. The heat of the desert can also cause dehydration.

Handler Jason Cannon realized that something was wrong when his dog started to act skittish while searching people crossing into Iraq from Syria. He and his dog were helicoptered back to base, where a vet prescribed two weeks of rest for the dog.

"We went out and played ball, pretty much hung out," said Cannon. "Mainly, we didn't do any work at all. 'Vacation' is a good word for it."

Less often, dogs on a mission have been shot or bombed. However, more than ten dogs have been killed and dozens have been injured—hit by stray bullets, blown up by roadside bombs, cut by broken glass, and scorched by the heat of the desert. Their services were valued so highly that wounded dogs were treated like wounded troops.

"They are cared for as well as any soldier," said Senior Airman Ronald A. Harden, a dog handler in Iraq.

Handlers were supplied with canine field kits containing medicine, syringes, and other items of first aid equipment. There were veterinarians on hand in country. Lackland trainer Trapanger Stephens, who did duty in Iraq, remembered seeing a vet rescue a shot dog with a breathing tube right in the field. The vet did surgery then and there. Some dogs were flown to Germany, or even back to the US, for rehabilitation.

Corporal Megan Leavey and her dog ended up back at Camp Pendleton after they were hit by a homemade bomb in Ramadi, Iraq. She suffered a concussion, while the dog was injured in the shoulder. The animal underwent a regimen familiar to athletes: The affected area was treated with ice, heat, stretching, and motion exercises.

Bulletproof vests are available for dogs, along with booties to protect their pads. They sometimes wear doggie goggles—called "doggles"—to keep blowing sand out their eyes. However, most handlers dispense with these for fear of the dogs overheating.

Cooper

Twenty-year-old Corporal Kory D. Wiens of the 94th Mine Dog Detachment, 5th Engineer Battalion, 1st Engineer Brigade from Fort Leonard Wood, Missouri, was so close with his Labrador retriever, Cooper, that when they were killed July 6, 2007, by an improvised explosive device while on patrol in Muhammad Sath, Iraq, they were buried together. They had been in the country together for six months.

The cremated remains of Corporal Wiens and Cooper were buried together at Salt Creek Cemetery in Wiens's hometown of Dallas, Oregon, at the request of his family. Man and dog had a strong bond in life. Master Sergeant Matt McHugh, the family's casualty assistance officer, said, "Kory referred to Cooper as his son, that's now much of a team they were."

"Most military dog handlers look at [their relationship with their dog] as a marriage," said Hans Freimarck, the military working dog coordinator for the Army Dog Program. "You give to the dog, the dog gives back to you. Every dog handler has a firm attachment to his dog and any dog in the military."

Cooper was Corporal Wiens's first military working dog, and Wiens was Cooper's first handler. They were part of a specialized search detachment trained to find firearms, ammunition, and explosives. Being on a specialized search team meant they had more training and, consequently, spent more time together before deployment. Cooper, who was four years old, worked off the leash.

Residents of Dallas lined the streets to honor the funeral procession, and thirty-seven dog teams from the Army, Air Force, Navy, Marine Corps, and local police departments attended the service, McHugh said.

Corporal Wiens was named Kory after his grandfather, who was a military canine handler during the Korean War.

Flapoor

On January 5, 2006, a suicide bomber blew himself up in the police academy in Ramadi. Marine Corporal Brendan N. Poelaert's arm was broken by ball bearings hurled so hard from a suicide bomb that they also became embedded in his gun. But his thoughts quickly went to his patrol dog, a powerful Belgian Malinois named Flapoor

The suicide bomber had detonated his vest in the thick of a crowd, and both US marines and Iraqi recruits were injured in the blast.

"The first thing I did was grab my arm because I thought it was missing," Poelaert said. "I saw another MP [military policeman] who was hit, heard machine gun fire, it seemed like there were bodies everywhere. I tried to lift my rifle but couldn't because of my arm."

As he surveyed the scene, he found that Sergeant Adam Cann and his dog, Bruno, were hit, and Flapoor was injured. The dog staggered a few steps along the Ramadi street with blood pouring from his chest. Then he collapsed.

"Flapoor tried to come to me, but he just laid on the ground and stared," Corporal Poelaert said. "I reacted the same as I would for any other marine, calling for corpsmen. Medics wanted to treat me, but I was more concerned with getting the dogs to a veterinarian."

Poelaert found himself bandaged from his neck to his wrist. But that was not his priority. "I didn't care about my injuries, my arm," he says. "I'm telling the medic, 'I got to get my dog to the vet!'"

Despite his injuries, Poelaert refused to be moved to Al Asad for treatment without Flapoor at his side. "Finally some other MPs got the K-9 truck to us and drove us to a hospital," he said.

Fortunately, Poelaert was trained in veterinary first aid and began care as soon as both were loaded into an SUV. He pressed his finger to his dog's chest to stop him from bleeding to death.

When they reached the base camp, a medic with veterinary training took over.

"There just happened to be a veterinarian technician at the hospital, so I felt better about that," said Poelaert. "They wanted me to get treated, so I was looking for another handler who could look after Flapoor."

The medic started Flapoor on an IV, while Poelaert was reluctantly taken way for surgery.

Corporal Poelaert, from East Kingston, New Hampshire, joined the Marine Corps in 2003, selecting military policeman as his military occupational specialty, and he volunteered to become a dog handler. He was with the 5th Battalion of the 14th Marine Regiment Provisional Military Police Battalion. Military police dog teams conduct vehicle searches, search open areas and buildings for personnel and evidence, perform tracking searches for lost or wanted persons, and can detect illegal drugs or explosives.

"It was something extra I was interested in when I went to [MP training]," Corporal Poelaert said. "I grew up on a farm, have been around animals all my life, and love playing with dogs, so it was pretty natural for me."

The name "Flapoor" means "droopy-eared" in the Flemish language of his homeland. The dog and Poelaert had been together for four months in Iraq. The team's primary missions there were to detect improvised explosive devices, provide crowd control, accompany patrols, detect narcotics, and ensure base safety. Corporal Poelaert and Flapoor had also seen action in Fallujah the previous November.

On the day of the incident, the pair were providing crowd control for Iraqis lined up for entrance into a police academy. With some three hundred Iraqis jostling for position, the working dogs had a calming effect on the crowd.

"People react to just the presence of the dogs," Poelaert said. "No matter where we are, here or stateside, the dogs have the same effect on crowds of people. Just being out, having that security presence de-escalates most situations."

That was when the suicide bomber struck. Poelaert was particularly concerned about the fate of his dog because he had lost one already during his time as a handler and was determined to do everything he could to save Flapoor.

"I lost a dog to cancer, so I had been through that helpless feeling before," Poelaert said. "They are like a best friend. It is hard to lose a dog, just as hard as losing a marine. I was determined to do what I could."

Flapoor was eventually flown on to Baghdad, where his punctured lung and belly wounds were patched up. Later he rejoined his handler

"It was great to see him," Corporal Poelaert said. "The relationship is what you make of it, but every handler I know goes out of their way to be with their dog. It is an unforgettable bond, something you never want to see end. Him pulling through really helped me deal with everything that happened. The hospital workers were great, I can't say enough about what they did for both of us."

Together, they flew back to the US in a cargo plane for physical rehab under the California sun at Camp Pendleton.

Flapoor was quickly back to his usual self in most ways—fast, friendly, eager-to-please. However he suffered a sort of canine posttraumatic stress disorder.

"He's really jumpy around loud noises now," Poelaert said. Nevertheless, he was eager to get back to work. "He hits like a ton of bricks and loves biting. You can tell he is missing it."

Poelaert insisted that the military working dogs like what they do and that checking a road for bombs in their idea of fun. He tried to put memories of the Ramadi explosion behind him. It killed dozens of people, including his best friend, fellow handler Adam Cann and his dog, Bruno. But he retained one inspiring image—the sight of the fatally wounded Bruno stretched over Cann's body, as if trying to protect him.

Rex

Technical Sergeant Jamie Dana's German shepherd, Rex, ended up on an Iraqi roadway when a bomb blew the door off the Humvee he was riding in with Dana in June 2005. The dog suffered little worse than a cut foot and a burned nose, but Dana nearly died, suffering a fractured spine, collapsed lungs, and brain trauma. The two were not parted for long, however. Rex visited Dana in the hospital a couple of weeks later. She whistled for him, and he jumped up on her bed.

Sergeant Dana's career as a soldier was over, but Rex was young and healthy, and the military did not want to let him go. Friends and family petitioned Congress, and the law was finally signed to allow even able dogs to be adopted under unusual circumstances. Rex now lives on a farm in Pennsylvania with Dana.

Fluffy

One of America's more unlikely war dogs was a German shepherd called Fluffy. During Operation Iraqi Freedom, Sergeant First Class Russell Joyce was with the Green Berets in northern Iraq. His Special Forces team wanted to get a dog for sentry and guard duties. Sergeant Joyce was against it, but the team said that they had used dogs when they were stationed in Afghanistan and they proved to be a very useful deterrent against people entering the compound.

The team enlisted the help of the Kurdish people they were working with in the north. A man named Kordo said that he knew of a German shepherd and a Rottweiler that might meet their needs. Joyce was more familiar with Dobermans, but was ready to try another breed. Feeling that a Rottweiler might be hard to handle at times, he opted for the shepherd.

A few days later, the Kurds brought a scrawny German shepherd who had obviously been neglected and abused. He had scars on his face and front legs. Plainly, the dog had been beaten, and had been so ill-fed that some of its teeth had fallen out. The dog was scared and nervous—hardly ideal material for a guard dog.

In Arab countries, dogs are considered unclean and are consequently not treated in the way that Americans are accustomed to. Dogs are not kept as pets or companions. They are only used for sheep herding or as a guard dog. The Iraqi people avoid touching a dog with their hands and will only touch them with their feet if they must.

The first night the dog was at the Special Forces' compound, he did not bark or make any sound at all. Instead, he cowered in the shadows. The Green Berets were not pleased. He did not fit the bill as a guard dog. But Sergeant Joyce felt that, as the Kurds had gone to a good deal of trouble to get them a dog, they had to give him a chance. He also thought the dog had been through some terrible trauma and that it would take him a while to get used to his new surroundings. A couple of nights later, the dog barked all night because there were a pack of stray dogs outside the fence, hunting for scraps of food. This did not endear him to the rest of the team.

Although Sergeant Joyce had been against getting a dog in the first place, he now realized that he was going to have to take responsibility for looking after it. He had been to dog-training classes in the past with the Doberman pinschers he had when he was younger. He had also attended some classes with the military, but he readily admitted that he had little experience training a dog for military duties. However, he realized that the first thing he would have to do was to gain its trust. Dog food was not commercially available in Iraq; the Iraqis would feed their dogs scraps from the table. So Joyce began sharing his own rations with the dog. He had learned the dog's name was Tera Kazez, so he called him Terror for short.

At first, Sergeant Joyce had no dog-handling equipment, so he used a piece of rope for a leash. But then he got in touch with Technical Sergeant Steven Smith, who was with the 506th K-9 unit in Iraq. Smith gave Joyce a leather leash, a collar, a muzzle, and some proper dog food. He arranged for Terror to have a medical examination by a US military veterinarian and get the right shots.

By using a system of rewards, Terror seemed to learn things very quickly. In just two weeks Terror learned walk patrol, staying on Joyce's left. He would stop when Joyce stopped and look in the direction Joyce pointed. He soon became protective of his American masters and, as a guard dog, he was aggressive with intruders. He also worked with other men in the unit. Sergeant Joyce encouraged them to repeat the commands that he had taught the dog to reinforce his understanding of English.

As Operation Iraqi Freedom progressed and the Green Berets headed south toward Baghdad, Terror went with them. He survived being shot at twice, and some members of the team suggested they change his name to Lucky. Instead, Joyce joked about changing his name to Fluffy. When he said the name Terror looked up.

"That's when it hit me that he seemed to like the name," said Sergeant Joyce.

His tour was drawing to a close. He was already thinking about taking the dog home with him and knew his kids would love a dog named Fluffy. So Fluffy it was. His fellow Green Berets did not like the sappy name though.

"The team was not happy with a guard dog named Fluffy," said Joyce. "But I liked it and so did he."

Fluffy and Joyce worked together the rest of his time in Iraq.

About four weeks before Sergeant Joyce was to return home, he heard about the law allowing the adoption of military working dogs. This gave preference to law enforcement agencies and the dog's former handler.

Sergeant Joyce got the permission of his commanding officer that the law required and the necessary certificates from a military veterinarian permitting him to take the dog home.

"Two weeks before my return home, I thought I had my T's crossed and my I's dotted," said Sergeant Joyce. "Boy, was I wrong."

When the time came for him to go, the US Air Force would not allow him to take a dog on the plane, because Fluffy was not an official war dog.

Sergeant Joyce again turned to Technical Sergeant Smith for help. But he could only keep Fluffy for three more days; there was limited room in the kennels and he was expecting a new delivery of dogs to arrive. Smith gave Joyce the phone number of Ron Aiello, who was then the head of the US War Dogs Association. Technical Sergeant Smith had been kennel master at McGuire Air Force Base, which was near Aiello's home in Burlington, New Jersey, and had met him there.

Joyce had to board the plane home without Fluffy. His wife and children came to meet the aircraft and were upset when they discovered that Fluffy wasn't on the flight. But at 8:30 the following morning, Sergeant Joyce contacted Ron Aiello.

Aiello said he could tell from Sergeant Joyce's voice that he loved Fluffy. It reminded him of the feelings he had had for his war dog, Stormy, more than thirty-five years before, and he agreed to do anything he could to help. The first thing Aiello did was write to the Secretary of Defense Donald Rumsfeld. He reminded Rumsfeld that, after the Vietnam war, the US government had put down or abandoned thousands of dogs that had given loyal service to the country. Fluffy had also done his bit protecting American lives. It was the Secretary of Defense's duty to bring him home. Three days later, a Mr. Stump phoned from the Pentagon. From then on, Stump and Aiello were in daily contact.

Sergeant Joyce had woken a sleeping giant: the dog handlers from Vietnam who had not been allowed to bring their dogs home. Word spread on the Internet. Petitions were raised, and Joyce's phone did not stop ringing.

On May 24, 2003, two weeks after Sergeant Joyce had returned from Iraq, it was decided that Fluffy could be brought home under the Military Dog Adoption Program, even though he was not an official war dog. The first thing that had to be done was to make him an honorary war dog and register him with the system at Lackland Air Force Base. Then he could be flown home with an escort. Once at back in the US, Sergeant Joyce and his family could then apply to adopt him.

On May 28, Technical Sergeant Smith called from Iraq to tell Aiello that Major Pompano of the USAF had been assigned to escort Fluffy onto the aircraft. He also said that Fluffy's plane would have already left if insurgents had not fired rockets at the airfield shortly before it was due to take off.

Later that day Aiello called Sergeant Joyce, telling him that Fluffy was airborne. On May 31, the dog landed at Charleston Air Force Base where Sergeant Joyce was waiting. Soon after, the two of them were on their way to Fluffy's new home at Fort Bragg.

"People wrote, calling me and Fluffy heroes," said Sergeant Joyce, "but we were not the heroes at all. It is the military dog handlers who serve and protect others. It's the search-and-rescue dogs that find lost kids, or attempted to rescue survivors from September 11. Or the police K-9 teams who put their lives on the line to protect us. It's the firefighters and medical people who work all hours to help you. It's the men and women of the armed services who leave their families to go off to foreign lands to free others. It's the families who are left behind to continue their lives while their spouse is away. It's the men and women who did not return or will not return. It's every American who owns an American flag and flies it with pride. And most of all its all the Vietnam War vets who never got a welcome home and were forced to leave behind their dogs that saved so many American lives."

Bodo

Explosive-detection dog Bodo saved the life of his handler, Specialist Joaquin Mello of the 98th Military Police. The German shepherd and the Air Force K-9 handler were on a route-clearing mission in the town of Najaf, Iraq, when Mello spotted a suspicious pile of rubble. But while they were searching there, Bodo began acting strangely.

"I had Bodo on the retractable leash, and while we were searching he started to get a little bit behind me so I tried to coach him ahead of me but he wouldn't go and I ended up getting in front of him," said Mello. "He was showing great change in his behavior."

Mello bent down and told Bodo to seek, but the dog ignored him.

"All of a sudden he jerked sharply behind me, and him jerking the leash jerked my head up," said Mello. "I heard a whiz and a loud ping like metal hitting rock. Sand started kicking up in my face and I'm waving my hands because I can't see because I have dust in my eyes. Then it hit me like a ton of bricks—someone just shot at me."

The bullet had passed within a foot or so of his head.

"It scared the crap out of me," Mello said. "I started thinking about it and I was like, 'Wow, my dog just saved my life.' It was a scary moment for me, like the war actually hit me. The war became real in that moment."

Mello put it down to Bodo's acute sense of hearing. His dog could hear things before he did.

"It's possible he did hear the round and thought, 'Dad's in trouble,' and pulled me back," said Mello. "It's not important to me how he did it. All I know is Bodo, without a doubt, saved my life that day."

When Mello returned to his base, he was asked whether he wanted to be put in for a Combat Action Badge, but he said no. "Bodo is the one who did something amazing...I just did my job."

CHAPTER NINE
AFGHANISTAN

GENERAL DAVID H. PETRAEUS, commander of United States forces in Afghanistan from July 4, 2010, to July 18, 2010, praised the contribution of canine commandoes in the war there.

"The capability they bring to the fight cannot be replicated by man or machine," he said. He is on record as saying that the military needs more dogs.

Technical Sergeant Kelly A. Mylott, the kennel master at Langley Air Force Base in Virginia, said that dogs are ideal for getting someone who was running away without having to shoot them. Malinois and German shepherd dogs are particularly useful, as they can run twice as fast as a humans, then bring a person to the ground. When the dogs go after a suspect, they are trained to bite and hold them. They can also grab people's attention in ways that weapons sometimes did not.

"Dogs can be an amazing psychological deterrent," Mylott said.

There were six hundred dogs serving in Afghanistan, including a number of Labrador retrievers that traveled off-leash a hundred yards or so in front of patrols to check out the safety of the route.

Dogs can be used to pacify an unruly group of people—particularly in the Middle East.

"There is a cultural aversion to dogs in some of these countries, where few of them are used as pets," said Major William Roberts, commander of the Defense Department's Military Working Dog Center at Lackland Air Force Base. "Dogs can be very intimidating in that situation."

After Operation Neptune Spear—the incursion into Pakistan to kill Osama bin Laden—the world discovered that the US Navy SEALs also employed dogs. Major Wes Ticer of the United States Special Operations Command, said the dogs' primary functions "are finding explosives and conducting searches and patrols. Dogs are relied upon to provide early warning for potential hazards, many times saving the lives of the Special Operations Forces with whom they operate."

In 2010, the SEALs bought four waterproof tactical vests for their dogs that, together, cost more than $86,000. They incorporated infrared and night-vision cameras so that their handlers could immediately see what the dogs were seeing on a three-inch monitor from as far away as a thousand yards. The camouflage vests also let the handlers talk to the dogs through a speaker that relayed their commands.

Cairo

The names of the members of SEAL Team Six who took down Osama bin Laden have been withheld for security reasons. Except for one—the war dog Cairo who accompanied the SEALs on their dangerous mission. His job was to track down anyone who tried to escape from the terrorist compound and to alert the SEALs to any approaching Pakistani security forces that might arrive to hamper their mission.

Additional roles included helping clear the buildings, sniffing for bombs and booby traps, searching for false walls or hidden doors where bin Laden could be hiding, or helping to keep curious neighbors at bay.

"Dogs are very good at detecting people inside of a building," said Major William Roberts. He said that Cairo could have checked the compound for explosives and even sniffed door handles to see if they were booby-trapped.

However, when it came down to it, bin Laden was easily located and neutralized by Cairo's human companions and, according to the *New Yorker* magazine, "The primary role that Cairo played in the actual raid seems to have been symbolic. He closed off the perimeter, stood watch—having a tough-looking dog around was probably a good way to keep passers-by at a distance, and impress on them that something vaguely military, a 'security operation,' was going on."

Nevertheless the dog traveled into Pakistan on one of the Black Hawk helicopters and risked his life in the defense of America.

Cairo was a Belgian Malinois, which are bred for detection, police work, search and rescue, and for work with the military. This highly intelligent and fearless breed is increasingly used by America's armed forces. Navy SEAL teams have trained to deploy out of helicopters with dogs. Cairo was trained to slide down a rope or jump from five thousand feet, wearing an oxygen mask, a parachute, and "doggles" to protect his eyes. Going into action with the SEALs in Pakistan, Cairo also wore special body armor. When President Barack Obama arrived at Fort Campbell, Kentucky, to thank the SEALs who had conducted the operation, he said, "Where's the dog? I want to meet the dog."

"If you want to meet the dog, Mr. President, I advise you to bring treats," said the squadron commander of the SEAL Team.

Cairo was quickly brought to meet to the president, though nervous Secret Service agents insisted the canine's warrior muzzle remained safely on while he petted him.

As with other SEALs, the details of Cairo's operational activities are kept secret, but it is feared that he was on the Chinook that was shot down by the Taliban on August 5, 2001, just three months after the raid on bin Laden. All on-board were killed. Within the Special Operations Command, some thirty-four dogs were killed in the line of duty between 2006 and 2009.

Target

US soldiers befriended stray dogs at their base at Dand Patan, near the border with Pakistan. They fed them and treated them as pets. One German shepherd mix they looked after was shot at by the Taliban and dodged explosions, escaping death so many times that the troops called her "Target."

The dogs on the base were eager to show their gratitude to the soldiers. One night in February 2010, a suicide bomber wearing twenty-five pounds of explosives approached the base, intent on killing Americans. Target and two other dogs named Rufus and Sasha snapped at the terrorist and barked at him, waking the sleeping GIs. The harassed insurgent made no further attempt to enter the building where soldiers were billeted, and blew himself up in the doorway. The dogs saved the lives of dozens of US soldiers. Five men were injured, but they all recovered.

Sasha was killed in the incident, and the other two dogs were badly injured. Nevertheless, with the attention of medics, their lives were saved. Afterward, the two dogs were treated like royalty. Rufus was taken by one soldier to live in Georgia, while Sergeant Terry Young, who figured he would have been fatally injured by shrapnel if Target had not intervened, took him home to the San Tan Valley, near Phoenix, Arizona, that August. There she became the pet of Sergeant Young's three children, aged fourteen, seven, and four, and appeared on the *Oprah Show* the following month in a show about amazing animals. But on Friday November 12, 2010, when Young went out into the backyard to feed Target, he found that the back gate was open and she had disappeared. Sergeant Young contacted local TV stations, which ran reports on the missing canine hero, and he put out notices online.

A neighbor had found Target wandering the streets and took her to the local dog shelter in Casa Grande. She had no tag or microchip. However, Sergeant Young saw her picture on a Website hosted by Pinal County's dog catchers for owners to find their lost pets. He assumed that the pound was closed over the weekend and that there was no hurry to pick up the errant dog. But due to a mix-up in the paperwork, Target was taken out of her pen and put down on Monday morning. By the time Sergeant Young got there it was too late. Target was already dead.

"My four-year-old son just can't understand what is going on with Target and keeps asking me to get the poison out of her and bring her home," Sergeant Young told a local CBS-TV station. "They can't grasp the idea that she's gone. They don't want her to go be with God yet...I just can't believe that something like this would happen to such a good dog."

Sergeant Young and his family were to be given the dog's cremated remains.

Sarbi

Australian special forces also had dogs with them in Afghanistan. One of these, Sarbi, came to worldwide attention when she was listed as missing in action. Then fourteen months later, she was found by a US soldier and returned to the Australians.

A black Labrador, Sarbi was trained in explosives detection before being deployed in Afghanistan. On September 2, 2008, she was out with the Australian Special Air Services Regiment in Oruzgan Province in a joint US, Australian, and Afghan convoy when they were ambushed. During the battle, SAS Trooper Mark Donaldson won the Victoria Cross; he was the first Australian recipient of the medal since the Vietnam War. A rocket landed near the patrol, and when the smoke cleared, Sarbi was gone.

The Special Operations Task Group made repeated attempts to find the dog. More than a year later, an American soldier spotted her with a local man. Suspicious, he used voice commands to ascertain that the dog had military training. He knew that the Australians were missing a dog, so she was then flown back to her Australian base in Tarin Kowt, where her handler, Corporal David Simpson, confirmed the dog was Sarbi.

George Hulse, a retired Lieutenant Colonel and the president of the Australian Defence Force Trackers and War Dogs Association, says he and many others gave up hope when the dog went missing. But Corporal Simpson, who was one of nine Australian soldiers injured in the ambush, never gave up.

"He wasn't going to let go of Sarbi," said Hulse. "He thought that he might one day arrive. I, on the other hand had abandoned any hope of that, and I was trying to console him. But he wasn't having any of it, so deep down I think he burned a candle for that dog and he feels very happy about her recovery now for sure."

Hulse described the dog as "an exceptionally good worker, a very gritty dog, and has found improvised explosive devices and she's saved quite a few lives in her work."

Sarbi was at Tarin Kowt when Australian Prime Minister Kevin Rudd and General Stanley A. McChrystal, who had taken over from General Petraeus, visited the base a few weeks later. This guaranteed worldwide media attention.

Sarbi was on her second tour of duty and had previously served with the Incident Response Regiment at the 2006 Commonwealth Games held in Melbourne.

Brigadier Brian Dawson, Head of Defence Public Affairs, said that Sarbi was in good health when she was returned. Obviously, someone had been looking after her. However, the *Australian* quoted a senior Australian military officer who asked not to be named as saying that the dog was wounded in the gun battle, and did return to a nearby coalition forward operating base shortly after the fight but was chased away by Afghan guards.

After six months' quarantine in Dubai, the ten-year-old sniffer dog was returned to Australia on December 9, 2010. Then on April 5, 2011, Sarbi was awarded an RSPCA Purple Cross, Australia's highest award for animal bravery.

Remco

A Silver Star, one of the Navy's highest awards, was awarded posthumously in 2009 to a combat assault dog named Remco after he helped save the life of a Navy SEAL when he and his handler, Chief Master-at-Arms Michael Toussaint, charged an insurgent's hideout in Afghanistan. Toussaint and Remco were assigned to the ultrasecretive SEAL Six direct action unit, also known as the Naval Special Warfare Development Group, or DEVGRU. They were part of a helicopter-borne assault force that came under small-arms and RPG fire as soon as it touched down. Toussaint and Remco began pursuing a group of al Qaeda and the Taliban insurgents. As they approached an enemy position, heavy automatic weapons fire erupted. The team began engaging the enemy fighters. The DEVGRU element leader, maneuvering beside Toussaint, was hit and critically wounded. Toussaint moved forward against the position where the enemy had dug in, eliminating the enemy from a distance of less than fifteen feet. But Remco was mortally wounded in the action and died soon after. Touissaint was also awarded the Silver Star. The dog's award is a break from tradition. Military regulations usually prohibit bravery awards being given to animals.

Eli

Bomb-sniffing black Labrador retriever Eli was so loyal to his handler, twenty-year-old PFC Colton Rusk that, when Rusk was shot in the chest by the Taliban, Eli snapped at other marines who rushed forward to help him, even biting one of them. He also climbed onto Private Rusk to shield him from enemy fire with his body.

When Private Rusk died, his family decided to adopt the dog. This was unusual because Eli was not injured in the attack and was still "operational"—he could have been given to another handler. There was already a bond between Eli and his new family because of Colton, who had grown up surrounded by dogs on the family's hundred-acre ranch in Orange Grove, just outside Corpus Christi on the Texas coast. Colton and his brothers had been brought up around Labradors and bulldogs, and "had 'em chewing on their diapers since they were little," said Colton's father, Darrell Rusk.

"Every time he called home, it was always about Eli," said his mother Kathy Rusk. "It gave me some comfort knowing that Colton wasn't alone over there."

Eli and been assigned to Private Rusk in May, seven months before he died. The two quickly grew inseparable. Military dogs were supposed to sleep in kennels on deployment, but Rusk broke the rules and let Eli curl up with him on his cot, even taking up the entire sleeping bag. And Eli foreswore dog food, sharing Rusk's ready-to-eat meals.

"Whatever is mine is his," Private Rusk confided on his Facebook page.

Darrell Rusk kept more than a dozen photos of Eli and his son on his iPhone. In one, Colton is letting his tongue hang out alongside the panting Eli. The family first met Eli at Camp Pendleton in California, before Colton deployed on September 23—his twentieth birthday. It was Eli's second tour.

The family were driving around when they spotted the two together.

"Colton jumped right in, and the dog jumped in, too," Kathy Rusk said.

The military say that Private Rusk came under fire after another vehicle in the marine convoy ran over a hidden explosive in Helmand Province. He was shot when the rest of the convoy stopped to secure the area. At the time, he was thought to have been trying to tie up Eli.

"The enemy is aware that the dogs are finding their stuff," said Doug Miller, who runs the Defense Department's Military Working dog Program. "So it's logical they would pick a dog or handler to take out."

Military dogs cost thousands of dollars to train, and taking a dog out of service needed the okay of the Secretary of the Navy. But when the Rusk family asked, permission was granted.

They picked four-year-old Eli up at Lackland Air Force on February 4, 2011, to take him back to their home in rural South Texas. Eli wagged his tail furiously when he first met his new owners in a small room in the 37th Training Wing. Marine Staff Sergeant Jessy Eslick tried to get the dog to sit while he read a letter of appreciation to the family.

"Eli will forever be remembered by the Marine Corps as a dog that brought marines home to their families," he began.

But he gave up after Eli kept leaping forward to sniff Rusk's mother, Kathy. When the leash was finally handed to Darrell Rusk, his wife and Colton's two younger brothers, Cody and Brady, crouched down to pet Eli. They were crying.

"I know that Colton passed his love on to this dog, and that's why he's so loving," said Kathy Rusk. "He'll just be one of us, part of the family."

Eli joins the three German shepherds at the Rusks' ranch. The family uses them to hunt hogs, a task Eli might find as easy as sniffing out explosives, as he was doing on the day Colton Rusk was killed. The Rusks' adoption of Eli marked only the third time that a US military dog had been adopted by his handler or the family of a handler killed in combat.

The first was adopted by a wounded airman. The second, a German shepherd named Lex, was handed over to the family of Corporal Dustin Lee, a marine from Mississippi who was killed in a 2007 mortar attack in Fallujah, Iraq. This took considerable effort. Although Lex was recovering from shrapnel wounds in Albany, Georgia, the family were not allowed to visit him. However, they got in touch with dog-handler-turned-author John Burnam, who wrote a story from Lex's point of view. The story moved North Carolina Congressman Walter B. Jones, who contacted the Pentagon. Meanwhile, Dustin's uncle began an Internet petition that collected 3,200 signatures. Then CBS News took an interest. Nine months after Dustin Lee's death, the Pentagon relented and handed over Lex. It was the first time a Marine Corps war dog was given early retirement and handed over to the family of a fallen marine.

Hobo

A black Labrador named Hobo was with Britain's Royal Gurhka Rifles and 29 Commando Regiment of the Royal Marines serving in Afghanistan when he came under fire. His unit was out on patrol in the town of Nahr-e-Saraj in the notorious Helmand Province on July 21, 2011, when they were attacked by the Taliban. Heavy small-arms fire and rocket-propelled grenades forced them to take cover in a compound.

Moments later, four grenades came flying over the compound wall. Hobo, who is trained to seek out deadly explosives, was blasted with shrapnel three times. He was hit in the neck, abdomen and rear with razor-sharp shards of metal. Some fragments were so hot they instantly cauterized two of his injuries, while another piece cut straight through his neck and left him bleeding profusely.

Captain George Shipman, serving with Plymouth-based 29 Commando Royal Artillery attached to A Company, 2nd Battalion the Royal Gurkha Rifles, leapt into action and struggled to keep the dog alive.

"There were four loud explosions, the dust was kicked up, and it was difficult to see what was happening," said Captain Shipman. "We realized quickly that Hobo had been hit. He was bleeding heavily from the base of his neck.

Shipman administered a blood-clotting agent normally reserved for soldiers and applied pressure to stem the bleeding, then bound up the wound with a field dressing to protect it from infection. Throughout it all, Hobo remained calm and just stood there while his handlers treated him.

"I found it hard, harder than treating a human casualty because I couldn't explain what was going on," Captain Shipman said. "Hobo's become one of us, bounding around the patrol base all the time, so we're very fond of him—I've also got a two-year-old black lab, Oscar, at home, and Hobo reminds me so much of him."

During the attack, other members of the patrol were injured by fragments of shrapnel and a US medical evacuation helicopter was summoned. Within fifty minutes three-year-old Hobo was on his way back to receive veterinary care at Camp Bastion, the main British base in Afghanistan, northwest of Lashka Gah.

Private Patrick Medhurst-Feeny, a vet with the Royal Army Veterinary Corps, had been alerted that they were on their way.

"When we got the news, we set up for surgery immediately and prepared all of the equipment because we didn't know the extent of his injuries," he said. "We planned for every eventuality."

The veterinary team met Hobo as he came off of the helicopter and rushed him into surgery. After checking his wounds, they got him straight onto fluids because of the blood loss. There was a danger that he would go into shock, so they chose not to remove the shrapnel.

Hobo astonished everyone with the speed of his recovery. Two days later, he was swimming and playing ball.

"The quick thinking of Captain Shipman and his patrol saved Hobo's life," said Private Medhurst-Feeny. Their first aid meant that no surgery was required. "Hobo has recovered fantastically well. He's an athletic thirty-three kilograms [seventy-three pounds] and is bounding around as if nothing had happened. He's in great shape."

The wound healed quickly, and with a week Hobo was back out on patrol, sniffing out IEDs and saving soldiers' lives again. The Royal Army Veterinary Corps, based at Melton Mowbray in Leicestershire, has been involved in every army campaign since its formation in 1796. For its first 150 years, horses were the main focus. But more recently dogs have come to play a crucial role in British military operations around the globe.

Nicknamed "The Luckiest Hobo," Hobo completed his tour in November 2011 and returned to England where he became an Army demonstration dog. Having been "battle inoculated" by training against explosions, it is thought that Hobo is unlikely to suffer from posttraumatic stress disorder after the attack.

Theo

Other dogs had not been as lucky as Hobo. One British Army sniffer dog was killed alongside his handler in July 2008 when their unit was attacked by insurgents while making a routine patrol from the forward operating base Inkerman in the Sangin district of Helmand. His master, twenty-five-year-old Corporal Jason Barnes, was the first British dog handler to be killed in modern times.

Then there was Theo, a record-breaking springer spaniel, who died of a heart attack when he returned to the British base at Camp Bastion only hours after his handler, Lance Corporal Liam Tasker, was shot dead while they were out on patrol together north of Nahr-e-Saraj in Helmand in March 2011. It was said that Theo, who was just twenty-two months old, died of a broken heart, as he and his handler were inseparable.

Twenty-six-year-old Lance Corporal Tasker served with the Royal Army Veterinary Corps, 1st Military Working Dog Regiment. He and Theo were attached to 2 Company, 1st Battalion Irish Guards, as part of a mission to secure an area soldiers referred to as the "shark's fin" near the village of Shingazi, when Lance Corporal Tasker was shot in the head. Theo was so distressed by the incident that his leash had to be cut before medics could attend to his handler.

"Theo was running about, he was all over the place," said Captain Charles Allman-Brown, who was leading the patrol. "He didn't know what he was doing,"

Private Michael Johnston, a medic who attended to Lance Corporal Tasker, said Theo was "clearly distressed."

The dog was caught and taken back to FOB Kharnikah, where he started having seizures. He was airlifted to Camp Bastion for veterinary treatment, but died less than ten hours after his master.

"My honest opinion on this is, when Liam went down, that Theo didn't have the comfort from Liam to calm him down," said Lance Corporal Tasker's father. "I truly believe when Theo went back to the kennel, that would have a big, big impact because Liam wasn't there for him."

"I would like to believe that he died of a broken heart not to be with Liam," Tasker's mother added, saying that the fact her son and Theo had "worked together and died together" brought her some comfort.

"Once it had hit home to me what had happened to Liam, I asked if Theo was okay, and they told me Theo was okay," she said. "And then it came back to me a short time later that Theo had died as well. To me, I took a lot of comfort in that, as sad as it is that Theo died as well, because then they were together."

"He used to joke that Theo was impossible to restrain, but I would say the same about Lance Corporal Tasker," said their commanding officer Major Alexander Turner. "At the most hazardous phase of an advance, he would be at the point of the spear, badgering to get even further forward and work his dog. He met his fate in just such a situation—leading the way that we might be safe."

Major Turner said he was "confident Liam and his dog were on top of their game," saying he was told they were the "best team" the army had to offer. "They were extremely brave and enthusiastic about the task and gave us the option to operate more aggressively," he added.

Lance Corporal Tasker was said to have a natural empathy with dog and the two of them "undoubtedly saved many lives." Theo was on his first tour of duty in Afghanistan and had uncovered so many IEDs that his stay in the country was extended by a month. In just five months, he had discovered fourteen weapons caches and hidden bombs—a record for both dog and handler. When Lance Corporal Tasker's body was returned to Britain for burial, it was accompanied by Theo's ashes.

Just a month before he died, Lance Corporal Tasker said, "I love my job and working with Theo. He has a great character and never tires. He can't wait to get out and do his job and will stop at nothing."

Theo was the sixth British military dog to be killed in action in the Middle East since 2001.

Tango

In the spring of 2011, a Labrador named Tango was leading a small group of marines on a dirt road leading into a village in Helmand's Garmsir District when the dog suddenly went down on all fours, wagging his tail. This was a sign that he had detected explosives nearby. The patrol froze as a marine explosives team investigated. No bomb was found, so the patrol continued, but the dog had good reason for being a little sensitive. The temperature was 102°F. Like most Labrador retrievers, Tango was a good swimmer. He abandoned his duties and leapt into an irrigation canal to cool off. Then he found he could not climb back up the steep bank. So one of the marines had to jump into the canal and rescue him. These days, more than ever, the value of these dogs is recognized.

A patrol under Captain Manuel Zepeda, the commander of Company F, 2nd Battalion, 6th Marines, were on a foot patrol in the Taliban stronghold of Marja, Afghanistan, when they opened fire on a local dog when it tried to attack their

Labrador. If the dog had been hurt, they would have lost their best weapon for detecting roadside bombs and would have called for a helicopter to medevac the animal out.

"We consider the dog another marine," said Captain Zepeda.

While American troops were being stood down from Afghanistan, more dogs were going in. The marines began a pilot program in Afghanistan in 2007 with nine bomb-sniffing dogs. There were more than six hundred by the end of 2011. By then, there were some 2,700 dogs on active duty in the American military. Before the 9/11 attacks, there were 1,800.

"Most of the public isn't aware of what these dogs add to national security," said Gerry Proctor, a spokesman for training programs at Lackland Air Force Base in Texas, including the Military Working Dog School. Dogs are used for protection, pursuit, tracking, and search and rescue, but the military is also increasingly relying on them to sniff out the homemade bombs that cause the vast majority of American casualties in Afghanistan. So far, no human or human-made technology can do better.

While other branches of the service prefer German shepherds or Malinois, the marines in Afghanistan rely on purebred Labrador retrievers because of the dogs' good noses. They are also nonaggressive and eager to please. Labradors accompany marine foot patrols in Helmand Province in southern Afghanistan, wandering off-leash a hundred yards or more in front as bomb detectors.

Some twenty Labrador retrievers out of the 350 deployed have been killed in action since the marine program began. Most were victims of IEDs. Those that survive repeated deployments, sometimes as many as four, retire from the military at the age of eight or nine.

EPILOGUE
THE "ROBBY" LAW

CONGRESSMAN ROSCOE G. BARTLETT learned about the Department of Defense's war dog policy in the September 2000 issue of *Stars and Stripes* magazine. The article he read mentioned a marine dog named Robby, who was sick and near the end of his career. Because the dog was no longer of use to the military, he was at risk of being put down.

Representative Bartlett went to visit Robby. The dog's handler, Lance Corporal Shawn Manthey, tried to put Robby through his paces to show off for Bartlett, but the eight-year-old Belgian Malinois was suffering from arthritis, a hip complaint, and a painful growth on his spine. The aging dog was unable to catch a "suspect" when his handler ordered him to pursue. When Robby did get in a bite, his gums bled. It was plain that the dog was in so much pain that the demonstration was cut short.

Lance Corporal Manthey was attached to Robby and wanted to adopt him, but he was not able to do so under the then-current law. So on September 27, 2000, Bartlett introduced a bill allowing military dogs to be adopted after they had retired from their service. To aid its passage, William W. Putney, the former Commanding Officer of the War Training School at Camp Lejeune, wrote a letter on October 18, 2000, to Senator John Warner explaining why the adoption bill was so important. He wrote:

> Our service dogs must be honored and treated as heroes because that is what they are. And they must be allowed to retire to loving homes, as any soldier is. They have served us with honor and distinction, and have saved countless American sons and daughters from injury and death. They have risked their own death and injury for no more than the love and affection of their handlers.... They would never, ever have left us behind, and they would never give up on us because we were too old or infirm to do our jobs anymore. If they can offer us this sort of service and devotion, how can we do less for them? We owe them.

On November 6, 2000, President Bill Clinton signed the "Robby" law (Public Law 106-446). It stated that when military dogs had reached the end of their useful working lives or were surplus to the requirements of the Department of Defense, they could be adopted by law-enforcement agencies, former handlers, or other people capable of humanely caring for the animal. Restrictions were put on prospective adopters because some military dogs have been trained to be aggressive. Often these dogs also suffer from medical conditions due to the hard lives they have led and need special care.

By the time the legislation passed, Manthey's wife was pregnant and he found he could not afford the expensive medication that Robby would need. After living through another bitterly cold winter, Robby could no longer even stand and had to be put down on January 19, 2001.

In April 2001, eleven-year-old Ronny, another Belgian Malinois, was being retired from the service and became the first dog adopted under the new law. He was given a home by Marine Sergeant Kevin Bispham, who had been his handler for more than three years. To give Ronny a good home, Sergeant Bispham moved from an apartment into a housing unit on the base with a fenced yard. Then he bought a large kennel and paid to have Ronny shipped to his home in South Carolina.

"I love Ronny, and it's so exciting to bring him home," said Bispham. "He's done his time. Now it's time for him to take it easy and not work anymore."

Although Robby was not as lucky as Ronny, he was honored as the dog that helped bring attention to the plight of older military animals. On June 24, 2001, he was laid to rest at the Hartsdale Pet Cemetery in Hartsdale, New York. Established in 1896, Hartsdale was the country's first pet cemetery. The first War Dog Memorial was erected there in 1923. It has since been the centerpiece of an annual memorial service to pay homage to the thousands of dogs who have given their lives in times of war.

FURTHER READING

Barber, Carolyn. *Animals at War*. Harper and Row, 1971.

Bauer, Nona Kilgore. *Dog Heroes of September 11th: A Tribute to America's Search and Rescue Dogs*. Kennel Club Books, 2006.

Biros, Florence W. *Dog Jack: The Heartwarming Story of a Runaway Slave and His Best Friend*. Son-Rise Publications, 2001.

Burham, John C. *A Soldier's Best Friend: Scout Dogs and Their Handlers in the Vietnam War*. Union Square Press, 2003.

Burham, John C. *Dog Tags of Courage: The Turmoil of War and the Rewards of Companionship*. Lost Coast Press, 2000.

Choron, Sandra and Harry Choron. *Planet Dog: A Doglopedia*. Houghton Mifflin, 2005.

Cooper, Jilly. *Animals in War*. Heineman, 1983.

Gardiner, Juliet. *The Animals' War*. Portrait, 2006.

George, Isabel. *Animals at War*. Usborne, 2006.

George, Isabel. *Beyond the Call of Duty: Heartwarming Stories of Canine Devotion and Wartime Bravery*. Element, 2010.

George, Isabel. *The Dog that Saved My Life: Sacrifice, Loyalty, Love Beyond All Bounds*. Element, 2010.

Gilroy, James. *Furred and Feathered Heroes of World War II*. Trafalgar Publications, 1946.

Gray, Ernest A. *Dogs of War*. Hale, 1989.

Hamer, Blythe. *Dogs at War, True Stories of Canine Courage Under Fire*. Andre Deutsche, 2006.

Haran, Peter. *Trackers: The Untold Story of the Australian Dogs of War*. New Holland Australia, 2000.

Kopelman, Jay. *From Baghdad with Love: A Marine, the War, and a Dog Named Lava*. Bantam, 2007.

Le Chêne, Evelyn. *Silent Heroes: The Bravery and Devotion of Animals in War*. Souvenir, 1994.

Lemish, Michael G. *War Dogs: Canines in Combat*. Brassey's, 1996.

Morgan, Paul B. *K-9 Soldiers: Vietnam and After*. Hellgate Press, 1999.

Putney, William W. *Always Faithful: A Memoir of the Marine Dogs of World War II*. Brassey's, 2003.

Rogak, Lisa. *The Dogs of War: The Courage, Love, and Loyalty of Military Working Dogs*. Thomas Dunne Books, 2011.

Sanderson, Jeanette. *War Dog Heroes: True Stories of Dog Courage in Wartime*. Scholastic, 1997.

White, Joseph J. *Ebony and White: The Story of the K-9 Corps*. Doral Publishing, 1996.

Whitson, Angus. *Sea Dog Bamse: World War II Canine Hero*. Birlinn, 2008.

ABOUT THE AUTHOR

NIGEL CAWTHORNE is known for his best-selling Sex Lives series, including *Sex Lives of the Kings and Queens of England* and *Sex Lives of the Roman Emperors*; the books are available in 23 languages. He is also the author of *Serial Killers and Mass Murderers*, *Confirmed Kill*, *Warrior Elite*, *Against Their Will*, *Daughter in the Dungeon*, and more than 60 other books.